Gunbird Driver

Gunbird Driver

A Marine Huey Pilot's War in Vietnam

David A. Ballentine

Naval Institute Press
Annapolis, Maryland

Naval Institute Press
291 Wood Road
Annapolis, MD 21402

Library of Congress Cataloging-in-Publication Data
Ballentine, David A.
    Gunbird driver : a Marine Huey pilot's war in Vietnam / David A. Ballentine.
        p. cm.
    Includes bibliographical references and index.
    ISBN 978-1-59114-019-1 (alk. paper)
    1. Vietnam War, 1961–1975—Aerial operations, American. 2. Vietnam War, 1961–1975
—Personal narratives, American. 3. Military helicopters—Vietnam. 4. Ballentine, David A.
I. Title.
    DS558.8.B354 2008
    959.704'3092—dc22
    [B]
                                                                    2008015579

Printed in the United States of America on acid-free paper

14 13 12 11 10 09 08   9 8 7 6 5 4 3 2
First printing

CONTENTS

WHY I WROTE THIS

An e-mail from Dick Boston triggered this outburst. After years of no contact while we each pursued our separate lives, it came slamming: "Old copilot checking in." It reminded me of an unusual mission we flew. Although Vietnam has been swimming around behind my eyes since I left, for the first time I began to set my thoughts to paper. As I wrote, a whole series of events and circumstances flooded back. And now that my hand is no longer strapped to some income-producing plough handle, I have time to give my mind free rein, to reflect, recall, vent, and record. It feels right.

This story is uniquely mine, but it is likely similar to accounts of dozens of young pilots in Marine Observation Squadrons (VMOs) and reflective in a general way of all air crewmen in those now-defunct units.

One reason I write is simply because I can. And because I can, maybe I owe it to the squadron, to everyone who was a member of "Klondike," the squadron call sign. Someone needs to get off his ass and testify and, as arrogant as it sounds and as marginal as my talent may be, I guess it's me. This record is warranted that we might whisper, if not shout, down through time: We were there, we did those things, and lived that way.

We were Klondike men, proud of it and attached to it in a way those who were not members cannot know. Men and women who go to war become part of their units forever. My story is about one experience in one helicopter unit, but hats off to all Marine helo bubbas, to Deadlock, Powerglide, Stationbreak, Bonnie Sue, Mohair, Whitegold, Clip Clop, Tarbush, Superchief, Barrelhouse, Northbrook, Switch, Buffalo City, Millpoint, Junkman, and any other Marine helo unit that flew in my war or any war.

An additional reason for this effort is probably vanity. I have hope this document will be retained in my family for the coming years, maybe even centuries. If it is, David A. Ballentine will be more than a forgotten name cast on a bronze plaque or carved in stone. He will be a person of some dimension, reflecting a life filled with human experience, a man, not just a name.

Finally, this record may be of some value in the montage of monographic personal experience accounts of the Vietnam War. I have read many; usually they are interesting and sometimes fascinating, but I see nothing about Marine UH-1E gunships. Yet they were of great value in prosecuting the war, misguided effort though it was.

LANGUAGE AND SITUATIONS

At the start of this effort I tried to say it nicely, to use words that would be okay in mixed company, although in this day that allows a wide swath of options. I tried, but I quickly threw in the towel. As I traced the episodes and personalities, including my own, the more the individual characters became vivid, the more I remembered how we expressed ourselves, and the more hopeless it was to "clean it up." I have simply allowed my mind to drift back, to lapse into the language of the Marines with whom I served. The vocabulary of the Marine Corps, at least the young officers, is here.

The words "fuck" and "shit" were in virtually every conversation longer than a sentence or two and it was often included in the briefest of exchanges. "Ross, what the fuck are you doin' there?" "Where the fuck did Bernard go?" "Whose shit is this on my rack?" These words decorated speech in a way that today might damage an officer's career. There is sizzling verbal shorthand in cuss words. For instance, in a group of junior officers having a splash of wine, some lieutenant might say, "This is pretty good shit," which is just the sort of to-the-point comment easily understood and accepted. If, on the other hand, he'd said, "This wine is pleasant, full-bodied with a fruity bouquet, having notes of chocolate and cherries and the slightest undertone of nutmeg," the response would have been much different. One in the group would surely have responded, "What kind of mincing, pussy bullshit was that?" Others would likely have chimed in, "Yeah, what the fuck was that shit?" A person had to get to the point and say it right. Cuss words were just the sauce called for and used.

One last thought, and I can think of massive exceptions, but the more dignified (senior) the officer's rank, the less likely he was to say "fuck." Maybe they'd outgrown it. Maybe they were taught in school to be a little nicer, to set an example for the kids and all, but none I knew seemed to be offended by it. I suppose they remembered their roots. Once they too had been at the rear of the ready room among the lieutenants, among the Buergers, Almidas, Almys, Bartleys, Wilsons, Rosses, Rankins, Pecoreros, Bodens, Andrews, Kufeldts, Motleys, Swinburns, Ballentines, and Petersons.

In addition to flying, I've included information on living conditions. Some of these topics are indelicate, but including them paints a more complete picture of our lives.

ACCURACY

This account of episodes and situations is my own, based upon my memory. If another, even in my own squadron and on the same mission, were questioned, his truth might be different. Although a truth exists, we each filter the same experience through a separate prism, use a different instrument, and with a different capacity to remember. Where it mattered, at least in my judgment, I've bounced parts of the manuscript against others in VMO-6. But when all is said and done, this is a memoir, not a history. It reflects my memory, opinions, and experiences. Though I have done little research and opinions vary, the events described in this book did happen.

On the small things, like whether our outhouses were six-holers or four-holers, and what the dimensions of a Southeast Asia hut actually were, instead of the size produced from my memory, I offer my neck to the headsman. That we had them and they were about the size I indicate is the point.

Also, I can't always remember who my air crewmembers were on all the memorable missions I flew. When memory failed me, I plugged in a name, but, except in one case, I always used the name of one of our Marines, a man who really was a gunner or crewchief, the people I flew with regularly. I've taken liberties here with pilots on some occasions as well. I can't remember, for instance, who was my copilot when I was forced down by enemy fire. I just know he was newer to the squadron than I and was likely junior to me. So I pulled out a name, John Boden, and it may well have been John. He and I flew together often. But regardless of crewmembers, the episodes and situations are true. They reflect the world of a lieutenant in a Marine Corps armed UH-1E squadron, in this case VMO-6.

Most of these missions, and they were many, merge into sameness. Like all helo pilots, I flew hundreds of missions. But some, the ones that were unusual for some reason or combination of reasons, stand out. I've written about the memorable ones in this book.

I have also written a bit about helicopters in general and the UH-1E specifically. Any helo pilot or air crewman who picks up this account will likely gloss over these parts, since the information will be old hat. But if someone other than a helo aviator chances upon this book, he or she will need more. I've given it.

The dialogue, ground unit call signs, grid coordinates, and radio-ICS chatter are invention. The only real quote I remember is Captain K. D. Waters' comment, "Who's givin' this fuckin' brief?" I've eased into literary license for all else. The words I've used are probable, but more importantly, I hope they capture the situations and breathe life into the people.

I've tried to avoid offense. If I have failed in this effort I can only offer that it was not my purpose. I've stayed true to memory and opinion, even though I know opinion can cause annoyance, even outrage.

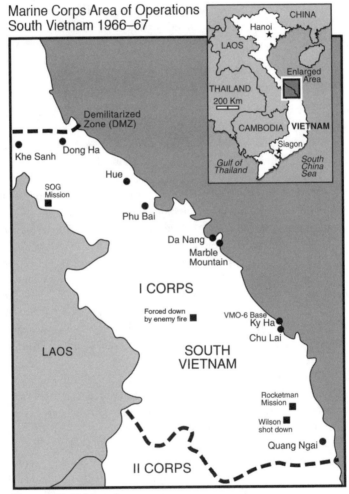

Map created by Rick Brownlee.

ACKNOWLEDGMENTS

This work might not have been possible without the support, encouragement, occasional nudges, and sweat-equity at a word processor of Dana Gayle (Sumner) Ballentine, a remarkable woman who loves me in spite of my flaws and who's agreed to spend her life with me. I'm a fortunate man. Thanks, Dana.

AGL	above ground level
AO	Area of Operations
AOM	all officers' meeting
CAS	close air support
CDO	command duty officer
CGFMFPAC	Commanding General, Fleet Marine Force Pacific
CO	commanding officer
COB	close of business
CONUS	Continental United States
CP	Command Post
CQ	carrier qualified
DASC	Direct Air Support Center
DME	distance measuring equipment (a component of TACAN; shows how far a pilot is from a TACAN station)
FAC	forward air controller
FAC(A)	forward air controller (Airborne)
FFAR	folding fin aerial rocket
FNG	fuckin' new guy
FO	forward observers
FOD	foreign object damage
FSG	Force Support Group
GCA	ground control approach
HAC	helicopter aircraft commander
HE	high explosive
HML	Marine Light Helicopter Squadron
HMM	Marine Medium Helicopter Squadron
HQMC	Headquarters Marine Corps, Washington, D.C.
ICS	intercom system

IFF/SIF	identification friend or foe/selective identification feature
IFR	instrument flight rules
JP	jet fuel
KIA	killed in action
LPH	landing platform helicopter
LZ	Landing Zone
MAF	Marine Amphibious Force
MAG	Marine Aircraft Group
MARCAD	Marine aviation cadet (a means in the 1950s and 1960s to become an aviator and receive a commission)
MCAS	Marine Corps Air Station
MIA	missing in action
MOS	military occupation specialties
MPC	military payment script
MSL	mean sea level
NATOPS	Naval Air Training and Operating Procedures Standardization
NCO	noncommissioned officer
NVA	North Vietnamese Army
ODO	operations duty officer
OIC	officer in charge
Ops O	operations officer (coordinates squadron flight operations)
PIC	pilot in command
PIREP	pilot report of weather
PMIP	post-maintenance inspection pilot
PQM	pilot qualified in model
QC	quality control
RADALT	radar altimeter
ROK	Republic of Korea
R-T	radio transmission
RVN	Republic of Vietnam (military forces)
SAR	search and rescue
SITREP	situation report
SLF	Special Landing Force
SLJO	shitty little jobs officer
SNCO	staff noncommissioned officer
SOG	Studies and Observation Group
SOP	standard operating procedure
SOS	shit on a shingle
TAC	tactical air controller
TAC(A)	tactical air controller (Airborne)
TACAN	tactical air navigation
VC	Viet Cong

VFR	visual flight rules
VMO	Marine Observation Squadron
WIA	wounded in action
XO	executive officer (second senior officer in a Marine unit)

The Aircraft and Training

THE UH-1E AND ITS ARMOR

The UH-1E was a remarkable combination of engine, airframe, and rotor system. As partial testimony, the twin-engine N model is still operated by Marines, and the Army continues to fly the older D model, though in a much-reduced role. Bell Helicopters and Lycoming Engines hit a home run with the whole series of UH-1s. The Army flew the B model as gunships and the D model for troop lift. According to Bell, the Marine's E model, the one I flew, "is an advanced version of the UH-1B with changes incorporated to insure Marine missions suitability."

The most notable differences between the B (Army) and the E (Marine) are the addition of a rescue hoist, the use of aluminum rather than magnesium in the tail boom, a rotor brake, and enhanced avionics for communication and navigation. All of these adjustments were driven by shipboard operational considerations: Aluminum is not as susceptible to saltwater corrosion as magnesium; a rotor brake is essential aboard ship to stop and hold the blades on a tossing deck; a rescue hoist allows pilots to pull people from the water; and the different comm-nav gear is installed so pilots can talk to the ship and navigate to it, even in bad weather. We couldn't just set it down at sea and wait for clouds to lift.

I flew a B model once at Hue with an Army lieutenant. I couldn't tell the difference in how it flew, though I was envious of the copilot's ability to swivel the side-mount M-60s from his seat. Ours were fixed straight ahead; we had to be pointed at the target. We relied exclusively on crewchiefs and door gunners to protect our sides and as we pulled off target. Army pilots could help themselves a little.

The UH-1E's main rotor swept a forty-four-foot disk, and the overall length was slightly less than fifty-three feet, measured from the forward sweep of the main rotor arc to the tail. It had no landing gear, tires, shocks, or wheels, but was perched instead on lateral cross-tubes attached to longitudinal skids. The Huey sat twelve inches off the ground. A yellow "stringer" protruded aft from the end of its tail boom to prevent a tail rotor ground strike on low flares. All Huey pilots have touched or even bounced that beauty down a few times; it's saved many asses.

The Huey was dual controlled; the pilot sat in the right seat (assbackwards from fixed-wing aircraft). Either a copilot or an "observer" sat on the left. It was set up for single pilot flying, but required a set of eyes on the left side to watch where the pilot could not.

Between these seats and directly behind a center console was a "jump seat," an ideal perch for recon by people we hauled. This seat was removed to accommodate ammo cans in gunbirds. The center console housed all the radios, navigation, ordnance control boxes, and miscellaneous switches to start and shut down the engine.

Along the rear of the cabin was a row of red nylon webbed seats stretched over tubular aluminum framing. The helo's interior was navy gray with some gray quilted soundproofing attached to the overhead and against the back cabin bulkhead. It offered some reduction in turbine and transmission whine and to rotor wop, but it didn't make much difference in a gunbird. They were noisy as hell because we flew them without cabin doors, but especially when we were in action with the M-60s. Flight helmets reduced the noise, but they didn't save us from the racket.

The first time I rolled in with guns was a real attention-getter. Although we trained with one M-60 machine gun on each side in the States, in Vietnam we had two. We also had a crewchief and gunner, each with a doormounted M-60. So, you might have six M-60s barking away at one time, each spewing 500 to 600 rounds a minute. All barrels were within five to eight feet of the crewmembers. It was loud and lethal.

We did not adhere to the "Die, motherfucker, die," three-second-burst mantra I've heard was taught at the grunt M-60 ranges. Supposedly by squeezing the trigger and slowly repeating the "Die, motherfucker, die" incantation, about three seconds elapsed. The shooter was then to give the barrel a slight rest and reapply as necessary; this prolonged barrel longevity. The M-60 range guys would shudder at a Huey driver's technique. We got on the trigger and marched the tracers around in the target area. Three seconds was rare, good thing our barrels were cooled in our slipstream.

Rocket runs were much more ear-friendly, though the crewchief and the gunner might still be cranking out the 7.62 ball and tracer ammunition. The rocket pods, one on each side, carried either seven or nineteen rockets. Most of us preferred the sevens, since they were lighter and offered less flat-plate area for the bird to drag through the air. The Huey behaved better with the small pods. Staying up with the flight might even be a problem with the big ones, and on especially hot, windless days, just getting airborne with the large pods required exceptional pilot technique. We had to skim and skip along the runway at max power, eventually nursing the bird into flight.

The rocket pods housed 2.75-inch Folding Fin Aerial Rockets (FFAR), the same ones fired from jets. Rockets were area weapons. Hitting anything you aimed at was more chance than skill. Their accuracy was substantially improved in 1966 when the factory ordnance guys cut tapers in the four rocket motor exhaust nozzles. Then they rotated the nozzles 90 degrees one nozzle to the next. This innovation caused the rockets to spin in flight, better stabilizing them and improving accuracy. This was by no means a panacea. Rockets had minds of their own.

The Huey's power plant was a reliable 1,100-horsepower Lycoming turbine engine. Fuel was metered to the engine by a fuel control, which responded to any perceived increase or decrease in engine RPM. If it failed, pilots could resort to emergency fuel control and meter fuel to the engine with a motorcycle style twist-grip under the pilot's left palm. We all practiced emergency fuel operations just in case, though I never had a fuel control malfunction in more than 1,500 hours of Huey flying. The helo carried enough jet fuel for two hours of flight and ferry tanks could be added in the cabin to extend range.

The bird was moved around on the ramp or in the hangars by fitting ground handling wheels to attachment points on skid tube pivot points. Then, using a tow bar and a tractor, the helo could be pulled and pushed as needed.

When I was in 'Nam, only VMOs flew Hueys. The name "observation" was a holdover from the Korean War when the squadron was heavily involved in adjusting artillery and naval gunfire and in controlling jet attacks on close air support (CAS) targets. We still did all that, but most of the work VMOs did in Vietnam was with guns and rockets. We aided the lift helos into and out of landing zones by providing suppressive fire. We also helped the infantry units when the opportunity presented itself, but usually we escorted the lift helos.

Aircraft composition in the squadrons reflected the mission; twenty gunbirds and four unarmed "slicks" were assigned, but we never had the full number. Battle damage held our numbers down and one or more were usually undergoing periodic "depot level" maintenance in Osaka, Japan.

During my part of the war, 1966–67, only two VMOs were in Vietnam, VMO-6 at Ky Ha near Chu Lai, and VMO-2 at Marble Mountain in the Danang area. Later in the war, aircraft and missions fragmented. What the

UH-1Es did in 1966 and 1967 was largely portioned out to AH-1s, a redesigned attack model of the UH-1, and to the OV-10A. The trusty Hueys were assigned to HMLs (Helicopter Marine Light), but they were still armed and dangerous.

The Huey's systems were reasonably simple compared to other turbine-driven helos. Later in my career I flew CH-53s, which were nightmares of complexity and redundancy compared to the UH-1E.

Hueys were versatile and well constructed with good crash-survivable cabins. I once had an engine failure on takeoff at nearly maximum gross weight. We slammed down, the tail boom broke off, the rotor mast snapped and tumbled forward over the cabin, the cross-tubes spread, the skid-tubes were nearly yanked from the airframe, but when the bird came to a rest, we simply turned off switches, unstrapped, opened the doors, and stepped out. Many lives were saved by the cabin strength.

The rotor head came in two variations, the 204 head, which we had in VMO-1 and VMO-6, and the 540 head, which the Corps went to in the 1967–68 time frame. The 204 head was lighter, fast enough to produce 120 knots, and less inclined to rotor RPM decay when power demands were rapidly increased. The 540 head was heavier and faster. Top speed went to 140 knots, but its heaviness caused rotor RPM decay if power demands were too rapid.

The 540 head also "flew" differently than the 204, and required new pilot techniques for autorotation. It was inclined to "balloon" on autos. The first three or four autos I practiced with the 540 were embarrassing. Although I could do these in my sleep with the 204, when I used the same stick and collective positions with the 540, I ended up fifty feet in the air. You're supposed to be at eight feet or so. But in VMO-6 we flew the 204 head. I was happy with that, since I'd trained on it in the States.

That the UH-1 series of helos was the workhorse of the Army in the 1960s and 1970s is apparent from any Vietnam War movie. Although the Corps had them in spare numbers, assigned only to VMOs, the Army had them by the hundreds.

Every military pilot is nostalgic about the aircraft he flew. I surely am. To me the Huey was simply a great helo, versatile, strong, simple, and fun. I always felt safe in it, but maybe I would have in any aircraft I flew daily. I look back on those days as the most rewarding in my life from a "job satisfaction" view. I wish I'd been a squadron pilot for life, but advancement and circumstance drew me away from the cockpit and the crews. Still a man can dream and long; I have since the Huey days.

EXECUTION BEATS THE SHIT OUT OF TRAINING

Stateside flying is and was training. It's essential and satisfying to a degree; you master the aircraft, learn its system, and get radio procedures down so you don't make a complete ass of yourself when you key the mic. But it's not nearly as satisfying as mission flying, especially combat mission flying.

Like all pilots new to an aircraft I studied, practiced, and was tested. This was not necessarily fun, but although I haven't been in a Huey cockpit for many years, I can still recite most of the aircraft systems lost if the main generator fails. I learned the aircraft well.

I flew the helo through a series of programmed instructional hops with some already-competent, more senior guy who showed me how to execute maneuvers and corrected my screwups until I fell within the pale of acceptability. Like all other pilots, I had "check rides" on which I demonstrated skill competence and systems knowledge.

I was prepared as well as the already-qualified guys could make me for the missions I eventually flew. But the heart and soul of Marine aviation, where it all comes together in a more meaningful way, where air crews actually provide some service to the greater effort, is in mission execution. And even though missions can be similar in type, they usually are made different by changing circumstance. Examples of these adjustments are: supported unit, geography, crew, flight leader, number of helos, enemy action at or near a landing zone, radio frequencies, and call signs. Variety, both internal to a mission type and in the ways the Hueys were employed, made flying them interesting.

Here is a list of the kinds of missions we flew in 'Nam:

- Armed escort for troop insertion/extraction, medevac, and ground convoys
- Medevac pickup
- Small unit insertion/extraction (recon teams mostly)
- Aerial reconnaissance
- VIP hauling
- Tactical Air Control (TAC) of jet attack aircraft and overall coordination of major aviation ops
- Spotting/adjusting for artillery/Naval gunfire
- Small units' resupply
- Admin runs for the delivery/pickup of people, aircraft parts, and supplies
- Test flights

Training was necessary and it continued in Vietnam for all FNGs (fuckin' new guys); we learned the terrain, the special radio procedures, and honed our helo tactics. We knew how to fly, but needed fine-tuning on tactical employment.

Execution makes for excitement, especially so in an environment of danger. At the end of the day, I felt a more solid sense of satisfaction from combat mission flying than from the CONUS (continental United States) training days. I believed I'd contributed something. It's like practicing on the violin for months, then someone tells you Itzak, who was supposed to perform, has the trots. All eyes turn to you; it's down to your sad and now fretting ass. But you go, you do, and it's well received. You can practice your ass off, but the real McCoy is in a different class. Execution beats the shit out of getting ready. Vietnam was virtually all execution.

PART 1

Early Going

CHAPTER 1

Geography and the CO

GETTING THERE

Permanent Change of Station orders come ultimately from Headquarters, United States Marine Corps. Downhill the missive came, out of the Navy Annex next to Arlington Cemetery in Washington from where the Corps was run, to Headquarters, 2nd Marine Aircraft Wing at Cherry Point, North Carolina, then to Marine Aircraft Group 26, at New River, North Carolina, and finally into my squadron, Marine Observation Squadron 1 (VMO-1). My ass was moving as a replacement pilot to a distant place, to the Asian war in Vietnam. They were kind. I received the notice a couple of months in advance of the March 1966 transfer, time enough to get my affairs arranged. I left my black 1963 Corvette coupe (doesn't every young man need one?) with my Dad. I stored the other accoutrements a twenty-five-year old doesn't need for war and reduced my trappings to a sea bag and a small locker box.

I, along with two lieutenants, Barney Ross and Steve Wilson, and Capt. K. D. Waters, received orders to the 1st Marine Aircraft Wing, which was at the time in Vietnam. We said our good-byes and headed for San Francisco aboard a civilian jetliner. A military bus took us to nearby Travis Air Force Base for a day or two of flailing around before a second commercial jetliner delivered us to Okinawa. We stayed a couple days at a Marine facility named Camp Butler on Oki for more processing.

If you're the kinda person who likes gamma globulin shots in the ass, you'd love Camp Butler. They were administered proportionate to a man's weight. These shots hurt like hell and I felt sorry for the big guys. We were told they helped counter hepatitis; we dutifully lined up and were poked.

The briefers lectured us on the importance of salt tablet regimen (I understand they no longer believe in this!) and other need-to-know topics for Vietnam-bound Marines. We signed documents, listened to talkers, and were herded around. Then, following a bus ride, we boarded an Air Force C-124. These have been out of the Air Force inventory for years, but in the 1960s they were still used for long-range, heavy hauling. They were powered by reciprocating, radial engines and droned along at a snail's pace. We read and napped, and finally arrived at the Danang Airbase in the northern part of South Vietnam.

I held my breath on our landing. I thought we'd at least be shot at; I was new to war and didn't know what to expect. I kept this idea to myself. I didn't want anyone to think I was crazy or chicken-shit before I even got into combat.

After a day at another processing center, we had our orders endorsed and all four of us were assigned to Marine Aircraft Group 36 (MAG-36) at Ky Ha. It was fifty miles south of Danang, along the coast and adjacent to the Marine air strip at Chu Lai. We got on a Marine C-130 for the short flight, and then into the ass-end of a truck for the fifteen-minute ride from Chu Lai to Ky Ha. We checked in with the Group Headquarters, and since the four of us were UH-1E pilots, we were assigned to VMO-6, the only UH-1E squadron in the Group. The call sign of VMO-6 was "Klondike." For the next thirteen months, whenever I keyed the aircraft mic to transmit on any of the helo's three radios (HF, UHF, and FM), I identified myself as "Klondike." In a way I still do.

The squadron guys welcomed us; the Admin people took our Officer Qualification Records, which reflected our past in the Marines. Mine, like those of Ross and Wilson, was damn short. The Operations people took our pilot's log books and aviation training records. Then someone showed us the ropes, where everything was, and assigned us our living spaces. At the morning officers' meeting we were introduced, and within three days we were all on the flight schedule, flying copilot to the seasoned VMO-6 pilots.

Barney Ross, Steve Wilson, and I were all still second lieutenants; our lot was copilot for about a three-month period. Captain Waters, since he was senior, began flying as pilot in command within a month. That was justice.

We lieutenants were assigned miscellaneous pop-up jobs, but Waters went to aircraft maintenance, since that was his background. Our lives and our educations began anew. But this time it was mostly about the procedures used in the spectrum of missions we flew: who and when we called on the radios and what to say; navigational aids that fixed our positions relative to airbases; the terrain in general; and map-reading skills.

Emphasis had shifted. It was no longer how to fly, it was how to do the mission. Through all this, we began learning the personalities of our new squadron mates, who was clever, who was all business, who was moody and short-fused, who you'd rather be around, and who you'd rather not. We humans sort each other, so we sorted away. The squadron had a fistful of lieutenants and I gravitated to them. It was nicer hanging out with officers of my own rank; I could relax and get out of the "sir" mode. Most of my hooch-mates were lieutenants or recently promoted captains. It was a good fit. Barney and Steve lived in other buildings nearby. I was the only FNG in my hooch, but it was okay. I was well accepted and soon felt at home.

We fell into the squadron routine of eating, flying, showering, reading and writing letters, sometimes hitting the bar, chatting, making meetings each morning, and otherwise doing what was asked. Some of life was boring, some of it interesting, and some of it way too exciting. But I had arrived, the end product of two-and-a-half years of training, first in Pensacola, then in VMO-1. It was show time.

CLIMATE AND TOPOGRAPHY

Anyone really interested can find a bunch of information on these boring subjects in books or on the Internet, so I'll keep this short. For openers, Vietnam is on the same latitude as Honduras, just 14 degrees above the equator. This says much; it was hot, and, since it borders a large body of water, it was humid. The average temperature was in the 80s. No wonder people living there are slender. A fat ass has to be a rarity in that temperature and humidity. Sweating is what we did for about eight months of the year. Then there was the fall monsoon season, during which it rained almost every day, often in sheets. We counted thirty-four straight days of rain in the monsoon season of 1966. Although it was not really cold in the monsoons and in the short winter that followed, at least not cold like a Kansas winter, we were chilled. We'd gotten used to the heat.

For the rainy season, we were issued hooded ponchos; these were fabric with a green rubberized coating. They leaked at both the shoulder and neck seams; soon the flight suit beneath was wet and uncomfortable. But ponchos provided some protection and, though we bitched and moaned, we were happy to have them.

Flight operations were often curtailed in the worst of this weather, but helos can go in pretty bad weather. We usually did. After the monsoons and the short winter, which ended in February, it heated up again in a hurry. We marched right back into hot, bright, and humid. Air-conditioning was not any place I was, except (wouldn't ya know!) the Air Force compound in Danang. At Ky Ha we just sweat, though we normally got a daytime breeze from the ocean that made life a bit less unpleasant.

Humidity caused rust; we had to be especially careful with firearms. If you're there to shoot, you need to be able to. Our ordnance men were busy fighting oxidation, assuring our M-60s were lubricated and operating, and we had a bunch of M-60s, four per gunbird, plus the door mounts for the crew-chief and gunner. I kept my sidearm, a .38 Smith and Wesson revolver, oiled and wrapped in plastic. It hung in a holster from my web-belt. Like the M-60s, it had to be cleaned and oiled frequently. This is just the sort of stuff I don't like to do. But it was essential and I did it.

■ ■ ■

The Marines were assigned to "I Corps," the northernmost military division of South Vietnam. Topography there was pretty simple. We had white sandy beaches and dunes and the South China Sea to the east, several wide river valleys, which slowly narrowed as they ran west from the coast, a sandy coastal plain four to six miles in width, followed by mountainous terrain. The mountains only rose to about three thousand feet and never jutted above the tree line.

Fishing dominated the coastal regions and the mouths of rivers; rice farming and other small-plot agriculture characterized the lowland valleys. The inland hills were covered with low growth and tall "elephant" grass and the mountains of the uplands were shrouded in jungle vegetation, sometimes triple-canopy.

The land we overflew was striking in color contrasts. Blue-green ocean and white sands on the east, deep red clay soil farther inland, exposed sometimes from artillery and bomb impacts, and a variety of hues of green from the vegetation. To set it off nicely, in the warm months we usually had white puffy cumulus-nimbus clouds over the hills and mountains. The view was spectacular, the kind especially rewarding to aviators.

Villages and hamlets dotted the countryside, and houses were mostly constructed of bamboo with thatched roofs. They were picturesque and deadly. The country was beautiful, worth seeing. I've toyed with going back, but I may run out of time.

THE SKIPPER, KLONDIKE SIX

For openers, the "Six" of any Marine Corps organization is the commanding officer. So, if I was ever on the radio and the "Six" (e.g., Roughrider Six) was on the other end, I knew I was talking with the decision maker.

Also, I need to offer a few words about the term "skipper." Before driven by curiosity to find out, I never understood how the Marine Corps and Navy came up with the word. I knew it went way back in history and was nautical in origin. For instance, "It was the Schooner Hesperus that sailed the wintery sea; and the skipper [see!] had taken his daughter along to bear him company." But the term "skipper" always made me smile inside a bit, never on the outside, I can avoid an ass chewing with the best. My mind, however, goes where it wants and down through the years my lips would curl ever so slightly at comments like, "Knock that shit off. Here comes the skipper." I would certainly "knock off" whatever shit I was doing, but my mind would drift into irreverence, to an image of a man skipping in our direction. Skipping fits with jacks and hopscotch. It has zero to do with commanding a military organization, with all the experience, dignity, and rank appropriate to the responsibility. Still, we have "skippers" and I suppose, since military institutions stand on tradition like few others, we will have nonskipping skippers well into the future.

I have since come to know, by the way, that a ship was called a scip in England in the 1700s. A scipper was a shipman, which over time mutated into "skipper" and came to mean the captain of a ship. The Marine Corps is a naval organization and borrows language from that nautical tradition; bulkhead, ladder, hatch, port and starboard, and skipper are examples. For most of my tour, VMO-6's skipper was Lt. Col. Bill Maloney.

Major Maloney, at least he was prior to his promotion in our squadron, joined the Klondike in July 1966, after I'd been part of the organization for about four months. Almost immediately a different, steadier, calmer atmosphere descended.

We'd had a series of three interim bosses, senior majors, good men insofar as my junior ass could tell, but not men hand-picked and sent to the squadron to command it. They were already part of the unit and just moved up a chair when the prior CO was transferred or, in one case, killed. The middle of these three majors, Bill Goodsell, only had the helm for six days before he was killed in action. From what I knew he was a super guy and a hell of a Marine. His death was a sobering sadness to all, even those of us deployed aboard the USS *Princeton*, as I was at the time. Even now, years later, the words "killed in action" cause me to look up, stare out the window, and try to understand the significance of what it must have meant to those who loved him. It's incomprehensible.

We in the squadron were stunned, but the flight schedules did not cease; we were distracted by demands and could only ponder these events in between other activity. This was probably good. I lost two hooch-mates in Vietnam, two captains, Leon G. Chadwick and Brook M. Shadburne, good guys, good sticks, gone. Their stuff was packed and within a month someone else was in their space. Although memorials were held at the chapel, the flight schedule didn't miss a beat. These were sobering but not debilitating events, unlike how they must have been for their families.

The rotational commanders' scenario happened way above the head of any lieutenant, but if stability is important in a command, we didn't have it for my first months in the squadron. I have no unsavory memories of our series of majors, nor any kudos to offer, but I served under Lieutenant Colonel Maloney for nine months, July 1966 to April 1967, when I rotated to the States. I liked it.

Even though he was senior, he made himself known to his squadron. And even though juniors assessing seniors is frowned upon, how can you avoid it? You can't just turn off your mind. From my sparrow's-eye view, I could tell he was a great commander: open, friendly, warm by disposition, approachable, willing to listen, yet strong and confident in his intellect and judgment, and a capable speaker. The ceremonial formations we had were marked by competence at the microphone, rather than an embarrassment of stumbling around, awkwardly searching for expression. He also had what the Corps calls "presence," an air of dignity and unflappability. He was not arrogant and presumptuous, nor was he inclined to throw his weight around or cow people. He was a sensible, bright, supportive commander who took a genuine interest in subordinates. Lieutenant Colonel Maloney learned our first names and used them, flew with us all regularly, often as copilot, and he led many flights. He was not the sort to say "sic 'em"; he was no shit in the cockpit at the controls of the Huey.

I never walked up to chat with him unless addressed or summoned. This lieutenant was a hair uneasy around rank, but he was open to all. He did a fine job and I was happy to have worked for him, albeit down in the pile somewhere and indirectly. I liked the idea that he represented Klondike guys at periodic meetings for squadron commanders with the MAG skipper and his staff. I respected and liked him, and the respect came not just from his rank; he'd earned it as a man.

As a side issue, I envied his herringbone utilities; they were holdovers from the 1950s and wearing them signaled to other Marines that he was no rookie. Rank might have shown that, but the herringbones stamped him for sure.

Lieutenant Colonel Maloney went on to become mighty in the Corps. He commanded an Air Wing and eventually achieved the rank of Lieutenant General (three stars!). He was the Deputy Chief of Staff for Manpower when I showed up for a Headquarters Marine Corps tour in the mid-1980s. I had not seen him for almost twenty years, but one day there he was in the ladder-well (staircase to the uninitiated) with three horse-holders in his wake. I was heading up; they were going the other way. But when he saw me, one of his old lieutenants, he slowed and stopped. I was flattered, almost speechless, yet I also felt remarkably comfortable. He and I had secrets the others could not begin to fathom: We were Klondike men. And these are not mere words; they were seared into our psyches with the branding iron of common experience in deadly circumstance. We chatted but briefly; much of what we communicated was nonvocal. It was a mutual salute, an acknowledgment of the past. Then we got on with our separate tasks. I will not forget the encounter.

He is one of four Marines for whom I worked who even today could ask me to dig a hole and I'd simply grab a shovel. He was and is, though now retired, a hell of a Marine.

CHAPTER 2

Capt. Steve Shoemaker, "Rocketman"

Since World War II, military aircraft usually fly either in sections of two, with one pilot designated as the section leader, or in divisions of four, with the overall flight lead pilot designated as the division leader. Within a division of four there are two sections of two aircraft each. So, even though the division leader is the "in charge" guy, he has two immediate subordinates, his own wingman and the leader of the second section.

In May of 1966 we were out on an escort mission for a troop insertion near the coast south of Chu Lai. Capt. Larry Wright was the division (four birds) leader, with Capt. Bill Huffcut his wingman. Capt. Larry Downey led the second section (two birds) within Wright's division. Capt. Steve Shoemaker was Downey's wingman and I was Shoemaker's copilot. Shoe and I were then dead-assed last in the flight of four. The call sign for our flight was Klondike twelve dash six. So Wright was Klondike twelve dash six "Lead"; his wingman was "Dash two"; Downey was "Dash three"; and Shoemaker was "Dash four."

As copilot, like other copilots, I helped by switching radio frequencies at the dictate of the division or section leader or whenever Shoemaker asked. I also followed along on the 1:50,000-meter map to ensure the lead bird (Wright) was taking us to the briefed grids instead of just somewhere in Southeast Asia. This also served to keep map-reading skills honed. In addition to radio and map-reading chores, I threw the necessary switches to select ordnance for the pilot in command when targets were attacked.

Sometimes I was given the controls. This happened with some regularity. Most of the pilots were good about sharing, as opposed to hogging, "stick time." How else were we junior guys to retain skill or get better? When, however, the helo was in a particularly demanding part of a flight, one warranting the skills of a more seasoned guy, the pilot in command usually and understandably kept the controls.

This time the inserted grunt unit was company-sized, short one of its platoons, and required twelve CH-34s. (A company had a small command element and three platoons of about forty Marines each.) The CH-34s were the older lift helos; most lift squadrons still flew them and I trained in them at Pensacola during the terminal stage of flight school. They were great but aging birds with radial reciprocating engines, spark plugs, carburetors, that sort of technology, but they carried less than the newer CH-46s, which were coming online in the mid-1960s. These newer helos were turbine-powered and able to carry more.

The squadron providing the lift CH-34s that day was Marine Medium Helicopter Squadron 362 (HMM-362). Their call sign was Clip Clop. The mission was briefed; we manned the gunbirds, launched, and rendezvoused with the 34s three miles south of the Chu Lai airstrip. No one expected trouble.

The VMO standard operating procedure (SOP) was to lead the lift helos to the zone and recon the zone with a low-level pass or two. Then, with the concurrence of the lift helos' leader on zone selection, the Huey crewchief in the lead gunbird often tossed a smoke grenade into the landing zone (LZ) to mark it and to show wind direction and velocity for the landing helos. Sometimes the lift guys preferred that the zone not be marked with smoke to keep any bad guys in the area from knowing where the flight was landing. This day they wanted smoke. Wright located and marked the zone and we all buzzed down for one pass looking for trouble. Nothing seemed threatening and a report was made to Clip Clop Lead that the zone was clear for the insertion. The LZ was only large enough for a division, and the first four CH-34s started down. Just prior to touchdown, as they flared to kill airspeed, came the transmission, "Clip Clop Lead taking fire from the left side tree line, 150 meters."

Wright and Huffcut were covering the right. Downey and Shoemaker (and me) the left. Since the heat was coming from our side, we were up to bat. When Clip Clop made his report, Downey was already in a run, though he was not delivering ordnance, just posing a threat. He was deep in his run, abeam the tree line and out of position to put suppressive fire on the trouble area. But Downey's crewchief started hammering with his M-60 from his left-side door mount.

"Dash three is past the target," Downey radioed. "Dash four, you got the tree line Clip Clop's talkin' about? Over."

"Klondike twelve Dash six, Dash four has it and we're in with guns," responded Shoemaker. The CH-34 flight had not waved off the landing, but pressed on into the zone discharging Marines, who quickly spread out and set up a perimeter to help protect the next division and the other Marines coming in.

Just before Shoe began his attack run, he keyed the ICS, "Dave, guns and go hot."

"Roger, guns hot," I countered and I turned a selector knob and threw a toggle on the lower part of the center console. We nosed over, sliding down the invisible hill, gaining speed. Shoe lined up the target area in the black crosshairs of a reticle he swung down from its pivot above the windscreen. He pulled the trigger and the familiar rattling barks of four M-60s filled the cockpit. I watched as the orange-red tracers found their way, first into the tree line nearest us, then up its length. Shoe made slight nose position adjustments with the cyclic (stick) and marched the bullets the length of the trees adjacent the LZ. When he completed hosing down the trees, he raised the nose, added full power, and climbed to the left. Both the crewchief and gunner had watched and heard, each vigilant for muzzle flashes. The crewchief pumped bursts into the tree line as we climbed left.

Shoe made the standard report when a gunbird finished its attack: "Klondike Dash four off target." I threw our arming switches, disabling the guns so Shoe, by mistake, would not squirt rounds into the countryside.

"Roger, Dash four," responded Downey. "We'll be in position for run shortly."

Clip Clop Lead left the zone during the end of our gun run. I watched the telltale dust and debris clouds created when helos add power. "Clip Clop Lead lifting." The other three helos from the initial wave made no report, but all four pulled up and nosed over as one. They gained speed and altitude, climbing to the right, away from the tree line. The door gunners and crewchiefs in the lift birds sprayed any suspect or threatening areas as they came up and out; the trees got special attention. Since there was not enough room to bring Wright's section into action on our side, he and Huffcut stayed on the right and made dummy gun runs on the side opposite the offending trees.

As the second division of CH-34s approached the zone, Downey radioed, "Klondike Dash three in hot with guns." Shoe and I were at one thousand feet above ground level (AGL). We'd climbed in a left arc and flew 180 degrees from our run-in heading. Our Huey strained to get back in position for another attack. I watched Downey's run. His bird nosed over; after a few seconds his guns blazed, a fine trail of brass casings and metal links spewing from the sides of his guns. Barely visible flashes came from the M-60 muzzles. Quick bursts came from his crewchief's door mount.

"Mighta scared 'em away," I offered.

"Probably," responded Shoe, "We'll just keep working it over until the last 34s are out."

"Klondike, Dash three off target," came the call from Downey.

"Roger, Dash three. We're about in position," answered Shoe.

"Clip Clop Lead to division, any damage? Over." A ripple of reporting followed from the first four CH-34s. Lead had taken some hits. No one else. But two other divisions had yet to get in and out of the zone.

"Lead has several hits high in the main cabin; no one's hurt. My systems seem okay." The metalsmiths at HMM-362 would fashion small patches, rivet them on, and paint them. To the unpracticed eye, no evidence of war would be apparent, but a helo guy in the late 1960s and 1970s would know at a glance the aircraft's history. All helos assigned to Vietnam had patches. Some had many.

We flew into position for a second run. The second division had landed and discharged troops. "Clip Clop Dash five and flight is lifting." As a unit, the second four CH-34s lifted, blew debris and sand, tucked their noses, and gained speed and altitude.

"Klondike Dash four, in hot," radioed Shoemaker. Down we went. I threw the necessary switches and he repeated his first attack, sweeping the tree line with bullets from rattling M-60s.

"Dash four is off target," he radioed again as he again pulled up and to the left. Once more the crewchief peppered the target area. The final division of CH-34s neared the LZ just vacated by the second four. These guys were pros, no piecemealing the insertion. They built up the forces on the ground quickly. "Clip Clop Dash nine on final," came the radio report.

Downey radioed the beginning of another run to cover the landing CH-34s and by the time we were again in attack position, the last 34s were coming out. "Clip Clop Dash nine is lifting." Shoe radioed another gun attack and we made our last pass. All birds were in and out; only one was damaged.

As we pulled up, a new voice came over the radio. "Clip Clop Lead, this is Roundup One Four. Over." It was a Forward Air Controller (FAC) assigned to the grunt company.

FACs were aviators on tours of duty with infantry units for the control of CAS. After the unit call sign, FACs had the numeral designation of "One Four." I was always comforted talking to one of my own, yet felt a hair of pity. Normally the only reason any aviator would go on an FAC assignment was to avoid an unpleasant boss or some other even less okay job. Although I don't mind camping out occasionally, lugging all my stuff and "living out" is another matter. I have great and abiding respect for the infantry, but mostly I need a cot when my work is done. A hot meal is a hell of a good idea as well, and fleas, chiggers, mosquitoes, leeches, and the like are depressing to even think about.

That was my attitude and, if pressed, the attitude of most aviators, maybe all. But some aviators had to be FACs and they performed super. They already knew the "aviator speak" and were used to jabbering on radios. Still, rather than volunteering, they were usually assigned.

"Roundup One Four, this is Clip Clop Lead. Go ahead. Over."

"Roger Clip Clop Lead. This is One Four. Can you tell us where the fire came from? Over." The FAC was good, unexcited, matter-of-fact. Just collecting info for the company commander.

"Roundup One Four, we landed on a heading of about 330 and took the heat on final. We think from the trees and about nine o'clock from our landing heading and maybe 100 to 150 meters from the LZ. We only took a few rounds. Over." Clip Clop answered.

"One Four copies. We'll be sweepin' in that direction shortly. Break. Klondike Lead, this is Roundup One Four. Over."

After a brief pause, Captain Wright answered, "Roundup One Four, this is Klondike Lead. Go ahead."

During this conversation we'd climbed out and followed Downey in a left-hand racetrack pattern over the suspect tree line. The lift helos were out of the zone and forming up to the northeast at 1,500 feet AGL.

"Klondike Lead, Roundup One Four. We're wondering if you can keep the guns on station a while? Over."

Wright responded immediately. "This is Klondike Lead, you betcha, Roundup. We've got thirty-plus minutes of loiter time and plenty of ammo. Break, Clip Clop, unless you have some heartburn, we'll stick around. If you need us on the drive home, we'll be up this freq. Over."

Clip Clop Lead answered first. "No problem, Klondike. We're takin' the beach route. If someone goes down, we'll call. See ya later. Out." The CH-34s had already turned northeast, heading for the coast, the white sand of the beaches, and the flight north, first to Chu Lai then Ky Ha. They'd debrief, talk to the squadron Intel guys about the small-arms fire, then head for their other squadron jobs, the hooches, other missions, or into whatever routine they'd fallen.

Then the FAC answered, "Roger, Klondike Lead. Roundup will be making a sweep toward the tree line where Clip Clop took fire. You might keep an eye on the area for us. Charlie could try to deedee [deedee means leave in a hurry]. Over."

"Okay, Roundup One Four. We'll be watchin'. Break. Klondike Dash three, keep your section over the tree line. We'll take position farther southwest. Over," Wright responded.

Downey acknowledged. We continued our watch of the trees. Wright and Huffcutt swung around our pattern to stations southwest of us but in the direction the grunts were moving.

Then it came. We were just turning through the 90-degree position to our previous run-in heading, perfectly in position for an attack into the same area.

"Damn! Captain Shoe," the crewchief, Sergeant Alexander, said into the ICS, "we got a runner."

"Where?" Shoemaker asked. But before Alexander could answer, we knew. There he was trucking down the paddy dike that angled away from the tree line to the southwest.

"He's there, sir, out in the open just west of the trees. He's smokin'. You got him?" Alexander responded.

"Yeah," Shoe answered. He was already turning the Huey in the runner's direction. "Rockets, hot, Dave." I turned the knobs and threw a toggle. Each time Shoe pumped the trigger a jolt of current would launch two 2.75-inch rockets, one from each pod.

"Klondike Dash three, this is Dash four. We got a runner. We're in on him. Over," Shoemaker radioed to Downey and implicitly to Wright; both had authority to deny Shoe's attack.

"We see him. We'll follow," responded Downey. Wright remained silent, which meant assent.

We were already sliding down the hill again, this time with rockets. Shoemaker later said he thought we were getting low on 7.62 after three gun runs. But, whatever the reason, we were in hot with pairs of 2.75s. He made sure the helo was in balanced flight and "wings" level, otherwise he'd be squirting rockets all over hell and back instead of where the helo was heading. He lined up the hatless man who wore the traditional black pajamas, and he had leaves from some tropical plants wedged in a belt. The leaves protruded both up and down. No one could mistake his effort at camouflage.

"You're on pairs and hot," I said.

"Sergeant Alexander, be ready to stay on this guy," Shoemaker said into the ICS.

"We're ready, sir," Alexander answered. Both the crewchief and the door gunner hunched over their M-60s.

As I've said before, and anyone with experience knows, 2.75 FFARs are definitely area weapons, not designed nor expected to be pinpoint accurate. But that day you would not have known it. That afternoon months of practice and experience and some blind-assed luck came together. Shoemaker steadied the UH-1E in its descent, led the running man the amount he judged necessary and squeezed. Two 2.75s came sizzling out of their tubes. We watched in rapt fascination as the rightmost of the two rockets made a beeline to intersect the advance of the runner. I thought for certain it would strike him. It didn't; it hit the dike no more that a foot to his front. He was blown into the brown, calf-high, fetid (they used human and animal offal in these) rice paddy water.

After a moment of stunned and reverent silence, "You're shittin' me," I said into the ICS and looked over at Shoe.

"Good shot, Captain Shoe," Alexander echoed my sentiment from the rear.

Shoemaker smiled. "Lucky shot," he responded; likely he was stunned like the rest of us. He adjusted the Huey's nose position and added power. We pulled up.

As we started our climb, Alexander came up on the ICS again. "Damn, sir. Charlie's gettin' up!" And Alexander started hammering away with his M-60.

The guy was up, first to his hands and knees, then to a standing position, and finally scrambling onto the dike. Water kicked up around him from Alexander's 7.62 rounds. The VC started hauling ass again. He was stroking, some of the green camouflage leaves he'd poked around in his belt had survived. They flapped and swayed vigorously as he ran. Although Alexander kept the rounds heading his way, the guy made it to the relative safety of trees, bushes, and brush at the end of the dike, and disappeared.

Downey came up on FM. "We saw most of that, Dash four. Klondike Dash three is in hot on the trees."

"Roger, Dash three," Shoe answered. "We'll come around for another pass."

We worked over that area for several passes using both guns and rockets. Shoemaker and I took turns on these attacks. The running man did not reappear. Wright held his section out of the action.

Finally Downey figured we'd done about all we could. "Dash four, let's give it a rest. We'll snoop around for other targets." We loitered and reconned making lazy patterns with occasional swoops over potential hiding places and trouble spots.

"Klondike Lead, Roundup One Four. We're on line beginning our sweep. Over."

Wright answered, "Roger, Roundup. We'll be on station a while longer. We had one guy movin' out smartly a few minutes ago. Probably the guy that shot at Clip Clop. Nothing else. He disappeared into trees and brush about one hundred meters past the tree line you're headin' for. Over."

We watched as the grunts moved forward, advancing on line. They were in the open, some slogged through the paddies, others walked on the dikes. They closed on the tree line from which Clip Clop had taken fire and disappeared into the foliage. Not a shot was fired.

After a few minutes they called again. They were continuing the sweep. We watched another on-line advance, and they slowly closed on and entered the copse of trees and bushes where our running man had disappeared. Downey called them to make sure they knew of the potential danger. They acknowledged.

Then "Roundup One Four, Klondike Dash three. Any evidence of our runner? Over." Downey called.

"We're still poking around, Klondike. Nothing yet. Over."

After a few more minutes Wright radioed, "Roundup, we're starting to run a little low on gas; unless you have something, we probably oughta head for the barn. Over."

"Wait one, Klondike, I'll check with the Six. Over," the FAC responded.

Within a minute came, "Klondike Lead, Six requests you work over the turf to our front, excluding the vil about two clicks out [a click is one thousand meters], wherever you see a likely place for Charlie, treed areas, brush, that sort of thing. A little recon by fire would be appreciated. Over."

"Roger Roundup, we'll look around and prep the area a bit. Over. Break. Klondike flight, maintain section integrity and make a couple of passes. Let's get rid of our rockets first. Acknowledge," Wright radioed.

Our sections made three passes each, rippling rockets into potential hiding places on the first two passes and expending most of our 7.62 ammo on the third. Wright and Huffcutt made a fourth attack run. We were almost out of ordnance, so Downey held our section high. It was over in fifteen minutes.

Wright's final call was, "Roundup One Four, Klondike's goin' home. We didn't flush anyone, but maybe did some softenin' up. Have a good day. Over."

"Okay, Klondike. Thanks for the support. Have a cold one for us. One Four, out."

Wright had already turned his gunship toward the northeast, the beach, and Ky Ha. We moved into a loose-as-hell fingertip formation, Downey and Shoe on the left and aft of the leader, Huffcut on the right. Before landing, we'd go into trail position (all helos lined up behind the leader), with about one hundred yards separating each. The rest of the flight was routine.

I've thought about that running VC many times. I'll never know if he made it or not. I'm a farm boy and I've repeatedly seen the menfolk wring a chicken's neck. Chickens make quite a few frantic headless circuits before flopping down and surrendering. The only way old Grandpa Travis Ballentine could keep one in an area was to trace a box in the dirt of our farmyard with a stick. Somehow the chicken knew not to leave that box. Maybe our running man was a goner, but his box was big. Part of me hopes he survived, that he has a great story to tell his grandkids about being knocked over by rocket blast, then running in a hail of machine-gun bullets until he reached the cover of some trees and his tunnel entrance. I'm ambivalent about this. Had he lived, he might have shot at our men and machines other times in that protracted war. This is not a good alternative.

My guess is the dike, made of dirt on top and mud underneath, absorbed much if not all of the shrapnel, and, although injured and suffering from blast concussion (bleeding and ringing ears, stomped chest, and disorientation), he somehow pulled through the rocket ordeal. Alexander's M-60 bullet hail was the second crisis, but if a guy is hit by a 7.62 round, he'd likely drop. The VC probably made it through that as well.

Shoemaker's remarkable rocket shot was the buzz of the ready room, the bar, and our hooches for a day or two. Then this small but amazing microcosm of war passed, overtaken by other activities, other feats, other missions, and the routine of our daily lives. Few would remember it today, maybe just Shoe and me. I remind him of it when I see him every few years at reunions.

CHAPTER 3

Embarrassments, Assessments, and a Job

FIRST LIEUTENANT MARTIN TEACHES US A LESSON

First Lt. Jim Martin (name changed to protect the guilty), like myself, had been a MARCAD. He'd earned pilot wings and a commission at the end of flight training and endured a year or so in a squadron as a second lieutenant before promotion. Second lieutenant is not a good rank to hold in a squadron. You are the junior guy, or at least one of them, and usually passed over as the pilot in command of aircraft in favor of officers with more rank. The Corps is rank-conscious, believing in its soul that the more senior guy has earned the nod and is less likely to fuck anything up. So, rank itself works against a second lieutenant. Then, of course, there is the simple truth that a guy wearing a brown bar *is* inexperienced. It's not just rank; it's fact. Second lieutenants are suspect; one must use caution, bring them along, nurture, ass chew, and watch them. They have not quite arrived, not yet. The world opened quite a bit when I was promoted to first lieutenant, and when I became a captain, well, there was little question that any cockpit-related job was completely within my competence.

Occasionally a junior guy, even a second lieutenant is thrown a bone; he gets a mission. Maybe no one else wants it, maybe it's so simple he can't screw it up, maybe the operations officer feels a tinge of fatherly compassion, or maybe the ops guys just made a typing mistake and decided to live with it. Who knows? But sometimes a really junior guy signs for the helo and launches as pilot in command, rather than as copilot to the more senior. And so it was with recently promoted First Lt. Jim Martin, the junior guy in VMO-6 before we FNG replacements began showing up. Yes, Jim was given a mission and my sad and even more junior ass was assigned as his copilot.

It was an easy task: Go to some grid coords, pick up a Korean general and party of three from a compound there, take them to an ARVN compound somewhere else, where they get briefed, feted, and fed. Wait there while all the hoopla was conducted and endured, until they got bored, until strained, pregnant silence descended, engulfing all in awkwardness. Then take the Koreans back to their compound, return to Ky Ha, give the ODO a quick dump of how everything went as scheduled, and hang out or head for the hooch. Piece o' cake!

Jim was just hauling people, so a slick was assigned. We went single bird, no chase. It was Jim, me, and Sergeant Bastien, the crewchief. Jim, as a gesture of efficiency, asked me to meet him at the aircraft and he took the details of the brief from the ODO. I went to the flight line and preflighted the bird, which was my practice even when I was not the pilot in command. I figured two sets of eyes were better than one, and, after all, my ass was strapping in too, not just his.

Jim arrived at the helo and gave Sergeant Bastien and me a quick overview of the mission. He looked the helo over as I had. We cranked her up, got taxi clearance, pulled into a hover, and headed for the runway. All was routine. I navigated us to the grid coordinates Jim provided from the ODO brief. He shot an approach to a large, clearly marked landing site in a compound. A flag was flying so we needed no smoke to show wind direction and velocity. If it's a small flag and straight out it's ten knots; straight out and popping is fifteen or more. Helo guys learn these little ass-saving truths as they move along.

Jim rolled the throttle to flight idle and Sergeant Bastien exited the helo to greet the Koreans. Once they arrived, he'd get them situated and strapped in on the red nylon web seats across the rear of the cabin. Even with my helmet on and through the noise of the helo, I could hear faint strains of music. I looked to our front right and about eighty yards across the LZ was a band, whistling and tooting away. Six apparent dignitaries, starched and puffed with importance, headed our way. They made a ludicrous effort to stay in step, the kind of failure that would cause any drill instructor, past or present, to moan, scream threats of violence, and start barking cadence. These guys were looking a hell of a lot like greeters, rather than folks coming to get in our bird.

Jim was closest to the oncoming entourage. After glancing at them a few moments, he turned to me with a look of mild concern. His look slowly drifted into bewilderment, and then, after a quick look at his kneeboard, epiphany! "Oh, fuck," he said with raised voice into the ICS. "I wonder if I got these damned coordinates back-asswards or something?"

We both knew the answer.

Sergeant Bastien looked expectantly into the Huey as if to ask, "What's my next move guys?" Sure enough, these were RVN bubbas, not the Korean Marines we were to pick up, and as they approached, it became increasingly known to them that the helo crew was in the aircraft, but no one else. They halted near our Huey; two came forward. They inquired first of Sergeant Bastien, who was having none of that shit. He motioned them to Jim's lowered sliding window and they walked over. Jim stumbled around verbally. He offered that there'd been some confusion an' all, but that we'd go get the Koreans forthwith. He fumed, made explanations, and waffled. You know, the sort of back-pedaling horseshit that many of us resort to when treed, a version of what I call the dancing bear routine.

I was amused. I probably should not have been, and I sure as hell could not let on that I was. Nope, I kept a steely visage, but inside I thought, "Oh shit, this is gonna be good when we see the ops officer." And I knew this gaffe would get around. For once I was thankful I was the copilot, navigator, radio freq switching helper, and not the pilot in command who'd received the brief and was responsible for the mission.

After a minute of pow-wow, the starched RVN guys headed back to their starting point; this time, mercifully, they made no effort to march. The band fell silent and Jim rolled on the throttle. Sergeant Bastien got back in the helo and we were off to right a wrong.

When we were airborne, Jim called Klondike Base on the Fox Mike radio to chat with the ODO. Sure enough, he'd screwed up or they had. Jim pulled in as much power as the 1,100-horsepower Lycoming could provide. We closed rapidly on the real pickup LZ. Unfortunately, when we had not arrived as scheduled, the Koreans inquired through their channels. In sequence, first our Air Group then our squadron was embarrassed.

The Group Operations people got a section of CH-34s on its way home from a resupply mission to divert and get the Koreans. They completed the mission. Klondike Base called us and told us to just come on home.

Although I commiserated with Jim during the flight home and after, there was no getting around the facts. As it turned out, the brief was accurate, but somehow Jim had screwed up the LZ sequence. Some "Ah, shits" from the Ops O followed and Jim explained his side of the rhubarb to anyone who'd listen. It died a slow death. The episode was the subject of many a ready room, O'club, and hooch rehash in the coming days. To his face the junior pilots were sympathetic and would say shit like, "It might have happened to anyone," and "It was perfectly understandable how a guy might screw up a brief and it was probably the ODO's fault anyway." But privately it was more like, "Damn, can you believe this shit . . ." We humans love to give a toe nudge to the down.

His blunder was hugely instructional. It demonstrated how a guy, even a pretty smart one, needed to pay damn close attention to all aspects of a brief, ask questions, think, and not just ease along in neutral. Otherwise he might fall victim to oversight. On this mission it didn't matter much; no one got shot up, hurt, or killed. On many missions, however, small oversights could result in huge consequence. Say a recon team is about to be overrun and you've been diverted from a mission to help, but you copy the wrong coordinates on your kneeboard and they *are* overrun. You'd feel the weight of that blunder all your days. It might destroy you. I like to think in the grand scheme there was a reason for Jim's episode.

Being mostly copilot was largely situational for Jim. He'd deployed to Vietnam with the squadron in 1965 and was the junior pilot. So, from a seniority view, the operations guys who scheduled pilots in seats had the entire list of aviators to work through before he was considered. That's a pretty good formula for a bunch of copilot time. I'm sure Jim flew other missions as pilot in command but I didn't pay much attention. I had other fish to fry; we all did. His rank relegated him mostly to second seat, not an ignominious assignment, just frustrating. It's best to make the decisions.

Unlike Jim, I and other junior guys joined VMO-6 as replacement pilots, swelling its pilot ranks and, like Jim, we usually played second fiddle. But our second fiddle playing had an end. In the late summer of 1966, the original members of VMO-6 completed their tours and rotated en masse back to the States. The squadron was left to those of us who'd been fed in piecemeal during the previous six months. All of us, including junior guys, got a full plate of pilot-in-command time. With the passage of time, I led sections. Indeed, my copilot often outranked me, but he was green, still learning the ropes of Vietnam missions, terrain, and radio procedures. This took a while, partly because we ranged all over I Corps from the DMZ up north to Quang Ngai in the south and partly because of the mission spectrum we flew.

We all flew virtually every day. The missions became routine, though we never knew when the routine would become nonroutine, when it required a man to draw on all his experience and make shit up on the fly. All helo drivers knew this. It truly was exciting stuff.

TRANSPORT HELO AND UH-1E VULNERABILITY

I've always had great respect for the helo air crews that did the lifting as a primary mission. VMOs did some of it, when it was a small unit (recon) insertion or extraction or when we were tasked to provide the medevac pickup helo and not just serve as its gunbird escort. But as a primary mission VMO guys did not insert, extract, and resupply Marines. That job was largely assigned to the pilots, crewchiefs, and gunners of the HMMs. They flew CH-34s and CH-46s.

The central mission of the lift helos made them more vulnerable. Helos are noisy; you can't "sneak up." When we flew into an area, people knew. If those people were hostile and armed, they'd grab a gun. Helos are also large and relatively slow moving. They are very slow moving on approach to or takeoff from an LZ. Worse yet, they are nonmoving, stationary targets while in an LZ. All of which is a formula for danger, excitement, and even disaster.

I could look it up, do some analysis, but I don't think I need to. I'm convinced the lift guys were hit more often than were the gunships. Sometimes my bird came home with bullet holes, but they were usually aft of the cabin area. Airspeed is responsible for that; they just weren't leading me enough. Conversely, the only time I was forced down by fire, I was on a medevac mission. I was a sitting duck, not a moving target.

So, hats off to the lift guys in the HMMs; carrying troops and stuff is a bit more risky than escorting the carriers, but nobody was home free: Every helo was holed, some did not come back at all, and many crewmembers were injured or killed. I've read statistics that reflect the hazards involved just for pilots. Among all Marine pilots killed in action (jets and helos), by a huge margin the helo community took the hit. And the most vulnerable rank was first lieutenant, officers like myself recently out of flight school. But no rank was untouched; generals were killed, as were sergeants major.

Although the lift pilots took more heat, their lives would have been even dicier without the help of the gunships. This is their opinion, one I've heard repeatedly at bars in Vietnam and at reunions. "Shit. Thanks for wadin' in on those bastards; they were hosing the hell outta us."

Stretching a single gunbird squadron over the activities of an entire air group required prioritization. Unescorted missions were gambles but the lift helo often flew these. This was sometimes bad news for those going.

WINGMAN TO CAPTAIN PERRYMAN, MY MAIDEN VOYAGE

In transport squadrons (CH-34s, CH-46s, and CH-53s), the pilots who signed for the helos and commanded the crews were Helicopter Aircraft Commanders (HACs). In Hueys, the pilot who signed for and commanded was simply a Pilot Qualified in Model (PQM). The different titles had to do with minimum crews. The lift birds required a copilot, crewchief, and door gunner. They required more of a "crew" than the UH-1Es. They had more of something to "command"; thus the title Helicopter Aircraft Commander. The Huey was a single-piloted helo, although it required an observer to give the pilot eyes out the aircraft's left side. So, Huey jocks were Pilots Qualified in Model and, when they signed for a bird, were pilots in command, not HACs, even though Hueys rarely flew single pilot, except on admin, test, or VIP hops. Normally we had a full complement of pilot, copilot, crewchief, and gunner. This is a good idea in combat. If one pilot is wounded, the other can bring the bird home.

Also, eight eyes are a hell of a lot better than four. Countless times the crewchief or door gunner reported we were taking fire or some other useful information, while I was busy with what was ahead of the helo. Finally, the door gunner and crewchief, each armed with a swivel-mounted M-60, helped protect the Huey from flank fire and kept the heads of bad guys down when we pulled off target.

As PQM, which I was well before arriving at VMO-6, I was qualified to sign for an aircraft. But I, like others just in from the States, was green. Not only was I green, I was a lieutenant, at the bottom of the officer food chain. So, for several months I flew as copilot, and, although I understand pecking orders, that shit got old. Reading maps, throwing switches, changing radio frequencies, and stirring the stick here and there at the pleasure of the pilot left me chomping at the bit. I was envious of Capt. K. D. Waters who, although we showed up in the squadron at the same time, flew as pilot in command soon after our arrival. I understood, bided my time, and flew as copilot, but my day would come. And it did.

I'd been recently promoted to first lieutenant, that is, from near ignominy to a person worthy of some trust. I had more that six hundred flight hours in the Huey, and I suppose no one could come up with a reason from observing my ability to hold me back. Then, of course, the old hands had to look to the future. It was May of 1966 and the original VMO-6 guys would rotate home in late summer. They'd leave the birds and missions to their replacements, to guys like me.

One afternoon I looked at the flight schedule for the next day and there I was, wingman to Capt. Jim Perryman. Ops had assigned us to escort some CH-34s on a resupply mission. My copilot was a guy with even less time in country than me. It was a good day; I knew this was the beginning, that breakout was at hand. If I didn't show my ass, I'd sign for helos and be in charge of a crew more often in the future. Once your cherry's broken, you're off and running, no turning back.

Of the original VMO-6 guys, Captain Perryman was one of the stalwarts. He had a good and well-deserved reputation for strength and level-headedness, someone who could stay cool when the shit hit the fan, one of the steady guys who did the hewing and carrying. We new guys looked to him and other experienced pilots for our in-country education. I viewed most of these men as founts of wisdom. They passed on the how-tos for combat. I knew the helo and how to fly it okay, but they knew Vietnam and the missions. It was nice in that respect; I fell in on an already up and operating squadron. I imagine they had some collective learning to do when, as a unit, they arrived in Vietnam with no one to hold school on them. But the old guys knew the whats and hows; we newbies learned and carried on.

At 1445 the next day, I met with Perryman and our copilots in the ready room for a brief. "Okay, gents, let's get started," he began, and we assembled in a small circle of chairs. The Captain covered call signs, frequencies, mission number, grid coordinates, and ground units, who we were escorting, rendezvous points, radio procedures, and the like. Then we moved to the wall map at the front of our ready room and he traced our route and identified the LZ. At the end of his thorough brief Perryman asked, "Any questions?"

I piped up, "This is my maiden voyage, Captain. Any special instructions?"

Perryman looked squarely in my eyes and said calmly but with emphasis, "If I go down, your job is to get me and the crew out. If my radios go bad, you've got the lead."

I nodded, "Yes, sir." I've never forgotten it. Oh, I already knew a helo section leader or his wingman's job becomes rescue if either bird goes down, but his direct address brought the responsibility home with perfect clarity. We were responsible for each other, period. When I started leading sections later in my tour, I made the Perryman instruction the last comment of my brief. Maybe it was needless, since implicit in the training of a Marine is a sense of communal responsibility. But stating to another man that he is responsible for you is both an awesome charge and a comfort. We were all in it together, each responsible to and for the other, duty-bound to our fellows, interlocking pieces of something larger, maybe something magnificent.

The Corps did a fine job of instilling this sense of duty, both to our current brethren and to a tradition. Marines well know of Daly, Baselone, Puller, and Wilson and the weight of their example. We were bathed in institutional standards at a young and impressionable age; expectations were ingrained.

I've pondered the notion of duty, bravery, and even love in the military. Where does one end and the other begin or are they somehow merged, inseparable? Why would a man perform a life-threatening deed for another? Humans have a built-in instinctual self-preservation response to danger, and this must be suppressed by choice, risen above, or we'd all simply run when threatened. Some greater good than the avoidance of injury or loss of life must become paramount. It may be love when it comes to a spouse or a child. And it may be at least partly love in close-knit infantry units.

An infantry acquaintance of mine, John Musgrave, was badly wounded in Vietnam. He tells me two of his buddies were killed and two others wounded when they tried to get to him after he'd been shot. He was rescued eventually, but at great cost to others, a cost that has weighed on him heavily all his days. Since I was not in the infantry, I can't fully appreciate the associations. But when it came to military brethren in our squadron, I've come to believe it was responsibility, duty to each other. This was fostered, not only from association in and identification with our unit, but through training to a standard and to institutional expectation. The closer the association, the greater the obligation. The benchmarks of the Marine Corps are revealed in the response-producing psychic formula: "Your job is to get me and the crew out." Simple yet powerful words transmitted to every man and every unit in the Corps. He'd said a mouthful. Bravo Jim Perryman.

My mission with the Captain was uneventful, though obviously impressive to me. We went out, escorted the resupply mission, delivered no ordnance, and flew home. But it was the beginning of my tour being in charge of my own helo. And when the old hands from the original VMO-6 rotated, I never flew as copilot again. That was nice.

As a side issue, during my tour a sense existed that one guy did not quite measure up to implicit/explicit expectations. He was ruined in the minds of the rest, a person to be tolerated but not fully accepted. He was not trusted in all circumstances and this was reflected on the flight schedule. In this area, one demonstration or suggestion of weakness and you were sunk. We all had to look the tiger in the eye and hold a steady gaze. Men in combat discover something about themselves; so do those around them.

NIGHT OPS

Often our night missions were under artificial light, illum as it was called. The best illum, the ones with the highest candlepower, were those kicked out of a circling fixed-wing transport aircraft, usually a DC-3 or a C-130. These beauties descended slowly suspended from parachutes and truly lit up the night. We could see it all. Of course so could every VC or NVA in the area. They cast a surreal, eerie white-green fusion of light and long shadows over the land. It was beautiful, dreamlike, and easily bright enough for our business, though danger lurked in the bright light.

We also worked under artillery-fired illumination, the next best light after those kicked out of aircraft. They were smaller, not as powerful, and burned out more quickly. The Marine artillery battery firing the flares, like those dropped from aircraft, could see when another round was needed, and, if requested, could simply keep them coming.

The third illumination option was fired from 81-mm mortars. They worked okay, but were even less long lasting and bright than the former two. Still, light was essential for providing suppression fire from an armed Huey on troublesome areas. We flew missions under illum occasionally, though most flights were during the day.

A downside of night ops under illumination was that the bright light destroyed "night vision." Night vision has to do with conditioning the eyes for optimum night acuity before launch and keeping them that way during the mission. It was the reason for red lights at night in the ready room, red lenses on flashlights for after dark preflight, red lights behind cockpit instruments, and our training in the use of off-center vision in looking for or at anything at night.

The aviation-medicine guys spent a bunch of time jaw-jacking about the physiology of eyes, about rods, cones, and an eye chemical named rodopsin. We all had to take tests in this stuff and the ins and outs of night vision. But the bottom line was this: Bright light, the kind produced from illum, ruined night vision. When the light went out, the dark was no-shit dark! Only with the passage of time in a relatively benign red light or dark environment, could you see much again. This happened even if a full moon was up and the night was clear. Although illum made it nice, once the flares were done, you had to get back on the red cockpit gauges in a hurry. It was dark, dark outside.

If you had to land, night ops without illum was a challenge. The Marine Corps had small boxes that sent beams of light up at a shallow angle, sort of like the mirror landing system on aircraft carriers. Some trained Marine on the ground placed the light box in a suitable LZ, he talked you to his area on the radio, and waved flashlights or wands to get the helo aircrew's attention. Then he talked you onto a heading and altitude that lined you up with the angled lights from his box. When you saw them, you flew down a green beam of light. If you started seeing a red light you were low; a white light meant you were high.

I only flew these hops in the States and they puckered my ass every time. Think about it. Blackness surrounds you outside the cockpit; and you're feeling for the ground following a light beam and instructions from a guy on the ground. You can't see that the tail rotor is clear of trees, if you actually fit into the selected zone, or how close you are to anything. You trust the judgment of others entirely. Down you go into the night, riding the green shaft, believing.

Turning on the landing or searchlight was a blessing and a curse. You could see, but your night vision was destroyed. And not just yours, but everyone else looking on. Also, every swinging Richard or Nguyen for miles around could see you. The Nguyens had a great target.

I preferred illum by a large margin even though it screwed night vision and it gave "Charlie" a shot if he wanted it. I just liked seeing, taking the guesswork out of my relationship to the ground, other helos, and obstacles. Working at night, either under illum or in the dark was different, interesting, and exciting. Nowadays, of course, the Marines use night vision goggles and can "do it in the dark," as they say. In Vietnam we had no such devices.

I will always be the loyal subordinate of four Marine officers. Two of these men (W. Maloney and N. Derickson) were my commanding officers at one juncture or another; one (L. Buehl) I worked for at HQMC, and the other was Kenneth David "K. D." Waters, a squadron mate in three squadrons, my boss in two.

My first squadron after Pensacola and flight school was VMO-1 at the Marine Corps Air Facility, New River, North Carolina. Waters was with that squadron when I joined. Earlier in his career he'd flown F-8 Crusaders but when that community shrunk in the early 1960s, he and other F-8 jocks were sent elsewhere. Some, including Waters, came to the helo community. He ended up in VMO-1 and worked in aircraft maintenance.

I, on the other hand, was a freshly commissioned, nugget aviator. As such I was assigned to an also-ran category job reserved for the brown bars of a second lieutenant; good enough for teeth cutting, but not a frontline task. As is often the case in the military, a sergeant saved my ass. My main responsibility, at least as I saw it, was to learn aircraft systems and improve flying skills. We operated the O-1C, a small fixed-wing tail-dragger Cessna, used traditionally for reconnaissance, controlling artillery and naval gunfire, and bringing fixed-wing attack aircraft onto ground targets. We also operated the UH-1E, which was new in the inventory of Marine aviation in 1965.

In those days, although an ocean of distance separated captains from second lieutenants, the span collapsed to some degree by imposed Happy Hours after work each Friday and by periodic squadron parties and social events. Unlike in the post-Vietnam era, at Happy Hour the Officers' Clubs were packed. Each squadron sent a small advance party. These men pushed a few tables together, ordered a couple of pitchers, and staked out turf for follow-on squadron members.

Beer flowed, wives and girlfriends were forbidden. We chatted about the week, the day, forthcoming events, the aircraft, who'd done the most impressive dumbshit of late, and generally got to know each other. Most of us got tipsy then we went home. First Lt. Bud Willis once said he liked to get naked on his back porch and enter through the kitchen to greet his new bride. It was a grand time and a good environment to learn from the old hands, mostly the captains, since none of us junior officers wanted to fart around with majors and above. We could and did get euphoric, say bad words, even scream them, and nobody gave a shit. Indeed, it was almost expected, especially of the juniors.

Those scenarios, coupled with a few parties at one or another officer's quarters, and the Marine Corps Ball, held that year in our decorated hangar, collapsed some of the separation imposed by rank and allowed me to get acquainted with Captain Waters. He was a smart, no-bullshit officer, and a remarkably competent aviator. He had a reasonable sense of humor, though one had to be careful. His body language was easy to read; if you pissed him off, he turned red. I discovered this and tried to avoid it.

As an example, one morning in Vietnam I was hanging out in the ready room. Waters was briefing pilots on a mission he was leading. Another captain, his wingman, interrupted him several times with editorial comments and questions. I could see him changing colors, a sure sign of danger to those of us who knew him. At about the fourth interruption, Waters, in a raised voice, with red face, and slightly bulging eyes, glared at his wingman, "Who's givin' this fuckin' brief?" he asked. To which the sputtering wingman stammered some shit like, "Well, I was just curious about, blah, blah, blah, humma, humma, frick-frack."

Waters countered with, "Well if you'd just hold on, I'm gonna cover all that shit. If I leave something out or any of you have questions, we'll get to it at the end."

"Okay. Sorry for the interruptions," responded the cowed captain.

The briefing continued uninterrupted and, not surprisingly, it was thorough. Nothing was left to discuss when he finished. "Any questions?" was met with general head shaking; the pilots had what they needed.

Waters was what a mid to senior Marine Captain was supposed to be: knowledgeable, dedicated, smart, practical, squared away, a fine aviator, strong to subordinates, loyal and obedient to seniors, and able to provide sound advice to those above him without being pushy. He was a capable, hard worker and never an ass kisser, a man you respected, partly because of rank, but more importantly because of his qualities.

As time rolled along in the first months of our assignment to VMO-6, it became apparent that, when the original members of the squadron rotated back to the States, K. D. would take over as the Aircraft Maintenance Officer. It also became increasingly likely that junior guys such as myself would be pressed into more meaningful jobs than the step-and-fetch-it miscellany that usually fell to us. We might indeed cease being Shitty Little Jobs Officers (SLJOs). The prospect was tantalizing.

One summer day while hanging out with other lieutenants in the ready room, bored, awaiting a mission later in the day, Waters called me to the ready room door. I stepped out into brilliant sunlight. "Yes, sir."

"Dave, since the original guys are heading out, the squadron's reorganizin', movin' people around. How'd you like a job in maintenance?" As usual, he was to the point.

"Damn, sir. That'd be good," I answered promptly. "I've been doin' mostly whatever's thrown my way. A no-shit job in maintenance would be great."

"Well, looks like I'll be takin' over Maintenance and I'll need a couple of officers. There's a hole in Quality Control. Later this became Quality

Assurance. Same shit, different name, conveying a more positive image I guess.] Maybe that'd be a good spot for you." He watched my reaction as much as listened to my response.

"No, really, whatever you've got is welcome. I'd be happy to have it," and I meant it. Not only was a job in aircraft maintenance a real assignment with specific work and a place to go daily, other than to just the ready room, but it would save me from other much less appealing options that might surface.

"We have some damn good Marines assigned there. They'll show you the ropes and I'll train you as a test pilot. You'd likely have long days and mostly over in the maintenance shop instead of here. You'd probably like it."

The words *test pilot* ricocheted around in my mind. I was floored, honored. I liked the sound of it and knew I would become more knowledgeable and competent on aircraft systems through the experience. Also, I'd likely become a better stick-and-throttle guy from flying test hops. It was one thing to learn the NATOPS manual, but quite another to get inside the minds of the aircraft mechanics. Their technical knowledge of the helo was levels above what pilot manuals provided. "Damn, sir, I'm your man. It would be great and I appreciate it."

"Okay. The admin people will cut a squadron special order soon and you'll be reassigned to maintenance as the QC Officer. Come in tomorrow mornin' and I'll introduce you around. Staff Sergeant Hillmandollar can start snappin' you in. He's the QC Chief and knows his business and the Huey like the back of his hand. You'll be primarily testin' birds comin' out of scheduled and nonscheduled maintenance. There's a bunch to know. We can get started in the mornin' unless Ops has you scheduled for an early flight. If they do, just come by after you're done."

"Okay, sir. I'll be there as soon as I can," I responded.

"Alright. See you tomorrow," and Waters turned and headed for the maintenance offices.

"Yes, sir. Tomorrow."

I had no idea, at least with any precision, what I'd be doing in maintenance but it beat the hell out of what I'd been doing to date. Beer procurement officer and the like was hardly what I had in mind as a Marine, but I did what I was told, as all of us did; it's all about survival. Anticipation and curiosity grew in me. The prospect of a job that increased my aviator skills, away from some paper-pushing alternative and the "little of this and little of that" bullshit I'd been doing was a liberating breakthrough. Whether K. D. chose me or the seniors drew straws and he got the short one, I'll never know, will never ask, and don't give a shit. I was going to maintenance; that's what mattered.

The next day, I was not scheduled early. My education as a more informed and better skilled UH-1E pilot began. Over the course of the next weeks, K. D. took me on test hops as they occurred, showed me the checklists, the maneuvers, what to look for in the cockpit, and what to notice from the feel of the bird. He then signed me off as a post-maintenance inspection pilot (PMIP). An entry was made in my logbook along with other designations such as carrier qualified (CQ) and Pilot Qualified in Model (PQM). I began testing the helos on my own. Excluding combat missions, it was my most rewarding job in the Marine Corps and maybe in my life. From my aged perch, I look back on it with satisfaction and longing.

The other part of my education was technical. Staff Sergeant Hillmandollar, "Buster" or "Red" as the staff noncommissioned officers called him, spent hours with me on the aircraft. He went over bearing tolerances, what the mechs looked for that caused a bird to be potentially dangerous, the flow paths of oils and hydraulic fluid, electrical parts and pieces, and how systems really worked. Between what he and the maintenance crews showed me, I learned the Huey again, this time through the eyes of the mechanics.

Testing was sometimes a slow process; for instance, rotor blade tracking was tedious. It required numerous starts and shutdowns. After each shutdown the crew made small adjustments on blade trim tabs or pitch change links on the rotor head. The process continued until both main rotor blades flew identical paths. Then K. D. or I flew the Huey to see if the track held during the dynamics of flight.

The most exciting test flight was checking for rudder authority. This was required any time the tail rotor or its drive train had been disconnected. The test involved a zero-airspeed, maxpower climb with the rotor RPM "drooped." One droops the rotor by pulling the collective up so far that the engine cannot sustain the induced blade pitch-angle. When this happens, the rotor RPM decays; it "droops." Straight up you go. It's a hell of an elevator ride, no forward airspeed, maxpower, heading up in a hurry. Once this is established, you feed in left pedal and turn the helo 360 degrees around its vertical axis, screwing yourself into the sky. If you can do this, the rudders are rigged okay in that direction.

The other direction must also be tested. For that, you stop the Huey mid-air, at three thousand feet or above. Once in the high hover, you lower the collective, roll the throttle to flight idle, and enter a zero airspeed autorotation. Stabilized in the auto, you feed in right pedal, turning the helo 360 degrees about its vertical axis, this time to the right. Like the maxpower ride up, it's a helluva ride down. You recover by rolling the throttle back on and feeding in collective as you nose over to regain airspeed.

The first time Waters demonstrated these bastards I was white knuckled, though I kept a professional exterior. I was thinking, "Oh, fuck, what other little *are-you-shitting-me* surprises are there in the test pilot's book of options?" But it became fun with repetition, and it was a confidence builder.

My newfound knowledge improved my preflights by a quantum leap. I really knew what a "downing gripe" was, and what just bore watching. I was a better pilot.

Our days were often long, since a helo might come out of maintenance late in the day or there might simply be too many to get tested during the normal working hours. On these occasions, we just stayed behind and worked with the bird(s) and the maintenance crews until the kinks were out. The helos often had to be ready to go in the morning and we had no place to go anyway. It was not like wives, children, or theater tickets beckoned. We had chow, the shower, the hooch, the club, maybe a movie, a book, a letter to write, and some shit-shooting with our hooch-mates.

My tour in Vietnam felt shorter after K. D. invited me to maintenance. I was a busy Marine; between testing and flying regular missions, every day I was in the air usually more than once, and I was interested in what I did. Job satisfaction was better than it ever got in my life.

MODESTY AND THE MARINE CORPS

Most of us are modest, notwithstanding Harry McGuire, a Harvard man and Navy Aviation Officer Candidate who, when in his cups, exposed himself at a crowded bar called The Schooner on Pensacola Beach. Unless driven by nature with such force that we have no choice, we'd usually prefer, for instance, not to pee in public or at least to turn our backs to the view of others. Yet, in the Corps at Ky Ha and elsewhere, peeing in public was inescapable. We did it by design.

Why my mind travels these roads remains a mystery to me. Maybe it's because my sensibilities were yanked around, bent, and offended by circumstance. "Piss tubes," as they were called, were nothing more than sections of pipe roughly twelve inches in diameter, though in heavily trafficked areas they could be small barrels. These tubes were buried some distance in the ground with eighteen inches or so protruding from the earth's surface. Covering the open mouth of the piss tube was a wire-mesh screen secured with clamps or safety wire. When the urge came you simply strode to the pipe, unzipped the bottom few inches of your flight suit, pulled out you-know-who, and relieved yourself into the mesh-covered opening. A yellow-white scum usually clung to the mesh, unpleasant at the very least.

The medical people periodically poured some oil in the tubes, confident in its sanitizing benefit and secure in the knowledge that the floating oil would mitigate the assault on olfactory nerves. It didn't work well, at least in this second purpose. On hot, humid, windless days, anyone within talking distance of a piss tube knew of its presence. Gentle breeze provided little relief; it just wafted the odor. A stiff blow was best. We were fortunate to be on the coast; typically the wind was up in the daytime. All suffered equally.

FNGs were especially astonished. "Oh, shit! That's the pisser?" followed by a nervous chuckle. One used to porcelain and flushing knew he'd arrived in a much different circumstance just from these "facilities." Piss tubes helped to dull down the senses, beat back any lingering presumptions of niceties from the civilized world. They aided in adjustments to new, harsher realities.

So, we peed in public; sometimes several of us at one time clustered around a pipe or small barrel. We tried to make casual conversation, but some small voice in the back of our heads was wondering, "Is this okay?" It was not, at least for a Kansas man.

You'd think there'd be no splatter or bounce-back from a screen, but you'd be wrong. A person learned this after his first trip or two to a tube. One needed to exercise caution; distance and aim were the answers. Gunbird drivers may have had an advantage here. Also, you never knew who might wander up and pee with you. The most senior to the most junior were all reduced to just men when it came to this. I always felt awkward at the tube and suppose others did as well. Standing next to the group commander with your crank out, for instance, was unsettling. And what about military courtesy? Does one change hands and salute? I figured if I was peeing, a verbal greeting would have to do.

Standing shoulder to shoulder with the piss tubes as stench factories and assaults on civilization, were the shitters. These were small, wooden buildings, probably eight feet square with slanted, corrugated metal roofs. For ventilation, which was much needed, screen covered a hinged door and a three-foot swath of screen ran around the building, two-thirds of the way up. Inside there were no stalls, no dividers that might have given a hint of privacy. Six holes, twelve inches in diameter, were cut in the seating surface, three on each side. When you sat, someone was often four feet away, directly across from you, or two feet away next to you. He'd often feign reading or engrossment in some document. What he was really doing was being uncomfortable.

Beneath the holes and accessible through hinged flaps at the building's rear were large receptacles to capture the feces. These were sawed-off fifty-five-gallon drums. They slid in and out through the hinged flaps for emptying. The containers were taken to a secluded area where the contents were mixed with diesel fuel and burned. Vietnamese had been hired for this task. We all knew when it occurred from the smell. The grunts did not use Vietnamese to burn their shitters; they did it themselves. I know this from a poem entitled, "Burn and Stir" by John Musgrave, another good Kansas man. His poem ranks up there with, "The Highwayman," "The Rhyme of the Ancient Mariner," and "Gunga Din." John says this duty was relegated to any junior Marine who'd offended the Company Gunny. I'm thankful Marines in the Air Wings were spared, but feel sorrow for those who were not.

When I was a young officer, I was rank-intimidated. I don't remember seeing a Marine lieutenant colonel until I'd finished flight school when one commissioned me. I may have glimpsed a major or two in Pensacola, but had no direct contact with them. First lieutenants and captains were sometimes instructors, but more often, both in the various cockpits and in ground school, they were Navy officers. The first real colonel I met was the MAG-26 commander, Colonel Baird, when I checked in after flight training in 1965. In my first year or so of commissioned service, I was all ears and no mouth in the presence of an experienced captain. Anyone above that was increasingly remote. Colonels were gods, lieutenant colonels just beneath. Generals were all grouped together, a *tertium quid*, a thing apart, strange, foreign, and powerful. It was almost like they gave us rank-and-file Marines orders and overarching direction, but they were not *in* the Corps. They just ran it. I got over some of this intimidation in Vietnam, not all, but some.

"You finished with that magazine, Garner?" I asked First Lt. Jerry Garner who sat on a chair in the ready room. I was plopped on the wooden bench the original VMO-6 guys had built around the ready room wall. Pilots sat on top and stowed their flight gear underneath. We kept our sidearms, for pilots a .38-caliber Smith and Wesson, on us, but flak jackets, helmets, gloves, kneeboards, survival packets, maps, and flashlights had to go somewhere. Under the ready room bench was the place.

Garner looked up from the flight schedule he was constructing for the next day. He was proposing a lineup of pilots for missions the group had called down. The Ops Officer would bless or modify it and get the CO's signature. A *Time* magazine was on the edge of Garner's ODO desk.

"I ain't done. You can read it if you don't take it."

"How 'bout to the shitter for a short spell?" I countered.

"Go for it," he said with a frown, "but air it out on your way back." I laughed. He wasn't smiling.

I grabbed the Southeast Asia edition of *Time* and stepped out into brilliant sunlight. Small black and gray dots appeared and danced in my vision. It was mid-afternoon, hot as hell, and bright to the point of brilliance. I pulled my utility cover low over my eyes and walked down the VMO-6 flight line, between parked Hueys on the right and the maintenance hooches and butler-building hangar on the left. Once past the buildings, I angled left for the squadron six-holer. Piss tubes were in several locations around the squadron working spaces, but we had only one shitter. That was my destination.

I opened the screen door and stepped up into the building. My eyes were still dazzled by the sun and the interior was dark by comparison. I knew I was not alone, but it could have been any Marine, even a civilian tech rep, since we had two. I nodded and spoke a greeting, "Howdy."

A response was made but I paid little attention. I was distracted unzipping my flight suit and peeling out of the top. I was about to make a critical maneuver. You might believe the hole cut in a shitter perch to receive the hindquarters of the needy and flight suit sleeves would hold no attraction for each other. But you'd be wrong; the two were in love. To avoid disaster, I collected my sleeves in front of me. I lowered my flight suit and shorts as one and sat back.

As my eyes grew accustomed to the relative dark of the interior, I became aware that Lt. Col. Bill Maloney, Klondike Six, my skipper, was the other occupant. So, there we were, ex-MARCAD Ballentine and a senior guy, *my* senior guy, taking a crap together. Several descriptive words come to mind; awkward is probably the best.

Civility, not to mention my own take on military courtesy mandated some response. "Oh," I engaged my mouth without my brain attached. "How're you doing, sir?"

Jesus! What the hell is a person supposed to say? Both of us were, good God, taking a shit. A powerful, senior man was a few feet away, sitting as I was, probably wishing as I did that some things could remain private.

"I'm staying busy, Dave. Paperwork, meetings, op tempo, and flying make my days full," he answered. We bounced the ball back and forth a little. Two conversations were going on, one spoken, one not—one the chitchat of common courtesy and military speak, the other subliminal, each wishing circumstance were altered, that our chat was being conducted by the side of the Ops hooch or near the line shack, not while relieving ourselves. Somehow it wasn't right, it was not okay. Officers way senior to me, and certainly he qualified, were objects of deference and respect. You stand up when they enter a room, initiate the greeting and salute. You say it nice and a bit tentatively with a "Sir" attached. So, how does one accommodate that sort of military psychic preconditioning with taking a crap together? You don't, you suffer mild, if temporary schizophrenia. We were reduced to common humanity by stark reality, yet ordered in a hierarchy by virtue of rank. Compartmentalizing is a partial answer but it's not fully effective. They ought to have had separate shitters and piss tubes for field grade officers or at least for commanders. They deserved it. But, as usual, no one consulted me.

Mercifully, the boss finished his business, stood and shrugged on his flight suit. "See you later, Dave," and he was gone.

"Yes, sir. Have a good day," was all I could muster.

*   *   *

One last comment on the indignity of circumstance: I must write about showering. As I do, I am reminded again of our infantry Marines who often went days between showers; their clothes actually rotted on their bodies. Because of their condition, I'll not complain. I'll simply report. (See John Corbett's *West Dickens Avenue* for an account of infantry living conditions.)

The company grade officers' (lieutenants and captains) shower, and they were all the same, was open to the world. We walked to and from them with a towel wrapped around our loins, soapbox in hand. The shower had some overhead pipes through which water was distributed to showerheads by the pull of a lever or the turn of a valve. The floor was pallets, wood, or metal wire. Shower shoes were a must, not only to keep your feet from getting dirty again on the way back to the hooch, but to protect them from the shower floor pallets. Standing on wire barefoot is no fun; neither are splinters.

The temperature of the water varied with use. If you were early in the evening you were in great shape. Later the temperature cooled and induced an embarrassing case of shrivels. When the hot water was gone, a person would endure a bracing, even paralyzing cold water experience, and had to resort to the old shipboard way: Get wet, stand away from the water and, while shuddering with nipples diamond-hard and heart near fibrillation, apply soap; then back under the water to rinse with alacrity, grab your close-at-hand towel, dry, and get the hell out of there.

I always figured shampoo was for pussies and just used my soap. I was happy to share this opinion with the lieutenants, but I had to exercise care; a senior captain luggin' a tube of Head 'n Shoulders or Prell might be in earshot.

While showering, once again you and others are exposed, like after gym class. Somewhere both my mother and grandmother were having sober conversations with me, not finger wagging, but close. The subject was modesty and propriety, the need to keep oneself covered and inoffensive. Group showers, especially for full-grown men, not to mention using either "restroom," would have met with their disapproval. The Kansas farm boy was once again at crosscurrents with his rearing. It was mildly unsettling. The Marine Corps was practical and efficient. The Corps did and still does what it has to, and I didn't croak from the experience. But, given the option, I like a door.

CHAPTER 4

Flying "The Brute"

One morning after a ready room all officers' meeting and after I'd been in the squadron several months, the Ops O, Major Walker, approached me. I stood outside making small talk with First Lieutenants Sipes and Ross.

"Lieutenant Ballentine, you got any experience flying heavies?"

My pulse quickened just a hair. "Not really, sir. The closest I've come to senior guys is haulin' the MAG-26 skipper to and from Cherry Point a coupla times."

I hadn't cared much for it, too much rank. I felt awkward, obliged to make up conversation instead of just letting it flow. But Colonel Baird, the MAG CO, had periodic meetings at 2nd Marine Aircraft Wing Headquarters at nearby Cherry Point; he liked to go in a Huey. Since they were early as hell meetings, one of the young pilots usually got the assignment to take him. I was in the rotation. If anyone thought he was screwing me, he was wrong. It was a chance to sign for the helo and be on my own. I preferred that to more time in the sack. Off we'd go, the Colonel, a crewchief, and me. We stayed at five hundred feet and followed the railroad tracks from Camp LeJeune to Cherry Point. I landed at the base of the air station tower, shut down, awaited the meeting's end, and flew the Colonel back to New River.

"Heavies" were VIPs. They could be military or civilian. In the military, VIPs began at the rank of colonel, not lieutenant colonel, but real colonels, the ones with eagles on their collars. These were Code Sevens. A brigadier general was a Code Six, a major general a Code Five, a lieutenant general a

Code Four, and so forth. On the civilian side a sliding scale of military rank equivalents existed, but civilian VIPs went all the way to Code One, the President and others.

When aviators make radio calls to controlling agencies, they make it known that a Code is aboard. It usually means that the aircraft flying the heavy is accorded priority handling. It also helps alert greeting parties and whomever else needs to start sweating and taking a last nervous shit, briefing officers for instance, that the Code-type guy is arriving. Our aviation controlling agencies in Vietnam were all military and it was pretty simple, no FAA folks to fart around with like in the States.

Walker continued, "I'm thinking of throwing your ass in the deep end of the pool tomorrow. Check the flight schedule real close this afternoon." He smiled and turned away heading for the Ops hooch.

"Okay, sir," I responded lamely.

"Oh," the Major offered over his shoulder as he eased away. "If I pin this rose on you, have a fresh flight suit, either a piss-cutter or squared away utility cover, and make sure you shine your boots with something other than a dog turd."

We snickered. "Yes, sir," I answered. "I'll look nice." Then, I started thinking, my mind only half on the Sipes-Ross banter. Shit, why me? Let one of the more senior guys fly whomever needed flyin' around. Some captain could do the bowing, scraping, and keeping a civil tongue on the VIP's boot.

"Fuck, I hope Walker rethinks that shit," I said to the guys. They didn't give a damn. Their ox had not been gored.

"Well, you'll know when the schedule comes out. No sense sweatin'. Your ass is either up to bat or it ain't," Ross allowed. I was not mollified.

But Barney was right. Wait and see. I inventoried my mind for any special alerts about which I'd need to be cautious. The only ideas that came to mind were to keep all the controlling agencies aware of what I was up to. I figured I'd have a chase helo following me around; since I'd have the VIP in my bird, I'd take off and land first. It was one thing to fly single bird taking Father Kelly on his Sunday morning rounds to outlying grunt camps and quite another to be out with a senior guy. It wouldn't do to have a general, for instance, stuck in the weeds because of an engine failure or some other inconvenient mechanical event. No, the Corps would want his ass out of there. I'd have a chase for sure.

The day continued in its routine including an early afternoon copilot ride on an uneventful recon insertion. Around 1630, fearing the verbal premonition of Major Walker, I walked to the ready room to check the schedule. Sure enough, at 0900 I was to take the CGFMFPAC plus three on Mission 1421. Tarbush, the call sign for HMM-361, was providing a chase CH-34. The ODO would provide details. Groan, shit, groan!

I was hauling around a very powerful officer, a man legendary in the Corp; none other than the Commanding General of Fleet Marine Force Pacific, a lieutenant general, three-star guy, who could eat lieutenant colonels and colonels for breakfast.

"Garner," I said to the ODO, who was as usual behind the only desk in the ready room, "Why me? General Krulak, are you shitting me?"

"I suppose we were down to your sad ass," came Jerry's answer. "Anyway you got this one. So quit bitchin'. Here's the briefing sheet. Looks like VMO-2's bringin' him in around 0700 and dumpin' him. He'll spend two hours or so having breakfast in our chow hall, gettin' briefed by the MAG. I expect Lieutenant Colonel Maloney and all the skippers will be involved. Then he'll come to the flight line, get in your bird and you'll take him to visit three grunt units." He pointed to the brief sheet.

"They're on the sheet with call signs and grids. You shut down and wait for him and after the three locations, you take him up to Danang, not Marble Mountain, but Danang. Drop him wherever the tower tells you, then return to base. Call Landshark if these units are not on the frequencies we have, and they'll unscrew it for you."

"Okay." I went to one of the benches around the ready room wall. I pulled out my kneeboard from among my stowed flight gear and began scribbling notes from the briefing sheet.

"It don't sound too complicated. I see Tarbush is following me around. Know who the pilot is?" Tarbush was one of the CH-34 lift helo squadrons assigned to MAG-36 and co-located with VMO-6 at Ky Ha.

"Beats the hell out of me," Jerry responded. "I'll ring 'em and see what's up."

He turned to a green field telephone behind his desk and cranked it, sending a small jolt of current into black lines that led mysteriously out of the ready room. After a short chat with someone, Garner turned to me, "They don't know yet, but your chase pilot will be in our ready room by 0730. You guys can meet and chat then."

"I got it," I said with resignation. This general was huge, a very, very big fish. I always felt a bit out of my element with senior Marines anyway and this was almost as senior as it got. At the time the Corps had only one four-star general, and a sprinkling of the three-star variety. The one I was flying was nicknamed "The Brute." All those senior men were veterans of both World War II and Korea, medals out the ass, no stranger to the nuts and bolts of combat, and this guy was a grunt, the heart and soul of the Corps. I maintained a calm exterior but had massive misgivings about being around such an embodiment of our tradition, one at the pinnacle of military success.

I suppose the Corps had built this sort of response into me. Rank was pivotal, the more you had, the more you reflected the winnowing-out process of promotion selection and the Darwinian idea of survival of the fittest. I was close enough to majors to notice they were not all uniformly capable, but lieutenant colonels were beginning to be a breed apart, not folks I usually enjoyed being around. It required special vigilance. The Corps had helped engender this awareness of rank, partly by insisting early on that I recognize rank emblems and stripes on sleeves, so I knew not only how to address a man, but where he stood in the pecking order. As a side effect, I knew where I stood in the order. I was low, low, low. By that time I was a first lieutenant, so I wasn't quite the lowest of the low, just right next to it. The Commanding General of the Fleet Marine Force Pacific, was almost the highest of the high.

I didn't sleep much that night. I was concerned about proximity; soon I'd be in the frag pattern of a man nicknamed "The Brute."

The next morning was fraught with activity at Ky Ha. Even the uninformed, casual observer might have known something was not quite routine. A little tension, some kinetic energy had been released, a bit more scurrying about was noticeable, more shine, starch, and spiffiness. A force was descending. Because I had a part in the drama, even though it was small, this energy affected me more than most. I was not quite my usual self. The shit on a shingle, a mixture of beef and white gravy, which normally I tolerated well, just sat on my plate at breakfast. I sucked down some black coffee and headed for the squadron.

I was the sort who liked to sit in the rear of the ready room watching the majors and senior captains do their thing at squadron meetings, as much an observer as a full participant, dutifully taking notes on information that touched me, but thankful my part was not at the front. We lieutenants could in private make fun of the gaffes of others, laugh at someone else's expense, his screwup. "Damn, Captain Marvel made an ass of himself this morning. The old man asked him two simple fuckin' questions and he couldn't answer either. An' he's s'posed to know that shit. I bet he has his act together tomorrow." That sort of "glad it's his ass and not mine" stuff.

But now I had a role, and an opportunity to screw things up with the world watching. I was temporarily no longer at "the rear of the ready room." Making some blunder, which might reflect poorly on the squadron or me, quickened my pulse a hair.

When I showed at the ready room around 0730, a strange captain was sitting there. The ever-present First Lieutenant Garner said, "Hey, Dave, that's Captain Grayson. He's your Tarbush chase with the General today."

I introduced myself, then asked, "Any update on our mission, Garner?"

"Nope, same launch time and itinerary. But, you never know about heavies. They show up early or late, sorta do what they want, when they want, like they were in charge an' all. You just gotta be flexible and hang loose." He smiled. "Oh, I have the passenger list. You'll have the General, his aide, his Sergeant Major, and a III MAF (Third Marine Amphibious Force, the headquarters that controlled Marines in Vietnam) colonel as escort officer."

I expected Garner was glad, for a change, that his ass was glued to the ready room ODO chair, while my ass was leaping off with General Krulak and his party.

I grabbed my kneeboard and went over a briefing with Captain Grayson. He already had the info. We agreed he'd turn up on VMO-6 squadron common FM frequency. I told him I'd make all the radio calls and made sure we agreed on destinations, call signs, and frequencies of the units we were visiting. In our chat I used "sir." I led the flight, but he was a captain. I told him we'd fly at 1,500 feet MSL give or take. His call sign was just Tarbush Chase.

"Well, sir," I concluded, "you can see me from your parking spot. I'll turn up as soon as Garner tells me they're on their way to the flight line. Jerry, you gonna call Tarbush to relay the here-he-comes signal?"

"Okay," Garner said. "Sir, when they call me, I'll call your Ops, in case someone else hasn't." He nodded at Grayson. "An' I'll get Dave hustlin' here."

That satisfied everyone. I had my mission; I'd briefed the chase CH-34 pilot. Now all I had to do was sign for and preflight the Huey, give the crew-chief a brief, and wait.

"I'm going to the line shack, Jerry. See ya later, sir," I said to Garner.

Garner mumbled something and Grayson walked out with me, but turned and headed up the ramp for his flight line. "Meet you on Fox Mike, Dave," he said as he walked away.

"Yes, sir. Later," I answered.

In the maintenance line shack I went over the records of the slick they'd given me, signed the yellow sheet accepting the bird, and walked to the helo where I met the crewchief, Lance Corp. Rick Ault. We exchanged greetings. The helo was as spiffy as could be expected and the VIP kit had been installed. This was a portable red-leatherette contraption that covered the rear seats. In large letters it announced VMO-6 to the dignitary being trans-ported. I gave Lance Corporal Ault a brief of the expected activities and told him we'd offer the General the copilot's seat. Should he decline, we'd make it available to the others in his crowd and if none of them wanted it, Ault would sit there.

He'd placed two headsets in the helo, one for the General in the copilot's seat, and one on the jump seat for whomever else wanted it. For those not outfitted with headsets, he'd obtained Mickey Mouse ears, which look like headsets without a boom microphone. Mickey Mouse ears, named for their appearance, didn't really remind me of Annette Funicello's headgear (I usu-ally don't think of headgear when I remember Annette) but they were close enough. The mouse headgear protected ears from the aircraft noise, but did not let the wearer hear the helo's intercom and radio transmissions, nor could the wearer talk to others. Folks with Mickey Mouse ears had to yell and gesticulate. I enjoyed it, damn me, when senior guys had to do this. Hueys could only accommodate four on the ICS. Others were left to shout and play charades.

Following the preflight, we waited at the aircraft. Soon enough Garner came out of the ready room and shouted to us from forty yards away, "They're on the way. Crank it up."

I ran through the reasonably short checklist, got the engine and rotor on line, but kept the engine at flight idle. Two jeeps pulled into the space between the ready room and the line shack. One had a three-star placard mounted on its front bumper. Several Marines got out, among them was Lieutenant Colonel Maloney. After a brief exchange, hands were shaken and Maloney and the MAG CO walked with the General and his party to my turning helo. They took off their covers as they approached, otherwise rotor wash, even at low RPM, would have blown them across the flight line. Lieutenant Colonel Maloney opened the copilot's door for the General and he climbed in. I guess it was never a question of where he was to sit. Lance Corporal Ault helped him strap in. I handed his headset to him when he was situated.

Once he'd placed his headset over his ears, I keyed the ICS, "Sir, I'm Lieutenant Ballentine. I'll be driving you around today." I pointed to a metal foot-button on the floor; it looked like the headlight dimmer switch on cars made in the 1940s. "Just step on that foot switch to talk, General." He probably knew that, since the guys from VMO-2 had flown him down in a Huey that morning. The others had piled in the back and attached their seatbelts and slipped on either Mickey Mouse ears or a headset, which went to the III MAF escort officer in the jump seat.

"I'm glad to meet you, Lieutenant," General Krulak smiled, extending his hand.

I thought for just a moment about removing my flight glove to be polite and really press the flesh, but decided it was too time-consuming. I reached over with my gloved right hand and shook "The Brute's" hand.

I made mental notes. Lt. Gen. Victor H. Krulak was not a large man, unlike, for instance, Lt. Gen. Louis Walt, our III MAF CG, who was a bear of a man. He was neat in his pressed utilities; the three stars on his lapel almost didn't fit. It was simply too much brass for the material. Maybe on a man who wore extra, extra large, it might have worked better. But he had a hell of a lot of collar stuff for the area. I was probably just not used to the emblems; maybe all collar lapels were the same size.

He carried a riding crop; a symbol of rank and a throwback to an earlier time when mules and horses were part of the system. A carved ivory horse head was inserted in the crop's thickest end. The mule-horse days were long gone, but he retained this vestige of rank, called a "swagger stick" in the Old Corps. Lieutenant General Krulak is the only officer I ever saw carry one.

They were no longer a uniform item. But, like Patton's pearl-handled (or was it ivory?) revolvers, who's gonna say no to that much rank?

The General had quick, penetrating eyes and a prominent nose, but he seemed pleasant enough. I ran the engine up from ground idle to operating speed; the rotor RPM increased with it.

"Tarbush Chase is up," came an FM radio call.

"Roger, Tarbush, Klondike's readin' you five square. You up Ground?" I responded.

"Roger, Klondike. I'm up Ground and I'm reading you five square too. We're ready when you are."

I switched to the ICS. "Everyone strapped in?" I asked. Everyone was of course. Lance Corporal Ault had made sure of that.

My temperatures and pressures were in the green and my RPM was where it needed to be. I switched to the UHF radio and keyed the mic, "Ky Ha Ground, Klondike fourteen dash three, taxi for two. My wingman is Tarbush Chase. We have a Code 4 aboard and we're on Mission 1421. Over."

Ground Control responded and cleared us to runway three south. I gave a thumbs-up to our taxi director who responded with arm signals, and I pulled the Huey into a hover. We were off.

Between my radio transmissions and the comments from the escort colonel in the jump seat, Lieutenant General Krulak engaged me and Lance Corporal Ault on where we were from, how long we'd been in the squadron, whether or not we had enough pilots and crews in general, and seemed genuinely interested in both personal and squadron information. Time passed quickly en route to each of the three stops. One was a Regimental Headquarters; the other two were subordinate battalions of the same regiment. They were all ready for the General. I contacted them easily on the FM; they popped smoke on my request to show where they wanted us to land and, from the smoke, I knew wind velocity and direction and could set up for the best approach. Grayson kept the 34 airborne until the General was no longer near my helo. That way he avoided blowing debris and sandblasting the party. At each site I shut the helo down and shot the shit with Ault and Grayson and his crew.

By the time I had delivered "The Brute" to the three locations and to Danang, I was reasonably comfortable in his presence. He'd made this happen by engaging Lance Corporal Ault and me. He was another man doing a job, maybe not a god after all. I was beginning to believe flying heavies was okay.

I especially liked the response of Danang Tower when I radioed that I was ten miles southwest with a Code 4. "Roger, Klondike, understand Code 4. Continue direct. Plan to land at the base of the tower. Report three miles. Break. Checkerboard four dash one and flight, hold your position on the runway. Expect three- to five-minute delay for takeoff. Acknowledge. Over."

"Checkerboard four dash one and flight holding. We're good at it," came the F-4 pilot's response to the tower.

"Danang Tower, Klondike four dash fourteen copies. We'll set up to land at the tower base, and we'll call three miles. Over," I answered.

We were so close to Danang that a chase bird served little function. I told Tarbush at his discretion I'd meet him at Marble Mountain and we'd refuel before heading back to Ky Ha. He responded, agreed, broke off, and headed for Marble Mountain, a few miles south and east of the Danang Airbase. I made a final call to Danang Tower at three miles. As expected, tower cleared us direct to the tower base for landing.

A taxi director met us and signaled us to set down. Nearby a small convoy of jeeps awaited.

"Well, Lieutenant, thanks for the ride. I enjoyed it. Have a good tour." Lt. Gen. Victor Krulak reached across the cockpit, hand extended.

"I enjoyed it too, General." I smiled and shook his hand. Lance Corporal Ault opened the General's door. All the passengers unstrapped and got out. They ducked under the arc of our turning blades and headed in the direction of the jeeps. They loaded and were driven away within thirty seconds.

Ault got back in our slick and this time strapped himself in to the copilot's seat. I got clearance to lift and departed southeast for Marble Mountain. We refueled, linked up with Tarbush Chase, and took off heading south along the coast at 1500 feet AGL, bound for Ky Ha.

It had been a piece o' cake. Look sorta squared away, know where the hell you're going, who you call, know the R-T procedures, be willing to converse if the General seems interested, and get priority treatment from tower and other control agencies.

I flew codes on other occasions in Vietnam, but Lieutenant General Krulak was my first and most senior passenger. I carried him on at least one other occasion. It required less planning than many missions. Of course, if you screwed it up, it'd be well known.

My experience with "The Brute" was anything but unpleasant. Oh, I could tell that he was not just another Marine, and who knows what life might have been like for a more senior officer working on his staff. A person doesn't likely get a nickname like "The Brute" from being soft. But my experience was good, and flying the slick was always nice; it was quieter, with cabin doors to close, unlike the gunbirds where they'd been removed. And slicks were faster, since you were not dragging ordnance racks, guns, rocket pods, and ammo chutes through the airstream.

When I returned, Major Walker came to the ready room. "Did you fuck that up in any way?"

"Sir, it went exactly as planned, three LZs, three shutdowns, then I dropped him at Danang. Tarbush and I got gas at Marble and drove home.

Lance Corporal Ault and I even chatted a bit with the General. He seems like an okay guy," I answered.

"Glad all went well; have a good afternoon," the Major answered and returned to the Ops hooch.

Like a lot of events and activities in life, ignorance makes a person insecure. My outing with Lieutenant General Krulak was a perfect lesson in this for me. I've relearned this one many times and probably still don't have it down.

CHAPTER 5

Ky Ha Miscellany I

SHAVING MANTRA

To moisten my beard in preparation for shaving, I dip my cupped hands ten times in water and pull them to my face. Not eight times, not eleven, but ten. I started this in Vietnam; I never counted before, never gave a damn. But since, it is a ritual.

In the early days we drew cold water from a "water bull," as water trailers were called. One was parked near our hooch. Eventually waterlines were run, so we had an outside spigot near the end of our hooch. A handy water source made life less a pain in the ass for brushing teeth and shaving.

Each of us had purchased, commandeered, or been bequeathed a small mirror and a shallow tin wash pan, the size of a World War I helmet without its brim. In the morning, I drew a pan of cold water and carried it to an area outside the hooch where some stands had been erected. First I brushed my teeth, then I wet my beard and shaved.

Through experimentation I knew ten dips of beard-softening cold water was enough to soak whiskers for a shave. Following the water came some shaving cream; I opted for whatever was least expensive at the PX. Then came the Gillette safety razor, not the plastic throwaway kind so popular later in the twentieth century, but a metal contraption with replaceable blades that could be disassembled and cleaned. Following the shave, I'd towel my face and ears, toss the water, rinse the pan, collect my stuff, deposit it inside, and go to breakfast.

During this sequence I had my flight suit on, but just to the waist. I held it in place by snugging down Velcro tape on each side of the waist or sometimes I tied the arms of the suit about my middle. What is remarkable about this memory, if indeed anything, is that I still do the ten soaks of my beard. Maybe it's just efficiency at work. But it is programmed in my mind and muscles, almost like touching the forehead, stomach, left shoulder, right.

It has hidden, subtle meaning, a commemoration of sorts, an unspoken, symbolic gesture acknowledging association and change, the men, the machines, the mission, the loss and gain. In short, it causes me to glimpse back into what this memoir is about: *Them* and *me* doing *it*. So I'll continue the ten at least until someone else has to shave me, heaven forbid.

THE VC BARBERSHOP

The VC Barbershop, as most of us called it, was near the northern gate to Ky Ha. The Viet Cong disapproved of the Saigon government and waged guerilla warfare against it and the South Vietnam and the U.S. military forces.

The VC Barbershop was operated through contract with local Vietnamese. Their shop was a standard hooch with several barber chairs and mirrors. Except that sweat might be trickling down your back and into the crack of your ass and the barbers were Vietnamese rather than say from Connecticut or Oklahoma, it all looked pretty familiar. For instance, they had little jars of colored sterilizing fluid in which combs rested. This fluid is supposed to suggest that the combs are okay, that even though the last fucker had head lice, it's all right, since the combs were quarantined overnight in red or green fluid.

I was always tempted to bring a comb, but figured the clippers and scissors were there too and you can't just show up with a bag of tools for the barbers to use. So I allowed the "sterilized" comb, as did everyone else. I don't think it was ever an issue. Besides, we were all pretty clean, showered daily, that sort of thing. If a hooch-mate's personal hygiene went off the chart in the wrong direction, someone would have piped up, "Hey, you're startin' to stink." Or, "Jesus, how 'bout gettin' your cheeks down to the fuckin' shower?" or "Hey, Jim, when's the last time you changed the oil in that flight suit?" These sorts of gentle, understanding, and persuasive inducements would have worked.

Anyway, the Vietnamese guys cut our hair, and a virtual steady stream of Marines came through their door. These barbers used straight razors to shave the backs of our necks and (are you shittin' me!) our foreheads and temples at the hairline. So here we have Vietnamese guys wielding razors around the heads of Marines. What if the barber decided to sacrifice himself for a greater cause, to do more than simply garner intelligence for the VC outside the base? What if he decided to cut a throat, say one belonging to a first lieutenant, realizing that this rank was at the very heart of Marine aviation? Oh sure, our guys would finish him off, but maybe my ass would be lying in a pool of claret on the hairy barbershop floor, pumping out my last.

They never injured anyone, at least not that I heard, or no more than dull blades can inflict, but I always wondered about their politics. And I was absolutely certain that the Vietnamese who burned our shit receptacles were Cong, if not when they accepted the position, then surely over time. Honey bucket work can make a man unhappy, spiteful. He'd need revenge. I think I can hear their thoughts: "I'll burn your shit today, but tonight I'm providing useful information to Pham."

THE PX

Nowadays, it's called the Marine Corp Exchange, but then it was the PX or Post Exchange. It was near the VC Barbershop and north gate leading to a village and the world outside the concertina wire of our perimeter. The PX is where a person could go to purchase "health and comfort" items like soap, toothbrush and toothpaste, soap dishes, cigarettes (more people smoked in the 1960s than today), and, eventually, a scattering of magazines, stationery, candy, nuts, and dried, processed meat, the Pemmican stuff one finds in convenience stores.

I came to believe years ago that these dried meats, heavily seasoned and infused with preservatives and coloring, are designed for penance. Individually and collectively, they offer such offense to the sensibilities, smell, texture, taste, take your pick, that they cannot be chosen except as punishment. If one is so riddled with guilt and fear for the destruction of his soul that he needs expiation; if he is convinced that some sort of denial or self-inflicted pain would make his wrongful acts worthy of indulgence; then he might reach for some of this meat.

Say you're at the neighbors' for a cookout, you happen to notice the remarkable tits and ass of the hostess, and you're on your usual clandestine but prolonged visual tour. Your soul recognizes this carnal and sin-filled preoccupation; it forces your body to speak, "Honey," you say to your wife, "Do we still have any of that disgusting dried meat?" See how it might work? But a person can only speculate on these matters.

Browsing in the PX was not a lengthy outing; our needs were basic and the PX sufficed. After I returned to the States, wandering through department stores or supermarkets was bewildering. I'd grown accustomed to no choice or choosing between two and I kind of liked it. I didn't and don't want to have to read a bunch of stuff, get briefed by smiling helpers, and spend time pondering. I like to say, "I'll take this one." That's a hell of a lot easier if you're looking at two or one. Department stores are all about options, many options. I pretty much leave this to my wife.

The laundry was also in the PX–VC Barbershop area. Without this service, life would indeed have been less good. As I write this, I am painfully aware that our grunts' utilities simply rotted on their bodies. Sweat, humidity, jungle rot, who knows. Every account I've read of our ground forces makes this abundantly clear.

But I was not a grunt, and, mercifully, we had people who did laundry for money. So we each kept a laundry bag in our hooch area and, when it was filled, we'd drop it off. A couple days later we retrieved it.

For most of the flight crews, the uniform was simple: shorts, T-shirt, flight suit, socks, flight boots, and utility cover. Change the unders daily, the outers every third, and you're in good shape. The laundry made this practical. If we'd washed our own, who knows what the schedule might have been. I bet we'd have gone longer between rotations. I'm glad I'll never know.

PERIMETER SECURITY

The grunts are good at this part of being a Marine, that is, at perimeter guard. When and if bad guys are probing the perimeter, grunts are well trained in alerting buddies and they're good at killing bad guys. Nongrunt Marines are not as good, and nongrunts were on our perimeter.

"What the hell was all that firing about last night?" might come the question over breakfast or in the ready room.

The response might be, "I heard it was intramural."

This implies that some guys from different units got their weapons, chambered rounds, and started shooting at each other, intramural style. I can't be certain this ever happened at Ky Ha, but it was rumored on several occasions.

Although every Marine is trained to fire a rifle, Lord knows I remember my days of "snapping in" and at the range, not all Marines are riflemen. Riflemen are infantrymen.

"Snapping in" is when you try to get your body used to four different uncomfortable, at times even excruciating, positions for rifle firing: standing, sitting, kneeling, and prone. For me that was no fun, but Marines *must* qualify with the rifle. So others and I snapped in under the watchful eye and care of a staff sergeant and a sergeant who took satisfaction in helping us position our skeletons and muscles into zones of distress.

"There, sir. That's where you need to be." But I'd gone way past where I needed to be. It started when I was assigned with Bud Willis, Barney Ross, and Steve Wilson to the range for rifle qualification. Where I really needed to be was around the helos, around the smell of hydraulic fluid, jet fuel, and engine oil. I did not need the smell of exploding powder while my elbows dug into hard-scrabble, I did not need the rebellion in untrained muscles, and I did not need to keep aggravating the small cheek bruise under my right eye. This formed, exactly as the sergeant said it would, from not seating the rifle snugly enough in my shoulder when I fired. Recoil got me about every fourth or fifth shot.

So, in my view, even though "every Marine is a rifleman" is a nice notion, the real truth is the grunts are "riflemen"; everyone else is not; everyone else is just "qualified" with the rifle.

A grunt lives with his rifle; his life depends on it. He cleans it and fires it regularly; he lives in a culture with others who do the same. But it's much more than just the rifle use. It's fire discipline and fields of fire and familiarity with a lifestyle, knowing, for instance, what is dangerous and what is not, and what to do about it if it is dangerous. They live it. In one way or another, the rest of us support it.

Try to imagine you're a cook, baker, candlestick maker, hydraulics man, admin clerk, or whatever, anything but an infantryman. The Gunny comes to you and says, "By the way, Lance Corporal Willard, you're detailed to the perimeter guard for four weeks. You'll be back before you know it." And you, Lance Corporal Willard, are an intel guy right out of school working at Group Headquarters.

It comes as no surprise to me that the Lance Corporal Willards of this world, isolated and frightened in the night, might not respond as a grunt would. Willard is, after all, only "qualified" with the rifle. On hearing the gremlins, and they are always prowling at night, he may first make a whispered radio call or alert someone near. If the gremlin noises persist or become louder, and usually they do, he might pop a hand flare, thereby destroying his night vision and that of those near. Then dark becomes truly black. Eventually he slips off his safety and, in a rush of adrenaline-charged fear, he cranks a few rounds in the direction of the imaginary bastards trying to penetrate his sector.

Other clones of Lance Corporal Willard, also temporarily assigned to the perimeter, jumpy and scared, peer into the darkness. They too are inclined to be safe rather than sorry. They crank off a few rounds into the blackness and maybe send a flare aloft. And the Ky Ha perimeter was anything but a straight line, which adds to complexity, potential confusion, and hazard. So it goes. Until some strong NCO or SNCO gets in the middle and sorts it out, Marines are cranking away, potentially in the proximity of each other.

I never heard that a Marine was hurt by our own in these rumored exchanges. And I only heard the "intramural firefight" rumor a couple of times, but it was there. With smoke, especially recurring smoke, there was likely a little fire.

JOHNNY CASH

We didn't have any Armed Forces Radio for most of my tour, no "Good Morning, Vietnam" greeting as portrayed in the Robin Williams flick, nothing in the background to lighten the day as we went about tasks. But we did have reel-to-reel tape-deck music, mostly in the officers' clubs. A lot of guys bought these reel-to-reel, state-of-the-art players, and sent them home during a five-day out-of-country Rest and Relaxation (R&R) trip. Akai was the brand of choice, though in the 1960s many of us were still suspect of anything made in Asia. In those days, if it wasn't made in the USA, it was simply inferior. That's changed.

Anytime I hear Johnny Cash, even today, I am once again in an O club in Vietnam. It might be any club, Ky Ha, Phu Bai, or Marble. But from a musical view, Mister Cash was, is, and will remain Vietnam to me. "I hear that train a comin'," or "Because you're mine, I walk the line," are deeply, indelibly etched. His music was as predictably present as it was depressing in its sameness. Right beneath Johnny was Kenny Rogers begging Ruby not to take her "love" to town. Of course the guy who's supposedly singing the song had gotten all shot up and become an invalid in that "old crazy Asian War." But the guy, injured though he was, heard the "slammin' of the door" anyway. Apparently Ruby needed more than the hurt guy could provide. I was always sobered by it. Once I heard a club filled with guys erupt into song on the chorus. I guess we all knew of the potential built into our circumstance.

After these two singers, the music world disintegrated into a chaos of individuals and groups. These others were rarely heard at the clubs, only sometimes in the hooches on private reel-to-reel players, but not in the clubs. I remember the Beach Boys, Bee Gees, Beatles, though a Marine had to be careful of longhaired, nontraditional assholes. The group that sang, "We gotta get out of this place, if it's the last thing we ever do," was on target for obvious reasons. I liked "G-L-O-R-I-A," but I rarely heard it until we started getting a radio station piped to us late in my tour.

At our club, like at others, it was reel-to-reel and the same shit evening after evening. No Beethoven's Ninth, never a Rachmaninov piano sonata, little to promote the soaring of spirit, the cultivation of humanity, or the instruction of soul. Sipping a Sambuca over ice with a few dark-roast coffee beans strewn in was out of the question. But a tallboy Budweiser, a shot of bar bourbon, and some gut-level, simplistic, straight-ahead country-western was infinitely and distressingly available. It was our staple. To say it got old is an injustice; those words are too pale. If I was going to the club, and I did often, I just braced myself and used chitchat with the guys to block out the music. There was usually something to discuss from the day's events that moved Cash and Rogers into the background.

"Eddie Kufeldt went out and got the shit shot out of his bird today.

Sounds like he was doin' everything right, he's just one unlucky bastard," or "This new guy Thatcher must have a magnet in his ass. Every time the guy launches, he comes limping home with holes. I gotta stay away from that guy. And, fuck, he just smiles through it all. Don't he know this shit is dangerous?" or "Jesus, we were out today escortin' Buffalo City on a company insert. They were landing a division at a time. The lead bird landed too short in the zone so the last two birds were hovering over some trees waiting for the first section to discharge and lift so they could get in. I bet the flight leader is in for an 'aw shit' on that one. Man, you gotta get forward in the zone or tail end Charlie is just screwed. He'll be wavin' off or hoverin' for sure. No choice there."

Three or four Klondike pilots could go on for quite a while, but if joined by friends from other squadrons, the mix of experience expanded geometrically. With the help of Anheuser-Busch we could truly sail through the evening. When I got involved in these discussions or was just listening in, Cash was less intrusive.

Eventually, late in my tour, when we received Armed Forces Radio, we heard the music played Stateside. I never listened in the daytime, too much was going on. But I bought a little transistor radio and sometimes in the evenings I turned it on and listened to upbeat news on how we were kickin' Charlie's ass interspersed with music.

After my return to the States, sometimes I'd hear a gal sing along with some song completely foreign to me. The music had come into the culture, enjoyed enough success for her to know its lyrics, but it was new to me. In Vietnam we were simply isolated from the popular culture for most of 1966. I was from the States, but not part of it.

PART 2

Shipboard Ops and a Trip to the *Repose*

CHAPTER 6

Dickhouse I

In June 1966 the squadron Ops officer, in cahoots with other senior guys and blessed by the CO on the advice of the XO, constructed a list of air-crews and support folks to deploy aboard the USS *Princeton*. I was among those assigned. Capt. K. D. Waters was the detachment Officer in Charge (OIC). The deployment was in support of the Special Landing Force (SLF), which at the time was the 3rd Battalion, 5th Marine Regiment, out of Camp Pendleton, California. Along with the battalion was a battery of artillery and various pieces of the Force Support Group (FSG), where supply, mainte-nance, transportation, engineers, and medical units resided in the Corps. Our squadron was to provide a section of gunbirds and a slick for three weeks.

Lieutenant Colonel Summerville's HMM-364, the "Purple Fox" of Ky Ha, was the transport helo squadron assigned. Their motto was "Give a shit" and it was proudly displayed on the squadron cruise patch. A cruise patch is one developed specifically for a deployment, not the one registered and blessed for the squadron by the Marine Corps. The Foxes flew CH-34Ds, the older lift birds. In 1966 these were still the main transport helos, though the newer CH-46s were coming into the inventory.

During flight training at Pensacola I'd carrier qualified (CQ) aboard the USS *Lexington* in the T-28C, a fixed-wing training aircraft. And I CQed in the UH-1E, aboard an LPH (Landing Platform Helicopter) off the east coast while assigned to VMO-1 at New River. But I'd never lived and operated aboard ship. This outing would be interesting and new and a relief from the Ky Ha routine. I was glad I was going along.

Six pilots went, half were ex-VMO-1 bubbas: Ross, Waters, and me. I'd known Barney Ross from flight school days and had come to Vietnam with both Waters and him. I not only liked but trusted Waters; usually he was the right man for the job, unless the job were political in nature, the kind in which a guy had to be duplicitous, ass kiss, deal in partial truth, and be a fawning toady who fucks around the edges instead of getting to the heart of an issue; then he would probably not be your man. Maybe I could serve well in those capacities, but not Waters; he was way too blunt and fiery for that shit.

Numerous lists flew about, who was going, which birds, what records and orders were needed, and what parts for the helos must be taken. The know-how guys also figured out how resupply would work if we did not have the right parts with us, and how to pass word back and forth to the Squadron and Group from the ship. This would be primarily through the naval message system, the stuff of the "Message Board" that officers and SNCOs became regrettably and increasingly familiar with as they move up in rank. The parts we took were a bit weighty so we enlisted the support of the Purple Foxes to take a couple of loads for us to "the boat."

Launch day came. Waters gave us a special refresher brief on shipboard operations, which included the landing pattern our detachment would use, the *Princeton*'s TACAN channel, and its radio frequency and call sign. We brought along some extra clothes, a dop kit, slipped into our flight gear and a "Mae West" life vest (named after the impressive boobs on a movie actress of the 1930s), and signed for our helos. After preflight and turn up, we leaped off the Ky Ha cliff one morning, Waters in the lead. We flew to a rendezvous with the "Bullhorn," the *Princeton*'s call sign. It was heading south twenty miles off the coast of Chu Lai.

After Waters switched the flight to the appropriate UHF frequency, he called, "Bullhorn Tower, this is Klondike twelve dash four, flight of three UH-1's, eighteen miles, two-niner-zero-degree radial. We're feet wet, inbound for landing. Over." Feet wet simply meant we'd left land and were over water. It was a required call, just as "Feet dry" was when you'd crossed the coastline after departing the ship.

"Roger Klondike twelve dash four, understand flight of three. Feet wet. Your signal's Charlie. You're cleared for the break. After the downwind, cross the ship's stern and land starboard side, forward of the superstructure. Over."

"Roger Bullhorn. Klondike's cleared for the break and starboard-side landings. Over," Waters answered.

K. D. called us on FM and put the flight in right echelon. We lined slightly behind him at an angle; the second helo stepped up above first, and the third above the second. He took us first astern the *Princeton*, then we flew up the deck at three hundred feet. At three-second intervals, one after the other we broke left into 45-degree angles of bank. We held the bank and the altitude until our aircraft had turned 180 degrees and headed opposite the ship's course. (The break is designed to create time and space interval between aircraft, so each can land and be positioned on the carrier deck before the next comes aboard.) After we passed the ship in the opposite direction, one by one we turned left again. Waters took us across the *Princeton's* stern. I watched the green-white water churn beneath the ship's rear from its massive propellers. Again we turned left and flew up the starboard side of the carrier.

"Klondike twelve dash four and flight, this is Bullhorn. Your flight is cleared to land. Pick up the landing signalman forward of the superstructure. Follow his direction to your deck spots. Over."

"Roger, Bullhorn. Klondike twelve dash four and flight cleared to land," K. D. answered. We followed the leader in a long trail. I was flying the slick, the third and last Huey, "tail end Charlie" in the small formation.

Waters slowed and lost altitude as he pulled along the carrier's starboard side. He flew just a few knots faster than the ship, one hundred yards abeam, and slightly above deck level. He picked up the raised arms of a landing signal director and, with the nose of his helo just slightly left of the ship's course, he started sliding his Huey almost sideways toward the Bullhorn. At sixty feet above the water, Waters maneuvered across the deck edge with six to eight feet of clearance. Still under the direction of the Bullhorn crew, he air taxied to the *Princeton's* most forward portside parking spot. At the signalman's directon, he set the gunbird down.

By that time the second Huey was sliding sideways under the direction of a second signalman. He cleared the deck edge and was moved forward to the spot adjacent to K. D. This sequence was repeated with me. I was parked behind K. D.'s wingman.

We become accustomed to this starboard-side landing pattern. The ship brought the 34s aboard from the port side; the difference helped reduce landing pattern congestion. After our first landing we didn't enter a break; we just went into a trail formation with one Huey a hundred yards or so behind the other and landed, one at a time, forward of the superstructure.

We got good at this, though it was tricky since muscle memory fought us. From land operations we were inclined to hold a higher nose position with a slightly aft cyclic compared to the forward airspeed required to set down on or lift from the moving platform. We had countless landings on a nonmoving surface, but the ship might be steaming at fifteen knots. Wind could add another ten, maybe more. So we were actually air taxiing at twenty-five knots, give or take, at touchdown. Like formation flying, shipboard ops is all about relative motion; whatever speed the ship was making over the earth's surface, that better be your speed at landing and lifting. Otherwise you'd be backing up or moving forward, a bad idea on a helos-filled flight deck with people walking around.

It was great fun, exhilarating stuff, with a hair greater potential for trouble. I developed a renewed appreciation for carrier pilots, and believed their adrenaline rush comes as much from takeoff and landing as from most missions. Since I was normally land-based, mine usually came from the mission. Still, I always felt a sense of satisfaction, maybe achievement, at taking off and landing aboard ship. I tried to keep my ego in check; usually I succeeded. But working off a carrier is a pride inducer if ever there was one. After that, you have to smack down the tendency to crow and thereby become even more boring.

Carrier operations is another of those experiences that cannot be described. Unless lived, it remains secret. I'll always cherish and smile inwardly at these memories. It's difficult to compete with it, and has little to do with "going to work or to the office" in the traditional sense.

After our initial landing and shutdown, a ship's company Chief Petty Officer, the glue of the Navy, met us and directed us through a hatch in the superstructure that led to a common area for briefings. They gave us some mimeographed sketches of the ship so we'd be oriented and could find our way around. They covered chow hours, shower hours, where we slept, where the ready room was, refueling procedures, radio stuff, and other need-to-know nuts and bolts.

For sleeping, lieutenants were assigned to the Junior Officers' Port Bunk Room. We joined some guys from HMM-364 already there. The bunkroom had some steel vertical lockers along one bulkhead for stowing clothes and personal effects. In the middle of the room a long metal table and mattresses on fixed metal racks lined two bulkheads. The place accommodated ten. After one night there, it became apparent that the bunkroom was misnamed. It should have been the Junior Officers' Port Sauna, Casino, Grab Ass, Shit-shooting, and Sleep-if-you-can parlor.

The *Princeton*'s ready room and wardroom were air-conditioned, comfortable, cool, and pleasant. Maybe all of the living spaces aboard were air-conditioned and ours had failed, or maybe we were at the end of the distribution ducts and screwed as a consequence. Maybe some perverse bastard had stuffed rags in behind our grill or diverted what was supposed to be ours to his own needs. I can't know, but we were sweating in there. Most guys either sat around in their underwear or at least slipped out of the tops of their flight suits, tying the sleeves around their waists. It was hot, too hot, but I made it through the night.

Summerville's lift guys were a hoot, full of youthful energy and humor, great fun to be around. All were experienced 34 jocks, able to maneuver the cumbersome-looking helo with precision and competence. They knew what the bird could do and they could operate at the edges of the flight envelope. This was my first experience merged in with a lift squadron; it was one hell of an enjoyable and informative time. That is, unless you wanted sleep.

Their operations officer, a major, was one of the funniest guys I'd ever heard give a brief. This was unusual. Normally the more senior the guy and the more responsible the job, the more serious and tight-assed he was. It was like they wanted to set a good example for the kids, implying from a sober demeanor that, "This shit is serious. So you guys back there quit fucking around and listen up." Soberness among seniors also reflects, I suppose, the pressure on them. After all, they were responsible for the overall mission and for the young'uns who were executing it. Still, their Ops O, although he wore gold oak leaves, was a very clever guy and didn't mind performing. Briefs were fun. Lieutenant Colonel Summerville's presence, however, kept the act well within bounds. He was a wise older man, probably in his late thirties, but he seemed old to a twenty-five-year-old. He was smooth and smiling, with the right mix of experience, intelligence, dignity, grace, and forbearance to be a good squadron commander. The Corps had done itself proud in his command selection. I admired him from the first all-pilots meeting, which the Klondike guys always attended.

Fun though the bunkroom gang was, they were fun too late into the evening, playing cards, being clever, and shooting the shit well into the night. After the first night of hot and noisy, I started looking for alternate sleeping accommodations. That meant a trip to see the Staff Noncommissioned Officers. I thought of sleeping in or under a Huey on an inflatable mattress, called a "rubber lady." I needed some quiet, and exposure to cooler, circulating air. An on-deck solution would be an improvement.

"Hey, Gunny Remp, I need some help." I spied him on the hangar deck, one level below the flight deck where maintenance was performed,.

"What's up, Lieutenant?" he responded with mild and open curiosity.

"Well, I'm thinkin' of bedding down in a Huey. It's way too noisy and hot where I'm stayin'. You know where I might come by a rubber lady?"

"We probably have some in the pack up. You might check with Sergeant White. He can probably shit you one. He was around here a minute ago." He glanced around the hangar deck. "There he is, over there shootin' the shit." The Gunny pointed to a cluster of four Marines not thirty yards away.

"I see him," I answered. "Thanks. See ya later, Gunny."

"Okay, Lieutenant. Have a good one." I eased off in the direction on the small group. They sensed my approach. First one, then another turned their gaze to me. "What's up, sir," asked Sergeant White, the senior Marine in the group.

"Sergeant White, I'm hopin' you might have a rubber lady I can use while we're aboard ship," I began. And so it went. I acquired a mattress and, although I had to huff and puff to get the damn thing inflated, once it got that way, I just left it rigid, laying it on my bunk in the daylight hours.

Although I was thinking of sleeping either inside or under a Huey on the flight deck, I snooped around for an alternative and stumbled upon the perfect place. I think it's called the fantail. This was a large open area, probably sixty feet or more square just below the flight deck, at the stern of the ship. It was exposed on three sides, so wind blew through. Several large mooring cleats and bolsters were located on each side to accommodate huge ropes called hawsers, which slid over these and secured the ship dockside. It was a low traffic area in the day and a no traffic area at night.

I wondered fleetingly if it was okay to be there, but decided not to ask, relying instead on the old adage that it's easier to get forgiveness than permission. I tried it that night and it was super. I smelled the ocean, saw the moon when it was low in the sky, and was protected from rain and dew by the flight deck above me. I felt the gentle motion of the ship and heard the drumming of its engines and propellers well beneath me. And the sun woke me. The next day I shared my secret with Ross. "I've discovered a better place to sleep, Barney."

"What are you up to?"

"I'm out on the fantail. It's cooler and quieter by yards and there's a lotta space. If you're not okay with the bunk room, I recommend it." And I explained it all.

"I'll check it out," he countered. He never came, nor did any of the guys, which was fine with me.

Thus began a serene stay for my duration on the *Princeton*: alone in the night, a pillow, a blanket, an inflatable mattress, and my thoughts. My sleep did not depend on the behavior of others; when I'd had enough "fun" in our bunkroom, I grabbed my mattress and headed for the fantail. Each morning I saw the sun come up scattering orange and red across the sea. I rousted myself, collected my gear, and headed below to shave, then off to breakfast and for whatever flight was scheduled. It was a mellow, tranquil time for the Kansas man, a memory I cherish.

■ ■ ■

The operation we deployed to support was called Deckhouse I, which the irreverent lieutenants and the troops immediately renamed Dickhouse I. The more senior guys probably wanted to call it that too, but their days of snickering were behind them. Some folks had to be in charge and that can reduce the fun. We sailed south from the Chu Lai Tactical Area of Responsibility down into the II Corps area where the Army was responsible for the war's prosecution.

On H-hour, D-day, the lift squadron inserted the battalion, which was new to Vietnam. Each of the battalion's three companies went into separate LZs. The gunbirds, led by Waters, escorted the insertions. I was a copilot to someone on the mission. We recon'd the LZs and made threatening no-fire passes on both sides of the lift birds as they landed, discharged troops, and came out of the zones. Even though we took off at 0800, insertions took all morning and into the early afternoon. Shipboard refueling was required between company insertions.

Contact with the enemy was relatively light during the entire operation. A couple of skirmishes occurred with local VC but I remember no serious engagements. I flew medevac escort on two days for one of the Purple Foxes. Although "Whitegold," their call sign, pulled three or four Marines out of the field on each of my days as medevac chase, they were mostly heat exhaustion casualties. It came as no surprise to me that heat exhaustion was a problem for our Marines. It was June, hot as blazes and, as always, humidity was high. As I've said, Vietnam is on the latitude of Honduras in our hemisphere. Even with training classes and frequent water stops, "water discipline" as it was called, the grunts were hard-pressed to adjust to these extremes. A number simply had to be brought back to the ship, some semi-delirious. The docs would slam an IV in them and cool their core temperature. Usually that did it.

Enemy action produced few casualties, and some of these were from pungi-stake booby traps on trails. The VC were good at digging small pits and lining them with slender sharpened bamboo stakes. These might not penetrate the sole of combat boots, but the pit's side-mounted stakes sure could fuck up a man's ankle and calf. Sometimes it took a buddy or two to help a Marine extract his leg without causing further and greater injury.

Some fire was exchanged but it was occasional and small potatoes compared with the serious combat this Marine battalion would encounter along the DMZ just a month later in Operation Hastings. Generally speaking, and from a helo perspective, this operation was exercise, not characterized by the serious shit and the trading of blows the Marines often faced. It was probably just right for a new battalion getting its feet wet.

CHAPTER 7

Fuel, Friendship, and Doctors

LOW-FUEL ASS PUCKER

"Hey, Dave, you're flying Brigadier General LaHue tomorrow in the slick," K. D. said one evening in the ship's cool ready room.

"Okay, sir. Any more details?"

"Not much. It's just him and his aide. He came aboard this afternoon. The Foxes brought him down. He's getting briefed today, but tomorrow 0800, you'll take him pretty much wherever he wants to go. He's visiting the units ashore. Make sure you have their grids, freqs, and call signs before you leap off. I don't think they've assigned a chase."

"Roger, I got it, sir," I answered. I had no idea why we would not have a CH-34 following us around. Maybe they thought the turf was relatively non-threatening. Who knows? I checked the flight schedule later that day and, sure enough, I was going alone.

That evening I found the greenside operations people, the ones still aboard ship who controlled and monitored the Marines ashore (green is Marine, blue is Navy). I made sure the grids I'd pulled from the wall maps in the ready room were still good for unit locations. I also verified the FM radio freqs and call signs for the ashore Battalion CP, the letter companies, and the artillery battery. I transcribed them not only on a sheet of kneeboard paper, but also on the trusty 1:50,000-meter map, which, like the infantry, all helo jocks used. I kept one in the lower right pocket of my flight suit. These pockets were in front of both shins, wide, and ten or twelve inches deep. A horizontal zipper crossed their tops below the knees; they were just right for flight gloves or a folded map.

In the morning, as required, I'd looked over the last ten flights in the assigned helo's maintenance log to see if it had any recent problems. It was clean. No gripes. I signed the yellow sheet on the hangar deck, which served as our line shack and went up the ladder to the flight deck.

"How's she look, Sergeant Hock?" I asked as I approached the slick. Predictably, the crewchief, Sergeant Hockenbury in this case, was already at the helo. He'd preflighted the bird and signed it off earlier. The morning was super, clean, bright sky, fifteen knots across the deck, and gentle motion from the huge ship churning away in tranquil water. It was a great day to be alive and to leap off a carrier.

"It's in good shape, Lieutenant," Sergeant Hockenbury responded. "What're we up to?"

"We're gonna do whatever a Brigadier General named LaHue wants us to. That's the short answer. Ops didn't have many details, except we'll take him around to the units ashore. I have the grids and how to contact 'em. I guess this one may develop as we go." I opened the pilot's side door and threw my flak jacket and helmet bag onto the seat.

"We're just takin' the General and his aide. We ain't got a chase," I continued.

"Okay, sir. It'll be a whatever-the-General-wants day," Hock responded. We chatted a bit as I went through the usual pilot's preflight, looking in access doors, checking cable tensions to the tail rotor, and clambering around on the rotor head to check bearing tolerances and stabilizer bar dampening functions. Just as the logbook had suggested, the bird seemed solid; I knew this partly from flying it several days earlier. We were ready when the General and his aide, escorted by two operations people, showed up at 0800.

I met the party as they walked toward our helo. "Sir, I'm Lieutenant Ballentine, your pilot today, and that's Sergeant Hockenbury the crewchief." I nodded at Hock who stood near the Huey and smiled with my best military courtesy openers.

"Good to meet you both, I'm Brigadier General LaHue and this is my aide, Second Lieutenant Bob Parker. What's your first name?" the General asked as he extended his hand to me, then to Sergeant Hockenbury who walked over. The aide shook our hands also.

"Sir, I'm Dave. We can put you in the copilot's seat and your aide in the jump seat if you'd like, sir. That way you can see better."

"That'd be great, but whatever you think best."

"Then we'll do it that way, sir. Sergeant Hockenbury can help you strap in and show you the ICS switch. There's a headset inside for you and Bob." I paused. Then, "We can go, unless you have questions," I said.

"No questions, Dave. We're ready," he answered.

"Okay, sir. Oh, one more thing. We're supposed to wear life preservers while over water. There's one for you both on your seats. You're probably familiar, but you just slip it over your head and secure it with the snaps and buckles in front. If we go in the drink, I'll roll the helo to the right so I'll be on the downside. When the blades stop flailing, release your seat belt, and exit on your side of the helo, but don't inflate your preserver until you're clear of the aircraft. You inflate the vest by pulling the two toggles hanging down in front. The only other thing is you'd best jettison your door before we hit the water. There's a yellow T-handle at the hinges. Just yank it and the hinge-pins are pulled, then turn the regular door handle, give the door a kick, and it will fall away. Sergeant Hock can show you, sir."

While the General and his aide settled in with the help of Hockenbury, I got my gear on and started the checklist. Then Hock went outside the rotor arc for turn up. He gave me a thumbs-up and I pulled the start trigger. He got back in the cabin after we were at operating rpm.

"Everyone ready?" I asked into the ICS. They told me they were, so I called for takeoff.

"Bullhorn tower, Klondike six dash one to lift from spot five. Mission 1213. I have a Code 6 aboard," I transmitted over the UHF radio.

"Klondike six dash one, you're cleared to lift on Mission 1213. Follow the director's signals for launch."

"Roger, Bullhorn. Klondike six dash one cleared to lift."

Our slick was on the starboard side of the flight deck, first spot forward of the superstructure. I gave our director, who stood immediately in front, a thumbs-up. He responded with the arm and hand signal for me to lift. I gingerly pulled the helo into a fifteen-knot air taxi to hold my place over the moving deck. The director tilted his left arm down and his right arm up, the signal for me to slide to the right, off the ship's deck. As we began sliding toward deck edge, he brought his right arm across his torso to join his left and pointed with both to the open water. I flew off the deck and over the blue of the South China Sea.

I pulled in more power and fed in compensating left rudder to hold the helo's course, then lowered the nose a hair and began gathering speed and altitude. At 60 knots, I began a right turn away from the ship, climbed to 500 feet, and accelerated to 110 knots on a westerly heading.

It was thrilling and this was routine, at least while we operated off the Princeton. My guess is that the General and his aide were awed as well. How could you not be? We had blue-green sea beneath with small white caps blown up, a clear blue sky, and a sandy beach and lush green landforms ahead. It was an unforgettable visual smorgasbord. The machine was behaving itself as usual, and we were off on an adventure.

The AO (Area of Operations) was not huge, unlike the large chunks of real estate around Chu Lai, Danang, Phu Bai, and Dong Ha. I believed fuel would be adequate for whatever might come our way. Without ferry tanks, the Huey had two hours of flight time, a lot more if you're at flight idle in some LZ. I was in great shape for whatever the General wanted, at least I thought so.

I took the General to five different sites. The frequencies, call signs, and unit locations were just as briefed to me by shipboard Ops. After initial contact, smoke was popped at each. The LZs were adequate in size, although trees surrounded the second zone, and I had to shoot a precision approach. But I had at least seven hundred hours in model at the time. All the skills and confidences were in place; it posed no problem. The system had worked its magic on yet another young aviator.

Our first landing was at the Battalion CP and I left the Huey's engine at flight idle, rather than shutting it down. Unlike the reciprocating engines, there was little danger of overheating a turbine or the fluid systems associated with it. Sergeant Hock and I sat there at low engine rpm shooting the breeze, waiting for the General. What the hell, how long could he take?

But the answer was, he could take a long, long, long time. General LaHue must have pressed the flesh and chatted with everyone at the CP and then been briefed on every jot and tittle, every tent peg and ammo round, and every family of every Marine. He must have had a detailed, inquiring mind, not easily satisfied with the one-over-the-world approach that briefing officers hope for. To say he was there longer than I'd anticipated is an understatement. But, eventually here they came and they'd added a passenger.

After they strapped in, "Dave, this is Captain Lassiter, the Battalion Three Alpha [the "Three" is the Ops O; the Alpha is his assistant]. He's coming along to help point out some details of the AO as we go," the General offered as an introduction and explanation.

"Yes, sir." I said. "Glad to meet you, Captain," I turned left, sideways in my seat and extended my gloved right hand. Lassiter, a big man, occupied the jump seat just to the rear of the center console. He'd commandeered both the seat and the headset once used by the aide.

After the greetings, Sergeant Hockenbury watched from outside as we ran the engine and rotors to operating RPM. Then he joined us in the Huey, checked that all the passengers were belted in, then strapped himself into the rear behind the General. "I'm ready, Lieutenant," he said into the ICS.

"Okay, Hock." I pulled in the collective steadily, not pausing in a hover to check gauges as I normally would. I just glanced at them as we were passing through ten feet. The helo was blowing too much crap around from hover power for me to be methodically farting around checking gauges in a cloud of debris. I wanted my engine out of the FOD-producing (Foreign Object Damage) debris, over with the nose, power coming, left rudder, altitude and air speed advancing together. After three hundred feet, "Where to, sir?" I inquired over the ICS.

"Well, Dave, Ops suggests we take an aerial tour of the terrain and our AO first. Then we'll visit the letter companies and the artillery battery," the General answered.

"Dave, if you could take us to the beach first, right here." Lassiter was talking. He leaned over my left shoulder and showed me a place on a map with his thumb. "Then we'll just fly this ridgeline as it goes inland and swings north. I can talk you along as we go."

I glanced from his map to the one on my kneeboard. It was apparent what he wanted. "Okay, sir. We can do that." I swung the Huey left and headed southeast back to the coast.

We traced the AO flying just inside its limits, drilling along at approximately one thousand feet MSL. The flight took fifteen minutes or so as the Captain described what was going on where, intelligence aspects of the operation, enemy encountered (not much of this) or anticipated, and the deployment of his companies. All informative military stuff for the General.

"Okay, Dave, if we can go to these coordinates, we'll visit Golf Company for their brief." Once again Captain Lassiter leaned in with his thumb on his map and I glanced at my own to assure his location was the same as I'd recorded earlier aboard ship. They were identical.

"Roger, sir," I responded. "Looks like we're coming up on 'em."

"Yeah, they should be just up that valley," he answered and pointed to our right front.

"Sword Golf, Klondike six dash one. Over," I called to their FM frequency.

After just a pause, "Klondike six dash one. This is Sword Golf. Go ahead. Over."

"Roger Golf. We're in a Huey approaching your position to land. Can you smoke your LZ? Over."

"Smoke coming, Klondike. It'll be green. Over."

"Klondike, Roger. Green smoke. Over." Within ten seconds I picked up the beginnings of the billows.

"Sword Golf, Klondike has the smoke. Any bad guys we should be avoidin' on our way in? Over."

"Klondike. It's been quiet today. No contact. Over."

"Roger, Sword Golf. I've a Code aboard. You probably know that. Over."

"We do indeed, Klondike. Golf, out."

We settled into the company's LZ. The General, his aide, and Captain Lassiter deplaned and were met by a captain and a gunnery sergeant, no doubt the Company Commander and Company Gunny. Off they went. This time I shut the bird down.

After thirty minutes we were off again, and we repeated this hopscotch for two more letter companies, Hotel and India. Each time we toured around a bit at the request of Captain Lassiter to show the General company boundaries and discuss terrain and intelligence information. Finally we visited the artillery battery that supported the battalion.

My forehead was beginning to furrow a bit at the end. On our way back to drop off Captain Lassiter at the Battalion CP, we were getting low enough on fuel for me to mention it.

"Sir, we're getting a bit down on gas. If we're gonna do any more cruising around, we'll have to go back to the ship and top off." One hates to interrupt the plans of senior people, but it's better than a flameout over the South China Sea or, for that matter, over land.

"Oh, we're done, Dave. As soon as we drop the Captain, we can head to the ship," the General answered smiling. "We've had a good and full visit with the units and I'll be able to brief the Division Commander tomorrow from a good platform of knowledge. Thanks for hauling us around and for your patience," he concluded.

"Oh, sir. We're happy to do it. This was a great outing and a nice day for flying. I've truly enjoyed it," I answered. He was a gracious man; he didn't need to say any of that. Klondike was tasked; we provided. It was what we did, what every Marine unit did. Yet, he'd thanked us like we'd done a favor. I was impressed.

When we landed at the Battalion CP, out came the Battalion Commander. The General went out for a short pow-wow. He "would only be a minute." I didn't shut down. This was getting less okay by the minute, but soon we left.

Four hours had passed since lifting from the Princeton. The winds were stiffer and onshore.

After handshakes, we all slipped on our life preservers again for the overwater flight. We'd removed them earlier to stay cool. I lifted the slick for its return flight to the ship and headed for the coast, climbing to one thousand feet. My TACAN needle and DME (distance measuring equipment) stopped rotating. The *Princeton* was twenty miles at one two zero degrees. Shit. The *Princeton* must have a large box to steam around in; we were only four miles from the coast when we'd launched. I could see the gray structure in the distance. We crossed the shoreline. I radioed, "Bullhorn, Klondike six dash one. Feet wet inboard for landing. I have Code 6 aboard. Over."

"Klondike six dash one, Bullhorn, Roger. Proceed. Expect landing from portside abeam the superstructure. Over," came the *Princeton*'s answer.

My mind focused; this landing would be just opposite from our normal approach and landing pattern. Usually the Hueys approached from the starboard and landed forward of the superstructure.

"Roger Bullhorn. Understand Klondike six dash one to approach portside and land abeam the superstructure. Over."

"Klondike six dash one, Bullhorn. That's affirmative. Call two miles. Over." They were changing my routine, but no problem.

"Klondike six dash one. Roger, Bullhorn. We'll report two miles. Over." I settled down to drive and monitor the gauges. Within thirty seconds, the twenty-minute fuel light illuminated, bright and telling, on the instrument panel. I was ten minutes away from landing.

Since the light might alarm my passengers, I felt compelled to say something mollifying, even though I was feeling a bit unsettled. You don't wanna say, "Brace yourselves, gents. We might be headin' for the drink." That kinda shit can be upsetting.

"We're warned of low gas, sir," I said pointing to the light, which I presumed he'd seen. "But we'll get to the ship, no problem."

"I'm not worried, Dave," General LaHue answered. Then he and his aide absorbed themselves in conversation about their experiences of the day and their plans for tomorrow. Time may have passed quickly for them, but it was damn slow for me. I knew I'd make it if all things were equal, but there was always the possibility that the gauges and warning systems were off, that I was lower on fuel than my gauge registered. I had an increasingly tight grip on the licorice (cyclic and collective). It was still a great day, sunny, visibility forever, and small whitecaps decorated the sea. But I was distracted; my ass was beginning to tighten. I was not at full pucker, but a snugging had set in.

In my mind I went over again ditching procedures: Auto to the water, roll to the right, exit to the left once the blades stop, swim clear, inflate, and, if the sharks don't get your ass, be ready with dye marker for the rescue helo; then be returned ignominiously to the ship, endure a round or two of hearings which detail your blunder, and then lose your wings. Oh, and if someone died or was seriously injured, I'd suffer guilt at the suicidal dimension for the remainder of my days. Shit, flame out with a General aboard, or just flame out period, and your name will be the topic of discussion for months. The only possible good would be the lesson it would offer others.

I descended to five hundred feet, then to three hundred. Two miles off the stern of the *Princeton* I called, "Bullhorn, Klondike six dash one, two miles astern for landing. Over."

"Roger Klondike six dash one, you're cleared for a port approach to spot seven abeam the superstructure. Pick up the landing signalman on final. You're cleared to land. Over."

"Klondike six dash one cleared to land port side, spot seven," I repeated then reached to the base of the collective and loosened the friction knob. I'd snugged it earlier to hold the collective in place.

I lowered the collective a little and raised the nose feeding in right rudder to maintain balanced flight. The Huey slowed. I swung to the port of the ship's green-white wake and descended to one hundred feet on the RADALT. Then I slowed further until the airspeed indicator dropped below sixty knots. I stopped looking in the cockpit. I started flying formation on the USS *Princeton*. It was all about relative motions, closure rates, and staying slightly above the flight deck.

Abeam of the ship's stern and at two hundred feet off the ship's port-side, I slowed to match the Princeton's speed and I picked up my signal-man. Predictably, he was near the port deck edge and adjacent to the superstructure. Keeping my eyes on him, and holding the Huey's nose on a course almost paralleling the ship, I began my sideways slide. I crossed the deck edge at whatever speed the Princeton was making with eight feet of deck clearance. I brought the helo over the spot signaled and held my position for a moment. Then the director motioned me to set the bird down. I did gladly.

When the collective was bottomed and we were firmly on the Bullhorn's deck, I rolled the throttle to flight idle. We'd made it. When I glanced at the General and his aide, I was relieved and smiley.

"Dave, it's been a good day for us. Thanks for your help." The General beamed and reached across the cockpit, hand extended.

We shook. "It's been nice meeting you, sir. We're happy to help when we can," I responded. Sergeant Hockenbury had slid the left rear cabin door open and the aide climbed out. Then Hock opened the General's door and collected the Mae Wests and headsets from the departing passengers.

Two greeters approached the helo from the base of the superstructure. They ducked as they came under the helo's sweeping blades, shook hands, swapped howdys, then wheeled and headed for a hatch, disappearing into the ship's interior.

I was starting the shutdown procedures when this came over the UHF: "Klondike six dash one, you are cleared to lift from spot seven, take off port-side, turn downwind at pilot's discretion, cross the ship's stern and land starboard side in Klondike's usual spots. Over."

Oh, shit. I'd just landed here to drop the General, to save him thirty steps. But me and Hock, we needed to take our bird across the deck and forward to its "usual spot." And they didn't want me to air taxi; they wanted me to launch!

I tried an option, "Bullhorn, Klondike six dash one, I've started my shut-down sequence. Can't we just put on the ground handling wheels and tow it into the Klondike spots? Over."

After a pause, "Negative, Klondike. We have helos inbound and will need that spot. You're cleared for takeoff. Over."

Here was the dilemma: I could simply confess that my fuel was danger-ously low and that further flight was unwise, sort of declare an on-deck emergency and refuse my instructions from the tower. Or I could gamble. I could follow the tower's instruction, take my ass in both hands, and Hock's too for that matter, leap off, and defy what my judgment dictated. If I did this I might end up in the drink, risking Sergeant Hockenbury, a perfectly good, though out-of-gas, Huey, and myself.

I could not ponder long. I inched toward full pucker. If I chose the first course of action, I'd be the subject of an inquiry. "You mean to tell us, Lieutenant Ballentine, that you were flying the General and others, including your crewchief, around with a dangerously low fuel state?" How the hell you gonna tap dance out of that shit? Nothing I could say could alter this fact. If I dropped the bird into the sea, of course, I'd also have some explainin' to do before a board. But I probably had enough gas to make it.

I tightened into full-on, cinched-down ass pucker. "Roger, Bullhorn we'll be liftin'." I motioned for Sergeant Hockenbury to get back in the helo.

Into the ICS I said tensely, "Hock, I'm flyin' this beauty, low fuel and all, around the fuckin' boat and landin' again. We could get wet. You ready?"

"Yes, sir," was all he said.

I rolled the throttle on and ran the turbine RPM up to 6600, gave a thumbs-up to the director and, at his signal, pulled the bird again into the air and slid left over the flight deck edge and above the sea sixty feet below. I dipped the nose, added power and almost immediately began a 180-degree left turn to a heading opposite the ship's. I started the world's tightest circumnavigation of the *Princeton*'s ass end. I crossed the ship's wake just aft of its stern and pulled to the starboard side. I slowed and picked up my landing director, but I also monitored the instruments and listened for unusual noises, like turbine wind down.

"Klondike six dash one is cleared to land. Over," came the cryptic call from Bullhorn. They'd no doubt watched and maybe marveled at my pattern.

"Roger, Klondike's cleared to land," I transmitted. But I needed no clearance, my ass was comin' aboard. The director was motioning and I kept the Huey moving. We cleared the deck edge, and I breathed just a bit easier. Now if she quit, I could shoot a hover auto. Might bounce a little on the deck, but I was fine with that. The other Hueys were out on a mission and the director moved me, wouldn't you know, to the most forward and port of the Huey spots! I thought, "Damn, guy, this'll do." But no, I air taxied and farted around for another whole thirty seconds before he was happy and gave us the land signal. I did and I shut her down.

After the bird was resting and quiet, I put my flight gear in my helmet bag and opened my door. Stepping out, I looked at Hockenbury. He looked back. We just smiled; mine was relief with a tad of sheepishness mixed in. His was just a smile. I'd dodged another bullet. Hock and I were dry and safe. My reputation was intact and my peers and bosses were none the wiser, unless any of them ever read this. But then, I don't get fitness reports anymore.

I'd love to have been a fly on the wall when Sergeant Hockenbury chatted later with the other crewchiefs and the flight line bubbas. Oh well, the

Kansas boy was still pumpin' air and blood. Life was good. I got a little smarter that day.

INFANTRY–AVIATION COMMUNION

One evening in the early days of our *Princeton* deployment, I went alone for dinner in the wardroom, rather than in a cluster of pilots as usual. No seat was available at the tables occupied by the VMO-6 and Purple Fox pilots. A seat was, however, open at a table of grunts. I eased over.

"Mind if I join you?" I asked from behind the empty chair.

"No, hell. Have a seat," responded a captain.

"Thank ya, sir," I answered and pulled the chair back, lowered myself, and slid forward.

My name, like that of all flight suits—wearing aviators, was apparent and in plain view. It was stenciled on a strip of white cloth tape, which ran parallel to the zipper top on the left-front of the flight suit. But most Marines did not wear flight suits. And unlike today, they had no visible reminder of names. This would be difficult. I felt the weight of all Marine aviators everywhere and of all times. I concentrated.

"I'm Dave Ballentine, here with the Hueys."

The captain, and he was obviously in charge, extended his hand, "I'm Captain Marshall. I've got Hotel Company. This is Fred Wilkins," he nodded at the officer on his left, "my XO and that's Jeff Compton, the second platoon leader." We shook hands and howdied around. They seemed like agreeable chaps, smiling, open, about my own age, though Marshall was slightly older and Jeff Compton, a second lieutenant, was likely a couple of years younger.

I settled in and between mouthfuls of this and that, drinks of the red Kool Aid, usually referred to as "bug juice," and later coffee, we had a pleasant meal. It started with the usual chitchat: where we were from and where we'd gone to college. They were a little amazed that I was not degreed but a commissioned officer. So I explained the MARCAD program. We talked a little about the training we'd received that brought us to this point in our Marine Corps lives and covered what we did in the Corps. They were especially interested in my impressions of the terrain and climate, since none of them had been in country yet.

We were working through mounds of vanilla ice cream with chocolate sauce (are you shittin' me, the Navy lives good) when Marshall said, "Well, gents, the XO and I have a pow-wow with the three (Battalion Operations Officer). We gotta go. Nice meetin' you, Dave. See you around."

Then to Compton, "We'll meet as usual at 2200, Jeff."

Compton and I responded. Captain Marshall and First Lieutenant Wilkins shook my hand and departed. Jeff Compton and I stayed on.

Jeff, a Virginia man, seemed under no pressure, nor was I. We continued our conversation. Talk ranged from how we'd gotten to Asia and what the crossing was like, to the shape of our typical days and how grunts stay in shape aboard ship. Since I didn't have to hump a pack around, I did little physical training; but the grunts were at it daily. We chatted about personal stuff a bit, home, the girlfriend, future expectations; neither of us was sure the Corps would be a career or if the Green Machine would have us. We talked easily, just two young men from different States, with different jobs. We learned about each other and were entertained and distracted from circumstance. *There is no rank among lieutenants,* goes the Marine Corps saying. So we were on a first name basis, with none of the mandated superimposition of rank titles to formalize the association.

I was especially interested in the training and life of a platoon leader. I was convinced the job entailed awesome responsibility, since the lives of a bunch of Marines might hang in the balance of his decisions. I reasoned the Corps was asking a lot of our most junior and necessarily inexperienced officers, but we've been doing it that way for decades. The seniors must believe "it ain't broke."

"Why'd you choose 0302, or did they just put your ass in it?" I asked. The Marines, like all services have developed a numerical system of Military Occupation Specialties (MOS). Jeff was an infantry officer, so he was an 0302. I was an aviator, all of whom were 75-something. My MOS was 7563, the number reserved for UH-1E pilots.

"Maybe I saw too many John Wayne movies as a kid." Jeff smiled as he answered. "But since I was young I've believed that being in the Corps would be a great idea and being in the infantry would be the greatest. I volunteered, though it may not have mattered. A bunch of guys were just assigned to the grunts." He paused then continued. "Combat in an infantry unit will be a hell of challenge; might cause me to grow a little, learn something about myself. I'm looking forward to it, but I'd be lying if I didn't admit it causes me to think at night. I sure don't want to screw it up and get someone hurt or worse from a dumbshit call on my part," he mused.

"I expect it would be a super challenge, as you say. I don't think it's a good fit for me. That shit of livin' outdoors has always troubled me. I suppose if the Corps was only grunts, I might have passed," I offered.

"It can get uncomfortable, and in the field, a night's sleep is almost impossible. You get punchy after a couple of days. I know that already just from exercises, and I haven't even seen combat. We trained our butts off getting ready, but I wonder if you can get ready. Getting shot at and shooting back has got to change things. I suppose I'll find out in a couple of days."

"Our Marines are in great shape," he continued. "They know their skills from manuals, instruction, and practice. You'd be surprised how everyone starts paying close attention when they know they're heading for war. We've digested the latest info coming back from country. They have field skills and are pretty good shots, but, except for the Company Gunny, who's a Korean vet, nobody's seen or heard a shot fired in anger. As a matter of fact, no more than six or seven Marines in the battalion are vets, the CO, sergeant major, and maybe four or five other senior Staff NCOs. That's gonna change shortly."

"Yep, you'll shoot, maneuver, shoot, coordinate, swat bugs, maneuver, try to sleep, and sweat. You'll be takin' it to Charlie, Marine Corps style. My ass will escort the lift birds for insertions, extractions, resupply, and medevac. When I'm not doing that, I'll be here awaitin' your call." I couldn't resist the comparison. "But it all fits together someway I guess."

"I suppose," Jeff countered. "But my ass will always be in the center, in the very heart and soul of the Corps, and your ass will forever be supporting my ass." He was smiling large, vindicated.

"You got a point. I'm okay in a supportin' role," I finished.

We drifted on. He was curious about flight training, what we'd flown, carrier landings, how we got qualified and stayed that way after getting our wings, and squadron life in general. Our conversation was pleasant and informative, the beginnings of a bond, two Marines, each with a different job, but joined in common cause, with a common tradition.

I liked the Virginia man and sensed that he more than just tolerated me. Jeff and I ran across each other from time to time over the next few days and in the wardroom. When possible we'd chat over a meal or play cards or Acey-Ducey, a popular dice game of the time. He could be serious, but had a great mischievous streak. He was, of course, in super shape, a fine example of a poster Marine, square, lean, and starched. Then Operation Dickhouse I kicked off. I didn't see him again until the night before the VMO detachment flew off the *Princeton* for Ky Ha as the ship steamed north.

"Damn, Compton, you survived!" I said as I walked up to his wardroom table.

"Shit, I reckon," he answered smiling. He might have lost a couple of pounds from a week in the bush, but generally he seemed the same.

"I can't stay, I got some packin' and overseein' to do. My boss has saddled me up for a change. My overseein' is pretty much reduced to checkin' with the Gunny to see if he's got any concerns and gettin' the hell outta the way. But how'd it go?" I asked. And we talked for a few minutes. Apparently they'd had little contact, though they'd been sniped at. Their casualties were from the heat, and not wounds; he was satisfied that the operation was useful in "shaking out" the unit, getting it used to the field conditions in Vietnam.

"Well, Jeff, we're haulin' ass in the mornin' and I got a thing or two to do. I gotta say good-bye. It's been nice. Watch your ass." I extended my hand. He stood and we shook.

"It has been good, Dave. Why don't you put in for a FAC job? I'll vouch for you," he offered.

"Fat chance. I'd have to lug shit around and camp out. Not my kind of work." He laughed and, after we shook hands again, I shoved off. I thought I'd seen the last of Jefferson Davis Compton, Second Lieutenant of Marines, but he and I would meet again in sad circumstances.

In the morning we were packed and ready, engines and rotors turning. And as the ship steamed north and we neared Ky Ha, Captain Waters radioed, "Bullhorn tower, Klondike four dash one, flight of three to lift. Starboard departure. Over."

"Roger, Klondike four dash one and flight, you're cleared to lift. Starboard departure approved. Have a good flight." One by one, K. D. in the lead, we followed a director's signals, first into a hover, then over the deck edge. We joined up in loose formation for a short twenty-minute, over-water flight to Ky Ha.

"Klondike flight go trail," Waters instructed as Ky Ha neared. We acknowledged in sequence and slid behind the leader at about one-hundred-yard intervals. Shortly thereafter we landed and taxied into the VMO line.

A chapter in each man's life ended. We settled back into Klondike life at Ky Ha. Most of us were on the flight schedule the next day. During our absence a dramatic event happened at the squadron: Maj. Bill Goodsell, who'd just taken command, was killed in action. He'd had the squadron less than a week.

MODERN MEDICAL SCIENCE VERSUS OLD-TIME REMEDIES

On the back of my left hand just below the wrist, a ganglion cyst sprouted, at least I think that's the name for the kind that develops on or adheres to tender sheaths. It was more unsightly than troublesome, although when performing some hand-wrist maneuvers I noticed a twinge of discomfort. I have no idea how cysts form, but I wanted to be perfect, not marred by this small unsightly knob I'd lugged around more than a year, so I acted. During a slow part of our steaming away from the Dickhouse I AO, I went to the *Princeton*'s sickbay and asked the docs to take a look.

The Navy doctor was fascinated; he even called a buddy over to check it out. After a little dual observation, he said, "Well, Lieutenant Ballentine, in the old days we'd just put your hand palm-down on a table, grab a large book, usually the Bible, and slam it down on your cyst, rupturing it. Eventually it would simply go away, although several treatments might be necessary." He smiled broadly.

He probably could not suppress the smile, since the term "treatment" was surely not the perfect word for beating a cyst into submission with a book. I saw little humor. I nodded, waiting for the alternative to the "old days" method.

"We could do the Bible thing or we could aspirate it and see what happens." The doc looked at me expectantly. Apparently "aspirate" is a regular medical term, but how's a helo jock, one with two years of college, gonna know what it means?

After a pregnant pause, "What do you do to aspirate it?" I asked.

"Well, we'd numb the area around the cyst, stick a hypodermic needle into the cyst itself and draw out the fluid. Then we'd shoot some cortisone in there to aid the healing. I recommend this procedure; the cyst would likely go away. Oh, and we'd have to ground you for a couple of days if we aspirate it."

No aviator wants to be grounded, but we weren't flying anyway. The Purple Foxes had their rotor blades folded on the rear of the flight deck. Our Hueys were chained down forward.

"Hum, I gotta check with my boss, sir. I'll go find out," I responded.

"Fine. It's slow today. Just come back and we'll go to work if your boss approves," the doc said.

I slid off my gray metal chair and headed out to find Captain Waters. "Go ahead. We probably won't be doing anything for a few days anyway," he offered.

"Okay. This is probably my best shot, since they gotta ground me a day or two. See ya later, sir."

I walked back to sickbay; I'd been gone no more than twenty minutes. I was drawn to the Bible "treatment," since hypodermics have made me uneasy, even chickenshit, from the age of twelve, when I endured the one-a-day, fourteen-shot rabies series. But I figured I should go along with the doc's recommendation and aspirate the damn thing.

The Navy doctor was in a chair, going over documents. He looked up as I entered. "My boss says go for it, sir." And he did.

It was horrible. I pride myself, being a coward at heart when it comes to needles and scalpels, at enduring this self-sanctioned torture. The doctors both worked the cyst and farted around with the back of my hand for what seemed an eternity. The mental agony was huge, but I was a man and I endured, at least outwardly. But no matter how I tried to think of other things, places, and activities, I failed. Ski slopes, sailing on broad waters with the wind in my face, inverted coming over the top of a loop, the warm, inviting smile of a caring woman, nothing worked. I was yanked back to present reality by a small tray of sterile pain-inflicting devices, instruments to which I had submitted my hand and, unfortunately, my mind. Cysts are not *that* bad. Oh sure, every once in a while someone would say, "What the fuck is that?" But that was small potatoes compared to this. What the hell was I thinking?

Eventually they finished. My hand and wrist were heavily wrapped and encased in an Ace bandage. I'd be explaining that hand repeatedly in the next two days.

"Lieutenant Ballentine, keep this dry. Put plastic around it in the shower. If it hurts, take a couple aspirin. Here's a small bottle. Come see us day after tomorrow and we'll take a look, and here's you downing chit," the doctor informed me as he handed me a paper, which temporarily removed me from flight status.

"Okay, sir," I responded. These men were Navy lieutenants, the Marine Corps equivalent of captains. So I was talking uphill, as usual, "I'll see you in two days." I slid off the chair, headed for the hatch and many opportunities to explain my bandaged hand.

After two days the doctors looked at the area and seemed satisfied. The assaulted spot was almost as flat as the surrounding area, although slightly swollen.

"We can go to this small bandage now, Lieutenant," the doc said as he covered the area with a two-inch square dressing. "Here is a box with more to use in the coming days and here's an up-chit for your ops people. You can fly again." He'd scribbled something illegible on a small piece of paper. I stuck it in my flight suit with the "down-chit" they'd given me two days earlier. Since they didn't matter, I showed neither to anyone.

"Thanks for you help, sir." I shook his hand and headed for the door. The docs seemed satisfied, so I was optimistic that my discomfort during the aspiration was worth it, that the cyst was behind me. It wasn't.

Two months later, there it was again, dime-sized and loving it. "What the fuck's that on your hand there, Ballentine?" the guys wanted to know.

Something had to be done. I got half drunk at the club, but instead of using the Bible "treatment," I beat the back of my hand against the side of our hooch until the cyst broke. I repeated this "old days" treatment as warranted over the course of my stay in Vietnam. When I left, my wrist was like everyone else's. No cyst. It has not returned for lo these many years. It wouldn't dare; it knows I can get drunk anytime.

I suppose the price of my learning about the Bible treatment was enduring the aspiration. We learn as we go; sometimes new ways are less effective.

CHAPTER 8

Sarcocystus Lindemanni: A Trip to the USS *Repose*

I felt like hell. The sun was high; most people had a slight sheen of perspiration from the heat and humidity, but I was dry and bleary-eyed, unable to think well, and, even though I'd wrapped a blanket around my shoulders, I shivered. I was sick; I knew it. Mercifully I was not on the flight schedule that morning. Although I'd gone to the squadron work area, after a while I knew it was a bad idea. I made my excuses to my boss, Captain Waters, and went back to my quarters to lie down. After an hour and a half stretched out on my rack the situation had not improved.

It was time to see the docs. I was still in my flight suit. I swung my legs off the cot and sat, pulled on my boots, grabbed my utility cover, and, clutching my blanket about me, I headed for sickbay. Mercifully the journey was only a hundred yards.

I lurched through the screen door of the Ky Ha medical facility, a large, triple Southeast Asian hooch and for a heartbeat I pondered options. I could sign in and take a seat, howl for attention and immediate help, or stagger into the back of the facility, where they administered to the needy, find a cot, and lie down. I chose the latter and, as I brushed past the sign-in desk, noticed the wide-eyed, questioning, slightly surprised look of the Petty Officer Second Class who manned the desk. I went through two wide strips of material, which hung vertically from the top cross-member of a door jam. This faux door separated the reception from the treatment area.

"Can we help you, sir?" came the Petty Officer's question as I moved into the rear.

"I'm sick. I need to lie down," was all I could muster. I found a canvas cot and flopped.

The Petty Officer followed me into the rear and came to my side. "What's wrong, sir?" He was concerned. He knew a sick guy from a malingerer.

"I'm down, man. I'm with VMO. Can you get Doc Moffitt?" I responded. Moffitt, a Navy Lieutenant, was our squadron flight surgeon. When he wasn't chatting with us at the squadron about salt tablets and eating, sleeping, booze, and other flight surgeon stuff, his place of duty, like the flight surgeons from other squadrons, was the MAG-36 sickbay. This is not my usual luck, but he was there that day. In a couple minutes he stood at my cot. I was near delirium.

He started checking me over, poking and prodding. A Petty Officer First Class arrived and took my temperature and my pulse rate.

"Well, he's running about 102 degrees and his pulse is up," the Petty Officer offered to Doc Moffitt.

"Let's get some blood and urine and take a look," Moffitt responded. Then to me, "Dave, can you sit up and slip out of the top of your flight suit?"

"Yep," and I did. I was shivering off and on in more or less rhythmic cycles.

Here they came with vials and needles and rubber tubes. The corpsmen, with their usual competence made the blood draw almost unnoticeable. I stood and gave them a small sample of the other fluid they sought. Then back down I went.

A few minutes later, "Dave, here's a couple tablets to pull down your fever," Moffitt said and handed me two Dixie cups, one with pills and one with water. I sat up and downed them, then flopped block and drifted off.

Sometime later, Doc Moffitt returned. It could have been fifteen minutes or two hours. "Dave, you need medevac. We're not perfectly sure, but you have some unusual organisms in your blood. They look like malaria gametes; we could be wrong. Anyway, we're sending you to the hospital ship."

I listened to this, weak, sick, trying to compute what this could mean: medevac, malaria. No one else in the squadron had it. I hadn't heard of anyone in the Group with it, though it was a problem about which we'd been briefed before arriving in Vietnam. I was too ill to care much and had little choice anyway. Once the medical guys decide, you're along for the ride.

Someone from the squadron threw some stuff in a bag for me: another flight suit, some T-shirts, shorts, socks, a paperback, shaving and teeth cleaning gear. The bag was delivered to sickbay. My medical records, a set of hastily drawn orders, my sick ass, and my bag were taken to the north Ky Ha runway where, within three hours of my journey to sickbay, a trusty CH-34 flew me to Danang Airbase. After a wait there of less than an hour, another

CH-34 took me offshore and landed on the stern helo platform of USS *Repose*, a Navy hospital ship.

I've always marveled at the efficiency of the medical folks. When they made decisions, shit happened. One can only guess at the number of lives preserved by that efficiency. Even though nonmedical guys called them "pecker checkers" and "quacks," we all knew the real truth. They were pivotal and we'd have been in serious, serious trouble without them. They did a hell of a job.

With someone's help I got out of the 34 and, led by a sailor, I walked below deck. I heard the helo pull in power and lift as we went through the hatch.

I remember the grayness, the coolness of air conditioning, the cleanliness, the green tile deck, and the antiseptic smell. I was led to a counter where I surrendered my records and orders, then to a bed in a room of several beds. I was shown the head and the shower, given a gown, some towels, a robe, and slippers. After showering I laid down; they took my temperature again and again gave me tablets to reduce my returning fever. Then more blood was drawn and urine provided. I slept, was given a meal in the evening, and I slept again.

In the morning I felt better even though I'd received no medications, no treatments. According to the corpsman who'd checked me that morning, my fever was down, though he also warned that it might return as the day progressed. A lieutenant commander came by later in the morning. After checking my chart and asking me how I was feeling, which was okay, he said, "Lieutenant, we're not convinced you have malaria. So we've sent a sample of your blood to Japan for more analysis. We should have the results in a coupla days."

"Okay, sir. What do you think it is?"

"I can't even hazard a guess, but our lab guys think it may be something else. Maybe one of the lesser-known bugs we're learning about from our involvement here."

"Well, since I'm feelin' better, can I move around the ship? I mean, do I have some limits of travel outside this room?"

"Stay here this morning, read, take it easy. If you're feeling okay this afternoon, mention it to the corpsman when he makes his rounds. I'll tell him to unleash you a bit, if you're feeling up to it." He smiled. "Anything else?"

"No, sir, thanks. I guess it's a wait-and-see scenario."

"I guess; I'll see you again tomorrow morning."

It was indeed a wait-and-see scenario. I had a slight headache, so couldn't read much, but I ate, rested, slept, enjoyed the gentle motion of the ship, and showered again. I relaxed in a nonthreatening environment, one in which nobody had any expectations of me. This was new. But with the return of my strength I began to have expectations of myself, like maybe I ought to be with the squadron, in a nice sweaty cockpit, doing the Klondike do.

Later that day, I still felt okay; my fever had not returned. I was approximately my old self and the corpsman gave me some roaming area, but not the entire ship. He also gave me the option of having dinner delivered bedside or eating in the wardroom. I opted for the latter and at chow time I slipped into my clean flight suit and headed for the officers' mess.

Damn, even though it had been only weeks since my *Princeton* outing, I'd already forgotten. Plates, saucers, nice silver, not the stamped-out kind used on Marine bases, also thick-lipped urns of coffee, the option of tea, red bug juice, ice water, milk, and attendants dressed smartly in white. The Navy is a great service with great traditions. "Damn the torpedoes, full speed ahead." You have to be moved by that sort of cheek. Farragut, Halsey, Nimitz, Spruance, King, the attack carrier gang, the destroyer and destroyer escort pickets against the kamikaze the Sullivan brothers; anyone who noses around a bit or sees the "Victory at Sea" series has to be impressed. The Navy also has nice amenities and is whistle-clean compared to the Corps, at least the Corps in combat. But each service has a separate purpose; each trains differently to handle its missions.

On my way back from a hot meal and casual getting-to-know-you conversation with others at my table, I was brought up short. A man in a wheelchair, slightly hunched over, gaunt with a half-filled pee-bag hanging at the side of his chair, was looking up at me from a wide place in the passageway. It was Second Lt. Jefferson Davis Compton, or at least his shadow, the grunt platoon leader I'd befriended aboard the *Princeton* from 3rd Battalion, 5th Marine Regiment.

"Shit, Jeff!" I blurted. "You okay?" This was foolish. He was obviously not okay.

He smiled a little more broadly and answered weakly, slowly, "Dave, good to see you. I'm hurt pretty bad." He was glad to see me, but had more important concerns, his injuries and the future, for instance.

"You goin' someplace? I'll push your ass around. We can swap lies or something." I wanted to be of some use to him and could think of no other way. I was still in mild shock.

"No, but thanks. I gotta go in there when it's my turn." He nodded at a hatch entrance from the hall into a medical room. Curtains were drawn across its entry. "They'll come and get me in a minute."

I couldn't resist, "What the hell happened to you?" Just as I got it out, a corpsman slid the curtain aside and stepped out and to the rear of Jeff's wheelchair.

"You ready, sir?" he asked.

"I suppose," Jeff responded. "Dave, maybe we can chat tomorrow?" he said, still looking at me.

"Where can I find you?" I asked.

"I'm in 242 A. At least I think that's the room. Maybe you can come by tomorrow?"

"You got it," I countered as the corpsman unlocked the chair wheels and pushed Jeff forward through the curtained entry.

"See you tomorrow," he offered over his shoulder as he was rolled away.

Stunned, I walked back to my room. Just a few weeks before, Compton and I had been joshing and ribbing each other in the *Princeton*'s wardroom. He'd told me what a candy-ass I was for avoiding the real Marine Corps, the infantry. I'd responded that I'd rather fall on my sword than spend my life camping out with chiggers, fleas, leeches, rain, ball-numbing cold, or sweat trickling down the crack of my ass. It was the standard grunt-aviator exchange. We'd smiled and laughed and got on to other subjects.

When I knew him aboard the *Princeton*, he was a poster Marine, around six feet, looking like he could run or do pushups all day, lean, trim, strong. He was as clever and smart and as fun to be around as any of the bubbas in the Klondike ready room. I genuinely liked him and was as curious about the life of a platoon leader as he was about the life of a young pilot. It was a good association. He was a fine and dedicated Marine, a solid lieutenant for our Corps, a credit to his family and our nation. But now he weighed no more than 135 pounds, down 50 from his *Princeton* days, and apparently he was unable to walk or control his bladder. Jeff was a hurt pup and a lesson to me in what can happen short of death to strong, young bodies in war. It was sobering.

I had a little trouble getting to sleep that night, but I was mending from some foreign microbiotic or viral intruder. Sleep came. I escaped the *Repose* into that other world, the land of merged myths and realities, where the mind is not oriented, fixed, and stabilized by sense, where it is given free rein to create, if only for a few hours.

I felt fine the next morning. "Well, Lieutenant Ballentine, we got the information back sooner than we expected. Looks like you have a rare parasite called Sacrocystus Lindemanni," the lieutenant commander began.

I waited and searched the inventory of my mind for relevance. Parasite did not sound promising, or maybe it did, but it was the foreboding kind of promise. The rest was new territory. From the name, Sarcocystus Lindemanni, I presumed some guy named Lindemann had named or discovered it. Something along those lines drifted out of murkiness from high school biology classes, genus and species stuff. I didn't know what to say, but more was coming.

"Sarcocystus Lindemanni produces malaria-like symptoms in its early stages, then usually, from a symptomatic view, it just goes away. You may have no further symptoms during your entire life. Your system could simply deal with the invader and that'll be the end of it," the doctor offered.

"That'd be good, sir." I liked that option.

"The worst that might happen is that it stays with you. Should it stay, although relatively benign, in old age you may see some long, pale, subdural streaking in your muscles. But it does not attack vital organs or the brain and should cause you no pain. So," the doctor beamed, "you're in no danger and when you're feeling up to par, we'll release you back to your squadron." (Isn't "relatively benign" a great medical term? "Relatively" means pretty good; "benign" means good. So, I was gonna be pretty good. Another of my favorites is, "You may experience some mild discomfort," when it might mean, "Brace yourself. This sonofabitch is gonna hurt like hell.")

The doctor seemed all right with the diagnosis; I was not so sure. "Damn, sir, you mean I'm okay, but maybe this will be with me all my years?" It sounded like oxymoron stuff to me, like "good" and "tuna fish sandwich." Somehow the words were contradictory. I'm "okay" but I might play host to parasitic organisms all my life. Is a parasite benign? I struggled.

"That's sort of it. We're discovering much about oriental diseases and maladies from our experience here. The one you apparently have is weird and unusual. In the short run there are no effects, except at the outset. In the long run probably not either, but you may eventually get some white streaking, visible just beneath the skin in your skeletal muscles." He was finished; a note of finality was in his voice.

"Okay, I guess. I'm feeling good, so anytime you can release me is fine." But my mind was still computing this new information, as it would often in the coming years. It was time to get off the ship and back to Klondike.

"I'll tell the administrative people to arrange your discharge. You'll likely be out of here tomorrow morning. Any questions?" the doctor asked.

"No, sir. Thanks for the help." We were done, but this gift from the war caused me to ponder. I'd have to look *Sarcocystus Lindemanni* up someday, but old age to a twenty-five-year-old is a vague possibility, somewhere distant, not real, the land of grandparents. I had before me an inexhaustible vista of life, days so numerous that they spread before me like separate wheat stalks on the Kansas plains. I had plenty of time to do things before I became a white-striped old fart. And who gave a shit anyway. Meaningful life ends at around the time social security kicks in. At least so I believed in those days.

"No problem," the doctor said as he eased away. "Take care of yourself, Lieutenant Ballentine." A flicker of concern crossed his eyes. He'd seen a lot, patching up our Marines and Navy corpsmen. The doctors knew the ravage war wrecks on humans. Their job was to tend the injured and ill. The injured far outnumbered the ill; especially in the wake of operations they were lined up for repair almost unendingly. The doctors and medical people in general must have developed calluses on their souls, suppressing emotion and empathy in order to concentrate on the task at hand, fixing people. But in their humanness, flickers of compassion surfaced as in, "Take care of yourself, Lieutenant Ballentine," accompanied by a glance that said more than the noises he made. I read it and a primitive part of me understood.

"I'm gonna try, sir," I answered. The doctor walked back into his world, so separate from mine.

After my morning chat with the Doc, I found Compton's room. "What's up, man?" I asked. He smiled a greeting as I eased into a straight-back gray metal chair. "You feel strong enough to talk or should I get the hell outta here?"

"It's okay, Dave. I'm hanging on," came his weak response. He was propped up through the cranking mechanisms at the foot of the bed. A pee-bag hung from his bedside as it had from his wheelchair. A clear tube disappeared under the covers in the direction of his groin. I didn't want to look at the bag or tube nor think about what it all meant.

"What the fuck happened to you anyway? Looks like you took some major hits." I wanted to know how a solid, in-shape Marine could be converted in short order to this condition, whatever the condition was.

"Alright, here goes." Compton took a breath. "A few weeks after you guys left the *Princeton*, they put the battalion ashore several miles from the coast, just south of the DMZ. I guess the NVA was crossing the Qua Viet in numbers at night and infesting the area. Anyway, in we went, lifted by helos." He paused and took a couple more breaths.

"We were unopposed on landing, but almost as soon as we deployed, things started happening. It was a no-shit hornet's nest. I was in the open trying to get to cover and got hit in the chest by a spent 12.7 round." (A spent round is one that was largely out of juice. It'd bounced around or been slowed in some way or ways, so its punch was reduced. A 12.7-mm is the Soviet answer to our .50-caliber. It shoots *big* bullets.) I nodded; he continued.

"The round found a seam in my flak vest, penetrated my ribs, and lodged right next to my heart. It felt like someone had slammed me in the chest with a sledgehammer. By rights, I should be dead." He paused and took a few more shallow breaths. Just the effort of speaking in paragraphs rather than in short sentences, was having an effect on him.

"Take your time, Jeff. Shit, we got plenty," I said.

"Okay," he answered. Then, "I just need a measured pace anymore." After ten or fifteen seconds, he continued.

"Anyway, the hit dropped me. I was bleeding, couldn't move, and I was in the open. I was barely conscious and we came under mortar attack. I had no cover and got mortar shrapnel all over, legs, stomach, and kidneys. You name it. The flak jacket saved my upper torso, but below it, I got chewed up bad."

"Jesus, you took it big time. But you're here," I responded in an effort to inject some optimism.

"Yep, I am. My platoon sergeant and one of my Marines dragged me to cover as soon as the barrage lifted, but I'd been screwed up pretty much by then. One of our corpsmen got some morphine in me and a medevac helo picked me and some other wounded up a little later." After another pause, "When I got here the docs had to open my chest to get out the 12.7 round. They're still digging metal out of my legs and lower insides. My plumbing's not working, at least not now," he added solemnly and nodded toward the bedside bag.

Unable to resist, I asked, "When they gonna get you fit?"

Jeff smiled a little. "Well, I'm no good to the Corps anymore, so they'll survey me. I'll be going home eventually, when they've done all they can. My war is over. They're not sure yet what, if any, my long-range problems will be." He stopped and breathed. "I might have the bag a long time. They think my ticker will be okay, though I'm still sore as hell and it hurts to take a deep breath. I'd have been better if I'd had some cover when those 82s started falling. But I didn't. I was exposed," he finished.

The 82s he referred to were the 82-mm mortars the Soviet bloc used. The tubes were just slightly larger than the US 81-mm mortars. That way, they could use our ammo, if they got their hands on it, but we could not use theirs. Clever bastards!

"Fuck, man, you took a drubbin', but you made it. You're young and you'll mend. The docs will work their magic and fix you over time," I offered.

"That's what I'm hoping," Jeff continued. We chitchatted a while longer. I told him about my parasite problem and that I'd be leaving soon. Then he had to go see the docs again. So I helped him into his wheelchair and, with the permission of a corpsman who'd showed up for the chore, I wheeled him to see the specialists.

"How 'bout this afternoon? See the docs, have some chow, get some rest, and I'll come by around 1430 and see you. Maybe we can take a stroll?" I said just before he was taken into a treatment room.

"Sounds good, Dave. Thanks and see you later," Jeff responded. He was pale and weak. I could not get over his transformation.

Later that day I was with him again. He seemed slightly stronger and, at his request, I wheeled him out onto the deck of the *Repose*, into the sun and breeze. It was a super aviator's day, bright and clear; the South China Sea was calm and gentle. Wind generated by the ship making way felt great, exhilarating. I locked Jeff's chair so he'd not be responding to the ship's motion with some wheelchair motion of his own, but in short order I could tell Jeff was losing interest. Perspiration formed on his forehead and upper lip. His head was beginning to sag. I began to think he belonged below deck in a climate-controlled environment.

Jeff reached the same conclusion. "I'm startin' to feel pretty weak, Dave."

"Let's get outta here," I responded and off with the chair brakes and through the hatch we went, back into the cool interior of the *Repose*. Although the sun and wind felt great to me, for Jeff the added work his body had to perform from the exposure was too much. He was weak and needed much more mending before he could even sit in the sun. I was further impressed by how much destruction his body had sustained. To say he was a reduced man does not do his situation justice.

I took Jeff back to his room and left him to rest.

That evening a corpsman came by. "Lieutenant Ballentine, you're scheduled out on a chopper for Danang at 0800. Please muster on the flight deck by 0730 with your stuff. Here are your medical records and endorsed orders transferring you back to your unit."

"Okay, Doc. I'm ready whenever," I answered. I grabbed the packet of documents he held out. I was feeling fine, as I had almost since arrival. Time to get back to the squadron, back with the bubbas.

I went to say good-bye to Jeff early in the morning. It was awkward. Neither of us had a certain future, I was heading back to the war; he was hurt badly, heading for repair, rehab, and maybe a full and unencumbered life somewhere down the line. I preferred my uncertainty to his.

"Well, Jeff, you're a helluva guy. I enjoyed knowing you and liked the little time we had. I 'spect you'll be okay over time. Watch your ass and take care of yourself," was all I could think to say. Smiling, I extended my hand.

"Dave, it has been good. Watch the little guys out there. Some of 'em mean you harm." He clasped my hand. I looked at him and just nodded a few times. Then, "So long, Compton." I turned and walked from his bed.

"So long, Dave," and Jefferson Davis Compton, Lieutenant of Marines drifted out of my life. Or did he? Shit, here he is forty years later on this page, as he is in my mind.

The helo, a CH-34 again, landed and five of us boarded. The crewchief made sure we were all strapped tightly to the nylon-webbed fold-down seats and that we had on our Mae Wests. When he was happy, I saw him key his mic informing the HAC we were ready. The radial R1820 engine was fed a greater volume of fuel-air mixture by the practiced left hand of the pilot. He lifted the bird and held it above the deck spot for just a second, then nosed the green machine off and over the sea. It was noisy, but the wind whipping through the cabin felt good.

Within fifteen minutes, we were over the Danang complex heading for a helo pad near the transients' center. Later the same morning, I was on a Marine C-130 heading for Chu Lai. At Chu Lai a truck met the C-130 to take parts back to Ky Ha. I jumped in back and within twenty minutes, I was walking into Ky Ha sickbay with my records and a return-to-duty endorsement. Doc Moffitt, wouldn't ya know, was off farting around somewhere and not there to show appropriate concern and inquire about my health. Someone else took my records, stamped my orders, gave me a copy for the squadron, and an "up chit" returning me to flight status. By 1400 I was in the squadron area.

I told my story countless times, first to Maj. Ed Sample, the XO, then to Lieutenant Colonel Maloney, then to the ODO, then to my boss, then to any swinging Richard who inquired. I was on the flight schedule the next day, which was fine with me. I'd been down long enough.

PART 3

The Middle and Late Months

CHAPTER 9

First Lieutenant Ballentine, Purveyor of Beer and Porn

Although I was not a regular skin flick–goer, like most men I'd seen a few. One I saw during a high school lunch break in Tommy Myer's garage. I think the term is dogwater; I did that a little in my trousers at seventeen there in Tommy's garage. Then back to school for classes in ceramics and the allotropic forms of carbon. I had more trouble than usual concentrating that afternoon, especially in ceramics where I sat next to Jeannie Corlew, the love of my young life. Distracting images and possibilities danced in my mind.

In my twenties I saw another. They were erotic, but with no willing woman handy to accommodate a guy, it made little sense, and if you had a live, willing woman, why would you want celluloid. It was perplexing.

Through casual bar conversation at Ky Ha with gents from one of the CH-34 squadrons, I'd been made aware that First Lieutenant X owned several of these movies. He'd obtained them on a recent Rest & Relaxation journey to Japan. This information, not sought but stumbled upon, was filed away with countless other tidbits, catalogued for who knows what reason. Maybe in this case, it was for my old friend, Lynn LaPort.

It's like the number of people who live in Salina, Kansas. Why would anyone care except those who live there, or perhaps a demographer? Maybe they don't even care. But I stopped once in Salina for coffee and somebody nearby made an inquiry of the waitress. So now I know: Salina's population is between 46,000 and 48,000. I don't give a damn; I don't want to know, but there it is, stuck in my mind, ready for the question. My mind sifts the jewels and dross of this world, selecting and retaining what it will. Does it remember important stuff like on what day Thanksgiving falls or the KU point guard in 2001? Not on your life. But ask me how many folks live in Salina or, in 1966, who had skin flicks at Ky Ha and I'm your man.

I was armed with this trivia when First Lt. Lynn LaPort, Frog (CH-46) driver extraordinaire with Bonnie Sue (HMM-265), approached me at the Ky Ha bar. He was a great friend who flew with me through the Pensacola training ordeal. Although his squadron was based at Marble Mountain, he was down our way on some major local event, one which required more lift birds than our Group could provide.

"Ballentine," LaPort almost shouted recognizing me at the bar. "Damn, how's your ass?" He and Jim Wilker and two others approached.

"Shit, I'm fine. Just doin' the do in the Ky Ha way. You guys look parched. Let me spring for a suds."

"You got it," he responded as the Frog pilots aligned themselves along the bar adjacent to Second Lt. John Boden and me. John, a newbie and a helluva guy, and I were getting acquainted over libations.

After handshakes, "What brings your sad asses to these parts?" I inquired.

"I guess the old man (commanding officer) likes to keep us busy, so we're lifting shit and folks all over I Corps. We're down just a few days to help put in some grunts out west. I don't know the details, and don't care much to know. We'll be haulin' Marines tomorrow. That's the long an' short of it. But that ain't the deal that's got me bouncing around."

He paused to order booze, which arrived quickly. (One of the nice advantages of few choices is it precludes hemming and hawing over Pinch, Crown Royal, Black Jack, Boodles, or Bombay. You look; you see; you pick. No farting around.) We watched the barman grab cans of beer, punch holes in tops with a church key, and place them on the counter. The Frog drivers, Boden, and I hoisted cans and took pulls.

"Thanks," Lynn offered. The others echoed.

"What's up?" I asked out of politeness. What the hell, everyone had a tough-shit story, a sad tale about how the world is mistreating him, but this was my buddy. I was unusually inclined to compassion or at least willing to feign it.

"Well, Major Yancy, who's in charge down here, wants a detachment shindig before we head back to Marble, and he's tapped me as the arranger, coordinator, and provisioner. The senior guys just pass shit down to us; this time the shit ended up in my lap."

"Do I have a recent example of that sorta action?" I answered. "I guess we're so brainwashed in obedience, we bottom feeders simply start strokin' when the seniors send us forth. Let me tell ya of my pallet-of-beer-getting experience."

Before he could respond, I continued "What the hell do I know about beer-getting?" I asked rhetorically. "Not a fuckin' thing. But about three months ago, Major Presson, our skipper, laid eyes on me, the FNG. "Lieutenant Ballentine," he says. "You're in charge of getting us a pallet of beer. The squadron's running low." I paused and took a sip of bourbon and followed it with a pull on my tallboy Budweiser.

"What'd you do?" LaPort asked, distracted momentarily from his own woes. He drained a little beer also.

"I had to find a way or make one. I asked the boss if he had a hint on how I might go about this. He said to chat with the Navy people. He was right about that." I paused again.

"This ain't gonna go on forever, is it? I mean, I'm trying to tell you my story and I end up listening to your shit." Lynn looked at me smiling. He was in no mood for the long rendition.

"I'll keep it short, but it's worth hearin'." And I continued. "You guys are parked up on the north ramp. Right?" I figured they were, since no visiting CH-46s were on the south ramp when I'd walked up from the squadron.

They nodded, "Yep."

"Did you notice the sailors and those boats up there farther north from the ramp?"

"Yeah, when we were on approach I saw some boats and a couple of short piers up there," Lynn answered.

"That's it. Well, I visited 'em. The sailors, it seems, make trips all the time to and from the Philippines. Those fuckers eat like kings, have as much beer as they want, and it's cold. Anyway, I nosed around and found this Chief. Wouldn't ya know? The Navy's like the Corps; you want something done you can go the paper route and wait for the second coming of Jesus or you can see a senior Petty Officer. The Chief allowed as how a pallet of San MaGoo (San Miguel) was doable. He provided the cost and said it could be delivered within three or four weeks, if I got the dinero to him within a week. I was happy I'd found a source and didn't give a shit about money. I wasn't gonna haggle nickels and dimes."

I took another hit and a pull. At least the Bud was cool and not that skunk piss Falstaff or Carling Black Label. The Corps must have gotten a good deal on those brands. It was available everywhere for a while, but no good.

"You're killin' me!" LaPort offered. "Will you get on with this?"

"Okay, okay. Anyway, it ended up that my beer-getting outing went pretty well. I stood up in the next AOM and quoted a price and parsed it out among the officers. I allowed the few nondrinkers to skate. I shared a piece of the expense with the First Sergeant, who squeezed the Staff NCOs. We let the sergeants and below off the hook. I got a check-off list with everybody's name on it and a cigar box. I started collecting MPC [Military Payment Script was used in Vietnam on bases instead of dollars]. Within three days I had it all."

I was starting to lose them, so I rushed ahead. "I bummed the Admin Officer's jeep, ran over to the Navy, gave the Chief the money, and we shook hands. I walked away wonderin' how much was in it for him, but I didn't give a damn."

"Our CO pestered my ass at every damn meeting, so I went back in two weeks to check with the Chief so I'd have something to tell him. Hell, the beer was already on station. He showed me to a connex box and there it was under a tarp, a whole pallet of San Magoo. We got a six-by and a fork lift and moved the beer to the squadron area where we divvied it up." I smiled, satisfied at my story of how the Kansas man had landed on his feet.

"Sounds like you did good," Lynn responded.

"Oh, one last thing," I added.

"Fuck, go on," he said with a tinge of reluctance. The other Frog guys were starting to glaze over too, paying attention more out of courtesy than interest.

My mind raced for a hasty ending. "Well, the San Magoo people make two kinds of brew. One is for export, which they have high standards of quality control on, probably better stuff across the board, hops, malt, yeast, whatever goes into beer. That's the kind you're used to seein' back in the States. This shit the Chief got us was the other kind, the domestic stuff. It comes in blue bottles instead of those brown ones you're used to seein'. After the guys started having a few, the reports started comin' in. On the blue-bottle stuff, QC was virtually nonexistent. They might check it for rat shit content, but not for alcohol. You could drink one and be on your ass or four or five and just be mildly mellow. It was a roll of the dice."

"I heard some bitchin' and moanin' on this one, but I just shrugged it off and told 'em that, short of makin' beer my own damn self, we were along for the ride. It died down."

"Oh, an' hardly anyone said, 'Thanks,' Sierra Hotel (Shit Hot) and all that. We quit having beer available in the ready room a couple of weeks ago anyway, and now brew is kinda plentiful in the clubs so it's no longer such a big deal." I was finished and smiled. I'd had the mic for a couple of minutes and knew it was time to surrender stage center.

"Sounds like you did okay, and I expect I will too," Lynn answered. "I just don't like the buck stoppin' with me on stuff like this. We've already got some beer lined up and some cokes. The mess sergeants here are coughing up a case of hamburgers, some buns, mustard, and some macaroni salad. And we picked up some paper plates, plastic knives and forks, napkins, and cups."

He paused. "I've been jumpin' through my ass since we landed, though we brought some of this crap with us. We got a hooch lined up and ice looks likely. Maybe we'll be okay. I think we will, but I still have to draw it all together. It's my ass hanging in the lurch an' I'm new at this bullshit." Lynn finished quickly. I sensed that, even though he'd been thrown a short-fused grenade, and was assigned as the worry guy, it was all going to fit. He just needed to stay on top of the details.

"I hope I'm just okay and not great at this. I sure as hell don't wanna be known as the squadron party coordinator guy." He had a good point; a man doesn't want to excel at stuff he'd rather not do.

I looked at Lynn. He was three years younger; I felt as much like an older brother as a friend. One uncontrollable eyebrow hair still hung straight down, bisecting his cornea. It was predictable. Over the years when I'd mention it to him, he'd slick it back "How's that?" he'd ask. "You're lookin' good." I'd respond. But it was temporary; within five minutes the hair was back in its usual vertical place. I surrendered to the hair with time. I accepted LaPort as he was but I smiled inwardly at the perverse hair, which Lynn either chose to ignore or simply didn't notice.

We chatted on about his forthcoming party. Then, it came.

"And catch this shit. Someone had the balls to suggest that I run some fuck movies to ground!" he said with mild astonishment.

"Oh." I responded immediately, eyes fully open, forehead raised and furrowed. My mind was already pulling from its inventory of all-too-often useless information; a wire had been tripped. "I think a Lieutenant X from Millpoint (HMM-363) has some. At least someone said so here at the bar the other night."

"You're shittin' me. That would be a coup," LaPort offered with interest.

"Yeah, you can drift over to their ready room and run him to ground or at least find out what hooch he's in and work it that way. Hell, there's probably some Millpoint bubbas here or will be shortly."

"Damn, I'll try him," Lynn responded.

Our conversation drifted to other topics for another hour. Lynn voiced some concern over the recent crash of a CH-46 up north near Phu Bai. "They're still piecing it together, but the damn thing sorta fell apart in flight. No one survived. They fell from a couple thousand feet. The helo exploded on impact. Scary shit. They need to figure that one out," he concluded soberly.

"No shit!" I countered in agreement. I'd heard the rumor, but Lynn was in the squadron. This is the kind of info no helo guy wants to hear. "Yeah, it's one thing to have to shoot an auto from a failed engine, but a bird that breaks apart in flight. . . . Well, you ain't got a fightin' chance. You're a dead man."

We talked on for a while longer about the accident. Then Lynn said, "Well, I'd better head for the hooch. We have a little meeting at 2130. We're bedded down over on the north side of the compound and just finding the fuckin' place will take some navigating."

He stuck out his hand. "It's good seeing you, and if you're just farting around tomorrow night, find our hooch. We'll give you a beer and a burger. The chow starts at 1830, but we'll probably be there into the evening. It'd be good to see you. Come see me next time you're at Marble."

We all shook hands. "I'll try to see you before you shove. Have a good flight tomorrow." They moved out; Boden and I were back to a duet, though other Klondikers had showed up and were seated at a table nearby. We joined our squadron mates.

I was not on the escort mission supporting Bonnie Sue the next day, though I noticed from the flight schedule that Klondike had a division of gunbirds assigned. I was with a gun section escorting a two-bird CH-34 recon insert mission in the morning. That afternoon, I flew a test hop.

That night, I found the Bonnie Sue party hooch and ducked in after dark. HMM-265 was well led. It was also populated with the sort of solid people you might expect for the first east coast CH-46 squadron in the Corps. No washed-up, burned-out field grades or senior captains without a future. They had bright, hard-charging officers and SNCOs, but many of the junior guys were, like myself, relatively new to Marine aviation. The young officers added a nice spice to the mix; rowdy at the outer edges, feeling their way along as officers and aviators, clever and hell-raising, but serious when necessary. The lift squadrons had more pilots than the VMOs since they always flew with copilots, unlike the Hueys. When they showed up at the bar en masse, they could almost squeeze you out. Almost.

The detachment guys were well into their cups when I arrived. I looked around for familiar faces, LaPort in particular. My eyes alighted on him about the same time he saw me. "Ballentine," he hollered over the conversational din. The guys at his table looked up and waved or smiled. "Get your ass over here and grab a beer on your way." Lynn pointed to a barrel at the end of the hooch partly filled with cans and ice water.

"Got it," I responded and went to the barrel. My heart sank as I pulled out a can of coolish Carling Black Label. I looked for options. There were none. "Horse piss," I thought. Reluctantly I opened it with a church key attached by twine to the barrel. I headed to LaPort's table of bubbas.

Someone slid over, patting an empty chair. "Sit your ass down," Wilker said.

"You been staying off the skyline, David?" inquired Lynn. His eyes were dancing and intent; he was well along.

"Yep, just another day in the barrel," I responded. I joined them in their shit-shooting about home, aviation, and operational topics. We tried to entertain each other with cleverness. I noted as we jawed and haw-hawed that a sheet hung from the wall at one end of the hooch. I also noted that some senior guys were present, field grade officers, not just from Bonnie Sue (HMM-265), but from the squadrons based at Ky Ha. I didn't know any by name; I just recognized them from the chow hall and around. I'd exchanged salutes with them. But they were ours, MAG-36 guys. Out of the corner of my eye, I saw that a projector was erected and film reels attached. Film was already threaded through the various loops and contraptions required. The movie or movies had worked out for Lynn. A man stood by the projector. "Here we go," I thought.

LaPort scooted his chair back, stood, and then shouted for attention. "Hey, everyone, hey, hey. Quiet a minute."

After some stomping, baying, and shouting, a relative quiet rippled through the hooch. One small group after another stopped jawjacking to hear what he had to say. I was curious too.

When it got passably quiet, he offered the following: "Gents, I just want you to know we have, at my request, an interloper here: Dave Ballentine from Klondike. I invited him to have a beer with us, partly because he's an old buddy, but more important, he's the guy that provided the skin flicks!"

My eyeballs glazed; my mind shuddered.

Just for a heartbeat there was no response, but Lynn began clapping and by stages everyone joined in. Some even shouted their approval. Me, I just sat there with a crooked smile. How's a person supposed to respond who's just been publicly branded as a pornographer?

Oh, it's one thing to watch the occasional skin flick, especially as a youngster, but it's quite another to *own* them. I tried vainly to protest, to ensure all knew I deserved no honor or credit, that I'd just provided a name. But I was in mild shock and did not recover quickly enough to offer a convincing disclaimer. Before I knew it, the switch on the projector was thrown. Groans, shouts, comments, and roars overtook the evening. The stars were Asian, the movie black and white and it was not a "talkie." I remember little else.

Out of civility, I stayed for the first reel, but as the second was loaded, I made my excuses. "Hey, I'd like to stick around, but I've got an early flight and I just dropped by to say howdy anyway. Thanks for the invite and the brew. Keep your turns up and all that. I'll see you guys at Marble, soon, I expect." I stood, smiled, and extended my hand.

"Shit, Dave. You gotta go, huh?" Lynn protested mildly. "Well, thanks for droppin' by and take care of yourself." We pressed the flesh, as I did with the others at the table. I slipped out into the night, cheeks stinging. Embarrass-ment choked out other emotions. I headed for my hooch. Shit! Pornographer! Shit! What would my mother say?

I could only hope their minds were unlike mine; that once exposed, they would not have retained the population of Salina or that Ballentine was a porn guy. This was my hope. But I suspect the world of humans is similar. I felt branded and probably was. If Lynn had lived, I wonder if he'd have remembered.

CHAPTER 10

First Lt. Steve Wilson
Is Shot Down

The following is an excerpt from "A History of Marine Observation Squadron Six," published by History and Museums Division, Headquarters, U.S. Marine Corps, Washington, D.C., 1982.

First Lieutenant Steve C. Wilson began what turned into a busy evening for VMO-6. Wilson was shot down while attempting to pick up a wounded Korean Marine in a "hot zone" and his crewchief, Lance Corporal Richard N. Soukup, was wounded. Major William E. Dodds and First Lieutenant David A. Ballentine were overhead in H-1 gunships and provided immediate suppressive fire for the downed crewmembers and the Korean Marines. Captains John C. Arick and Charles Swinburn arrived on station in time to escort a CH-46 helicopter into the zone to pick up the crew and the wounded Korea. . . . Later in the evening Captain Kenneth D. Waters led another flight into the same zone and successfully evacuated 10 wounded Korean Marines.

We were a cobbled-together, pickup team that afternoon and that meant an emergency of some sort. Not only were we hastily assembled but Major Walker himself was giving the brief, not the ODO, another telltale indicator of trouble.

The call came in to the ODO on our squadron common FM radio from First Lt. Steve Wilson. Steve was out as gunbird chase, escorting a "Buffalo

City" (HMM-165) CH-46 southwest of Ky Ha on a medevac pickup of wounded Korean Marines. During the pickup, the Frog was badly damaged by small-arms fire. It managed to get airborne again even though several of its systems were out of commission. Unable to fly back to Ky Ha, the CH-46 limped into the nearest safe haven, a compound at Quang Ngai. Wilson escorted it there and on his way he called Klondike Base to report the incident and to ask for a section of gunbirds to support him in an effort to get a wounded Korean still in the LZ. He headed back to the area to await squadron response. To compound difficulty and increase hazard, weather was crappy around the pickup zone, with intermittent rain and, in places, ceilings between three hundred and five hundred feet.

As soon as the ODO received Wilson's FM transmission, he went for the Ops O, Major Walker, who came immediately to the ready room where the squadron FM radio was located. Walker satisfied himself through additional FM chats with Wilson. Once he knew all there was to know, he turned to the ODO, First Lt. Jerry Garner. Klondike started to move.

"Jerry, call Group Ops, tell them what's happened; see if they have heartburn with us sendin' support to Steve. Then call maintenance and have them rustle up a section of guns, the crewchiefs, and gunners. After I brief the Old Man and get his blessing, I'll work the pilot side. Make sure it happens in a hurry."

"Okay, sir. I got it," Garner answered. He reached for the field phone at his desk as Walker strode from the ready room.

"I'll be right back," he said on his way out.

Garner turned the hand crank on the green field phone. MAG-36 Operations picked up the other end. The squadron's relay of Wilson's request was approved. He made a second call to squadron maintenance. After another chat, he was satisfied that the necessary helos were available and crewchiefs and gunners could be provided. Maintenance projected fifteen minutes to crew and preflight two gunbirds.

Maj. Bill Dodds rounded the corner of the admin hooch; he almost ran into Walker. "Damn, Bill, just the guy I was lookin' for," said the Ops O.

"What's up?" Dodds answered.

"Well, you got real important stuff going this afternoon?"

"Nah, at least nothing that can't wait," Dodds countered.

"Steve Wilson just called on the Fox Mike. He's down south as medevac chase for Buff City. The 46 he was escortin' got shot up bad gettin' wounded Koreans out of a zone. The Frog made it to Quang Ngai, but a wounded guy is still out there. Wilson wants to get him with his gunbird, but he needs cover. If the boss and Group don't object, we'll send a gun section. I'm thinking of you leadin' the flight," Walker said.

"Sounds good to me," Dodds answered.

"Okay. Grab your gear and meet me in the ready room. Does Ed have a full plate?" Walker referred to Maj. Ed Sample, the squadron Executive Officer.

"Don't seem to. We been shootin' the shit in there. But he'd better answer that for himself. Like the Skipper there's always a pile of stuff in his in-basket, but he can probably work on it later. I expect he'd rather be flyin'. Meet ya in the ready room," Dodds concluded. They parted.

My favorite Major, Bill Dodds, was up to bat. I'd flown with him in VMO-1 while he was still a captain. He was strong, practical, had vast experience, an easy disposition, and a sense of humor. He was well respected among Marines of all ranks, a solid, reliable aviator. From my low perch, I never knew or heard of him making horseshit or even marginal decisions either in the cockpit or in his nonflying assignment. I would willingly follow him, not just out of duty or as a result of rank, but because he was a competent, level-headed helo driver.

I was in a Huey cockpit going through the tedious process of blade tracking. Although the whole family of H-1s had a built-in hemorrhoid-inducing vertical beat inherent in all two-bladed helos, out-of-track rotor blades made it much worse. And, allowed to go unchecked, it could damage, even destroy the rotor head. The blades had to fly the same path, otherwise flight could be unpleasant at best. Patience was necessary for the task, since it required numerous starts and shutdowns. But in Vietnam we had time, no place to go, no one waiting. Blade tracking was time-consuming and necessary, just not fun.

I'd run the bird up several times, when the line chief emerged from the line shack and walked out to our Huey. He came to my side of the helo and through my door window, which I'd lowered for ventilation, he announced with raised voice, "Lieutenant Ballentine, Ops wants to see you. It's a hop."

"Okay, Gunny. Thanks. I guess this shit can wait." I unstrapped, pulled off my helmet and collected my stuff as Remp told the check crew guys I'd be out of the loop for a while. They seemed okay with the news. I headed to the ready room, helmet bag over my shoulder. I eased through the screen door and was met by three majors, Dodds, Sample, and Walker, and the ODO, Jerry Garner.

"Dave, we're pressing you into service," Walker said in a matter-of-fact tone. "I've already chatted with K. D."

"Okay, sir." What's a good lieutenant to say? Besides, missions were more interesting than blade-tracking.

"We're gonna launch a gun section to help Wilson do a hot zone medevac. I'm sending you up as Major Dodd's wingman. The XO will fly with Major Dodds. Tom Peckham will be your copilot. He'll be here any minute. I'll brief once he shows. We've thrown this together and we'll launch as soon as we're able."

The crew assignment made perfect sense. The more Vietnam-experienced pilots, Major Dodds and I, were pilots in command signing for the helos. The less Vietnam-experienced, the XO and Tom Peckham, were co-pilots. Since Dodds was going, it would not have done for the XO to fly as my copilot; the majors would fly together as would the lieutenants.

I rummaged in my helmet bag and extracted my kneeboard, then pulled a folded 1:50,000-meter map from my left-shin flight suit pocket. I sat and listened to the more senior guys chat. Within two minutes the screen door swung open and in walked First Lt. Tom Peckham.

"Good. We can get going," Walker said.

Tom had a questioning look, but he collected his map and kneeboard and joined us as we clustered on metal chairs around Ops O at the wall map.

Walker had everyone's attention. "Okay, guys," he began. "Here's the deal. Steve Wilson is down south as gunbird escort to a medevac of some Korean Marines. The medevac bird got the shit shot out of it during the pickup. It's a Buffalo City Frog. He limped away, but we still got at least one wounded Korean out there. Wilson thinks he can get the guy with his gunbird, but wants a section to cover his ass. That's you guys. Major Dodds will lead and, Ballentine, you'll fly wing. The XO is goin' with Major Dodds." After a short pause he added, "Tom," he nodded at Peckham, "you'll be with Dave. And gents, the unit is no-shit in contact, or it was twenty minutes ago."

"The grids for the pickup are BS756473. Your contact is Red Dragon Three on Fox Mike 43.1. Wilson is on that freq also, though sometimes he checks in here on squadron common. They know a Klondike flight is coming. Your flight call will be Klondike six dash six. The mission number is 4213."

"Bad guys are in the area and are especially thick to the north of the LZ. There are tree lines and brush along about here," Walker pointed to an area on the wall map. "You'll know more about what's going on when you get on station and chat with Wilson and Red Dragon. They'll spool you up."

We all looked closely at the wall map and had opened our 1:50,000s to the area. I made a small circle on mine around the location from which we'd most likely take heat. It included the pickup LZ coordinates.

"This vil," he pointed again to the map, "may cause you grief as well." Again we looked at the map. I made grid coordinate notes on my kneeboard. The vil, like the LZ, was already in my drawn circle.

"I have no idea what arty fans are going, if any. The DASC [Direct Air Support Center] can tell you when you check in. I think that's about it. Any questions?"

Major Dodds looked up from his map. "Any guess on the size and number of the bad guys and whether they're VC or NVA?" These were great questions. VC, Victor Charlie, Viet Cong, take your pick, were typically from local cells, committed to a cause but less well trained, equipped, and disciplined than the North Vietnam Army guys. The VC were good. Predictably, the NVA was much better. They were committed and dangerous; some were even tattooed, "Born in the north to die in the south." Many did.

"They gave us no details on that, but since they've been in a fight for quite a while, it's probably NVA. As you guys know, VC are more apt to hit and run than stand and fight," Walker answered.

"Okay," countered Dodds. "They got an American adviser with these Koreans? We gonna' have any trouble talkin' to 'em?"

"Red Dragon is supposed to have an adviser, and some of their officers are English speakers. You probably won't have any trouble. Wilson's on station and he's apparently had no problem. At least he didn't say anything," Walker answered.

"Alright," Dodds said. Responsibility began shifting from the Operations Officer to him.

"Anyone have any other question?" Walker asked. I rummaged around in my mind, as did the others. We thought of nothing. We were going to escort Wilson in and out of a hot zone. This was not new; it was what we did.

"Okay, Ops. I got it." Dodds said to Walker.

"Alright. We'll be up squadron common as always; call if you need us," responded Walker. He stepped away from the map and joined Garner in the background.

Dodds turned to us. "Turn up on squadron common Fox Mike and check in. I'll make all the calls. Stay with me on the radios. Each time we switch freqs, acknowledge and check in. I'll wait to hear from you before I make any contacts. We'll fly loose as hell en route, same-way, same-day. But stay close enough for my crew to keep you in easy sight. Don't go trail."

In trail position, the second aircraft flies in a cone behind the lead, tracing similar, but not exact, paths over the ground. In trail, the leader might not be able to keep a wingman in view.

"Ops says we have a backup bird. If either of us goes down in the chocks, we'll just switch to the other helo. But I want to go out as a section. So, if one goes down, he'll wait for the other."

He continued with what had become a standard brief covering the routine of any flight, routes and altitudes, radio discipline, and lead change parameters. It was apparent from his brief that Dodds was smooth and knowing, a competent, experienced Marine helo pilot.

At the end we broke up and headed for the line shack, signed for our birds, met our crews at the helos, gave them the highlights of the mission, especially where the assholes might be, preflighted the birds, and turned up. I checked in on the FM radio. "Klondike six dash six, Dash two's up and ready."

"Roger, Dash two," Dodds answered.

Then he called on the UHF, "Ky Ha Ground, Klondike six dash six, flight of two for taxi. Mission 4213. Over."

"Klondike six dash six flight is cleared to three south. Switch Tower at pilot's discretion," came the reply.

So a section was drawn together, briefed, and was lifting within thirty minutes of Wilson's call. Two armed Hueys were air-taxiing, heading out. What had started as a mellow, routine day was now interesting. It would be especially interesting for Steve Wilson and his crew.

After the usual series of radio calls to and from Chu Lai Tower and Landshark Alpha, our DASC, we flew to the area. No Savaplanes were in effect; we could fly direct without skirting artillery.

As we neared, "Klondike six dash six, Dash two, go Red Dragon Fox Mike," Dodds directed.

I acknowledged, switched, and checked in on 43.1, the frequency Walker had briefed. The SOP was to avoid giving a frequency over the air. The intel folks said it might compromise operations. I always wondered about that possibility, but I was a good boy and did what I was told.

"Klondike Medevac Chase, this is Klondike six dash six. Over," Dodds radioed.

No answer. After a short wait, he tried again. This time, "Roger Klondike six dash six, this is Medevac Chase." It was Wilson. "We read you five square and have you in sight. Over."

Dodds answered, "Roger Chase. Two guns headin' your way. Estimating your position in seven. Can you give us a SITREP? Over."

Another short pause followed by, "Roger six dash six, we still have a wounded in the zone. Buff City got laced pretty good gettin' most of 'em out about thirty or forty minutes ago. He's at Quang Ngai. With gun cover, I could probably get this last guy. I'm orbiting at one thousand feet just west of the zone. Red Dragon is still up this freq and they're still in contact with the enemy. It's NVA for sure. Most of the fire is coming from north of the zone. Trees, brush, and a vil are up there. That whole area is infested with bad guys. Over," Wilson responded.

The cloud cover was broken to overcast, with occasional rain. Ceilings varied from three thousand to three hundred feet, but the area Wilson was working was okay for now. We were closing, just a few miles out. Tom pinpointed the vil on his map and came up on the ICS. "Dave, that vil is right there coming up on our left about three clicks away. On this heading, we'll pass north of the vil. The LZ's gotta be over there to the south someplace. You got Wilson?" He pointed down at the small hamlet we were approaching as he spoke. I glanced at his map, which he'd held up for me, and then at the ground. I had a good image of the situation, and I already had Steve's helo in sight.

"Okay. I got it, and I see Wilson."

"Medevac Chase. We have you, the vil, and the general area of the zone in sight," radioed Dodds, "Break. Dash two, you got a tally on vil and the area? He must mean the one ahead and left. Over."

"Roger Klondike six dash six. Dash two has the area and Chase in view." I was comfortably aft and to the right of Dodd's helo, drilling along at 110 knots and 1,000 feet. Since we were over the coastal plain, AGL and MSL were virtually identical

"Red Dragon, Klondike six dash six, Over," Dodds radioed.

"Klondike six dash six, Red Dragon, Go ahead," came an immediate response in perfect English.

"Roger, Red Dragon. Klondike six dash six is a section of armed Hueys here to help get your wounded. Could you mark the front trace of your Marines with smoke or give us grids to stay north of? We don't want to shoot up your people during the extraction. Over." Dodds was wise. If the good and bad guys were in contact, without some idea of where one group ended and the other began, we could easily hurt the wrong people.

"Red Dragon copies, Klondike. Wait one. Over." We hung around in loose orbit west of the ROK (Republic of Korea) Marines and recon'd the LZ and the general terrain.

"Klondike, this is Red Dragon. We can mark our forward positions. We'll use yellow smoke on your call. Over."

"Roger, Red Dragon. Understand yellow smoke on our call. Break. Medevac Chase, can you be in position to begin your approach in two minutes?" Dodds asked Wilson.

Pause. "Medevac Chase will be ready. Over," Wilson answered. He was loitering at our altitude, just south of us and west of the LZ.

"Roger, Medevac," Dodds responded. Wilson moved a little farther south positioning himself for an approach.

"Dash two, take interval," Dodds radioed to me. "We'll make our runs on a southeastern heading. Use guns. Over."

I answered and simultaneously reduced power and held my altitude, slowing my Huey to put more distance between me and Dodds. We'd moved east and flew over the Korean positions.

"Red Dragon, Klondike would like the smokes along the front trace sixty seconds from my mark. Mark to come in thirty seconds. Over," Dodds radioed.

A short pause, then, "Roger Klondike. We'll be ready for your mark," responded Red Dragon.

In twenty-five seconds, Dodds called again, "Red Dragon mark coming." He began counting slowly, "Five, four, three, two, one. Mark. Over."

Red Dragon responded to Dodds and radioed the sixty-second notice to the frontline Korean Marines. We drilled along. Both Dodds and Wilson got into position for runs; Dodds with heat, Wilson to the LZ for pickup. Shortly and within five seconds of each other, first two yellow smokes, then a third blossomed from the terrain below. By drawing an imaginary line between these, we knew the area to avoid in ordnance delivery. Steve was well familiar with the LZ; he'd witnessed Buff City get hammered there an hour earlier. He needed no LZ smoke.

"Medevac Chase, call when you're headin' down. I'll begin my run then. Over," Dodds radioed.

"Klondike six dash six, Medevac Chase can start down now, if you're ready. Over."

"Klondike six dash six copies and is in hot with guns." And so he was. From my position over the Koreans in a right-hand racetrack pattern, I watched the familiar nose over of a Huey at work. Down he went and so did Wilson. I pulled in a little power to position myself for a run as soon as the Major was off target.

"Tom, guns and hot when I start down." Then to our crewchief, "Sergeant Corning, you're cleared to hammer the shit out of anything that even looks suspicious and to cover us coming off the run."

I had to hold the door gunner in check, "Corporal Croft, the good guys will be on your side. You gotta hold fire unless it's no-shit sure someone's shootin' at us. Then just return the fire at that specific target; don't rake the area. You guys see the front trace yellow smokes, right? Left of the smoke on our run-in heading is fair game. South of it, we got friendlies. We'll climb out to the right, over the good guys."

"I got the smoke, Lieutenant," Corning answered.

"Me too, sir, and I'll hold fire," Croft responded. Both Corning and Croft were experienced bubbas. The last thing I wanted to hear was silence when I pulled up at the end of a run. I knew Corning would be slamming the area on his side of the helo with 7.62 ball ammunition, and probably not just as I pulled off target but on our way down as well. Croft, the door gunner behind me, would have to hold his horses unless he had an indisputable target, one shooting at us.

As usual our run was roughly parallel to the front trace of "friendlies." Steve made his approach on the same general heading, not perfectly into the wind, which the smoke showed coming from the northeast. But one beauty of a helo is you can make an approach from almost any damn direction and hook into the wind when you near the ground. This is especially a piece of cake for a single bird; it can get difficult, even dangerous if you're leading a flight into a zone. A lone bird has many options compared to a group, but this multiple-bird problem was generally isolated to the lift squadrons, not one VMOs had to contend with much. I glanced at Wilson's helo. He was nearing the ground, nose high, bleeding airspeed for his landing.

I closed on the attack initiation position, 90 degrees from the run-in heading and slowed the Huey even further. A low speed at the beginning of the attack was best. The bird gained speed rapidly once power was reduced and its nose was pointed at the target area. I reached up, grabbed the aiming reticule and pulled it down from the overhead, then glanced through its wire crosshairs at a grease pencil mark on the windscreen. When the crosshairs, the grease mark, and the target lined up, it was trigger-squeezing time. The reticule, primitive and Rube Goldberg–like though it was, provided a good starting point for the first burst. If I wasn't on target, I could "fly" the orange-red tracers from four barking M-60s into the area I wanted. The same was true for the rockets: line up; shoot a pair; adjust the nose; shoot again.

Dodds bottomed out on his run and pulled up to the right. "Klondike six dash six is off target," he called.

I glanced again at Wilson's bird. He was almost at the LZ, his speed increasingly slow. I raised the nose of the gunbird slightly to bleed off a little more speed and I turned to the target heading. "Go hot, Tom," I said into the ICS and Peckham threw a console toggle, arming the M-60s. Dodds climbed over the ROK Marine's positions.

"Dash two's in hot with guns," I radioed and lowered some of the collective, fed in compensating right rudder, and pointed the nose of the Huey at the target area. I flew the crosshairs to the base of the tree line about which we'd been briefed and checked the ball on my instrument panel to assure balanced flight. I squeezed the trigger. The loud but familiar chatter of guns erupted and echoed through the cabin; orange-red balls spewed out at great speed. I began walking tracers through the trees, raking down their length.

In my run, Steve's excited voice came over the FM. "Medevac's takin' fire." I wondered how these rat bastards could be shooting at Wilson, when I was hosing them, but I was already committed, already doing what I could. I pressed the attack further than usual, closer to the ground.

"Medevac, Klondike six dash six, where's the fire coming from?" Dodds radioed.

While Steve was killing off the last of his airspeed, an AK-47-toting NVA soldier stepped from behind trees and sprayed the landing Huey. Bullets struck Wilson's bird along its left side. Some of the rounds found the engine. Shrapnel in the whirring turbine blades broke first a single blade then another. In a split second a logjam of metal shards and pieces developed. A perfectly good Lycoming turbine engine was lunched. A load wham sounded from the exploding L1100; Steve flew an unpowered helo to a slam-down short of the intended landing site.

The helo came to rest on uneven ground, which caused the Huey to tilt awkwardly to the right, not belly up, but with a pronounced list. The rotors still turned, but with no power source, the RPM decayed steadily. Although the engine was a basket case, the Huey's battery still powered the FM radio. Wilson made the call none of us wanted to hear.

"We're down, Medevac is down. We're shot down just short of the zone." His voice was tight and excited. This transmission was his last on that radio. He threw switches and exited the tilting Huey. The other members of his crew were already unstrapped and getting out, except for Lance Corporal Soukup, the crewchief. He was gut-shot; he needed help.

First Lt. Kimo Andrews, Steve's copilot, grabbed the first-aid kit attached to the Huey's cabin wall. He and Steve helped Soukup and, once out of the helo, with bandages from the kit, they applied compression to the bleeding wound.

"Roger . . . evac . . . stand you . . . zone," came a garbled, broken transmission from Dodd's FM. No response came from Medevac Chase.

Again an effort from Dodds, "Med . . . Klon . . . Do you . . . Over."

I pulled up, off target. "Dash two's off target. Klondike six dash six, you're breaking up," I called over the FM. Sergeant Corning peppered the target area as we climbed right; we curled to a course opposite our run-in heading.

"Dash . . . you . . . six. Over." It was Dodds again, still not understandable.

I keyed the mic, "Klondike six dash six, your transmitter's bad. Over."

"Dash two, you . . . lead, you . . . Over," came the response.

Still climbing to the right, I keyed the FM again. "Klondike six dash six, if you read Dash two, key your mic twice."

Two clicks came rapidly into my headset. "Roger, six dash six. If you've passed Dash two the lead, key your mic twice again. Over." Here they came, two clicks.

"Roger six dash six. Dash two has the lead. Klondike six dash six, make another gun run. I'll drop down and look at the crash site. Over."

Two clicks came. We had an initial reaction, a short-term plan. I leveled the bird, bent it around, and headed for Wilson's crash site. They had just passed lower left on my climb out. I set up for a low pass.

"Keep a lookout gang, bad guys are probably near this LZ, not just out by the tree line we were attackin'. Be ready to shoot, but don't shoot first. The Koreans are around here."

I slowed as we approached Wilson's bird. I put it slightly off my right so they would not pass beneath my helo and I could get a good look. We flew by at fifty feet and thirty knots. The downed Huey's blades were stopped; the bird tilted awkwardly on sloping ground. Then I saw Wilson and the crew; they were dragging a man and moving in the direction of a paddy dike that separated them from the intended LZ. One of the crewmembers waved. I added climb power and swung to the right skirting the Koreans' landing zone and considered options.

Then good news came. "Klondike six dash six, Red Dragon. Over."

"Red Dragon. This is Klondike, Dash two. Klondike six dash six has radio problems. He's passed the lead to me. I just flew over the downed Huey and your LZ. Over."

"Roger, Dash two. The Huey crew's almost to our position. We'll have them with us in just a minute. Over."

"Roger, Red Dragon. Give us a SITREP [Situation Report] as soon as possible." Then I added, "Red Dragon, were we attackin' the right area? Over." My curiosity was tweaked; either an NVA had been lucky with a long shot or some guys named Nguyen and Pham were near the LZ.

After a short pause, "Klondike Dash two. The crew's here with us. They're banged around; one is wounded. Over."

He quit talking, so I interjected, "Red Dragon, this is Dash two. That's pretty good news," was all that came to me.

"Dash two, Red Dragon, you're working the right area. Keep it up. We estimate the enemy at battalion strength. Maybe more. Some have leaked through our lines and are between our forward units and the command element. They got the Huey. Over."

Shit I reckon, I thought. We're hosing the right area, but these guys are so numerous and spread out that we can't keep all their heads down. The ones not under attack are hammering away. At least Wilson and his crew were with the Koreans and were relatively safe for now, though Soukup's condition was an unknown.

I climbed back to attack altitude. Major Dodds was just out of his gun run. We had a bird down and a wounded man; I'd have to alert Klondike Base.

Then, "Klondike six dash six, this is Medevac Chase. Over?" It was Wilson on the Red Dragon radio. He was panting.

"Yeah, Medevac. Six dash six, Dash two's readin' you five square. How's the crew? Over."

"Dash two, Medevac Chase, Soukup's hit. Took a round in the belly. The rest of us are okay. Over."

"Roger, Steve. Does Soukup need immediate evac or can he hang on? I'm gonna tell Base what's happened, but they'll wanna know about Soukup. I'll make another gun run; then call Ops. Over," I radioed.

"Dash two, Roger. Wait. Out." Wilson answered.

I was in position for an attack; Dodds was well clear, climbing out. The yellow smoke from the grenades had largely dissipated, but I knew where the front trace was from the earlier marking. I pivoted the helo to the right in a tight turn, lined up, balanced the Huey, and headed for the target again.

"Go hot, Tom." He threw the switch and held out a thumbs-up with his right hand.

I'd just started hammering when the audio warning horn, shrill and undulating, sounded in my helmet. The instrument panel low RPM warning light glowed. I got off the trigger and glanced at Tom. He looked back, eyes large. We both knew the horn signaled engine failure.

I looked back at the instrument panel and was perplexed. The horn was still blazing away in my helmet, but the engine and rotor RPM needles were holding steady. I raised the collective a little to see if the engine responded. It did.

"Fuck, what else?" I thought. I reached down and threw a toggle on the upper center console, disabling the audio warning system. The horn shut off; the engine still cranked out its power. The horn is a serious attention-getter, "a varying oscillating frequency heard in the pilot's headset," as NATOPS puts it. This is sheer understatement; it's a screamer. My plate was pretty full without that shit.

"We're okay, guys. The warning system is just screwed up." I got back on target and continued what was left of the gun run. Sergeant Corning covered us again on the left; Croft's M-60 remained mute.

Jesus, I thought. Medevac Chase is down, we got two wounded in the zone and one of them is ours, Major Dodds' radios are on the fritz, I got the lead, and I'm likely taking hits, which explains the warning horn. Now I gotta get Steve and company from a hot zone or coordinate it, and, in the meantime, keep slamming Charlie so he stays on his side of the playing field.

As I climbed out, Wilson called. "Klondike six dash six, Dash two. This is Medevac chase. Over."

"Roger, Steve. Go ahead."

"We can't tell about Soukup. He's awake and talkin' but a belly hit can't be good. I don't think we're in danger of being overrun. Over." His breathing was more measured. Some of the adrenaline surge was behind him.

"Okay, Steve. There's a bunch of bad guys out here. The Major and I might pull you out ourselves, but I'm gonna call Base and let 'em know what's happened. I'll get back with you on Red Dragon freq in a few minutes. Over." Wilson acknowledged. My Huey was in a full-power seventy-knot climb. Major Dodds began his third gun pass as I climbed out.

"Klondike six dash six, this is Dash two. I'm switchin' Klondike Base Fox Mike. Recommend you join me and listen in. Acknowledge with two clicks. Over," I radioed. Dodds was busy trying to make life hellish for NVA soldiers. Then two clicks.

After Tom switched us to squadron common, I called. "Klondike, Base, Klondike six dash six, Dash two. Over."

Immediately a response came. "Klondike six dash six, Dash two, this is Base. Go ahead." It was Garner.

I was back in touch with the world and it felt good. Ops could rattle cages and make shit happen, not only in the squadron, but through our majors and the CO, the whole MAG could be moved off center. I liked that.

"Base, Klondike six dash six, Dash two. Bad news. Medevac Chase is shot down in zone; repeat Wilson is down in the zone. One man is wounded; all are safe with Red Dragon. Klondike six dash six has radio problems and Dash two has the lead. Over."

"Dash two, Base copies. Wait. Over." Garner was going for Major Walker. This one was too damn hot for the ODO. In less than a minute, Klondike three (the Ops O) was on the horn.

"Klondike six dash six, Dash two, this is Klondike three. Understand Medevac Chase is down in the zone with one wounded, and six dash six has bad radios. Over," Walker summarized.

"Base, Klondike Dash two. That's Charlie. There's a lot of bad guys here. We're deliverin' ordnance. The LZ is hot. We can either try gettin' the crew and the wounded Korean out with our gunbirds or a medevac bird will have to be launched. We can remain on station quite awhile. Over," I answered.

"Roger, Dash two. How much time do you have on station and what's the nature of the crewman's wound? Over."

I glanced at our gauges. We had just under nine hundred pounds of fuel. Major Dodds had to be close to that.

"Base, Dash two. We have about fifty minutes of time on station. The crewchief, Soukup, is wounded. He's gut-shot with small arms. Wilson says he's hangin' on okay, but it can't be good. And Klondike six dash six has a good receiver; he's listenin'. He just can't transmit. Over."

"Base copies, Dash two. Fifty minutes on station, the wound is a gut shot, and six dash six has a good receiver. Wait. Over."

I could guess what Ops was up to. He'd have Garner or himself brief the CO, put a call in to MAG 36 Ops to inform them, and to see if a Medevac helo might be available from another squadron. Then call the line shack to check on another section of gunbirds and maybe a slick to get Wilson's crew and the Korean. Then they'd look into the possibility of another ad hoc crew to man the birds.

We stayed in a racetrack over the Koreans, loitering for what seemed an eternity, but in reality it was less than five minutes.

"Klondike, Dash two. Base. Over." It was Walker again.

"Base, this is Dash two. Go," I answered.

"Roger, Dash two, we're scraping together another section of guns and a medevac bird from our squadron or another. Conserve fuel. We'll be in touch again in five minutes. Have Wilson monitor Soukup's condition and if it changes for the worse, you guys get him out. Over."

"Roger, Base. I'm switchin' to Red Dragon. I'll be back your freq shortly with any updates. If you need us, you can call on the Red Dragon freq. Over."

"Roger, Dash two. Call when you're back up Base freq. Over."

"Roger, Base. Dash two, out. Break. Klondike six dash six. Let's go Red Dragon Fox Mike. Over." A pause, then two clicks. Dodds was with me.

Tom switched us to Red Dragon, and, after Major Dodds checked in with his double clicks, I briefed Wilson on developments. Then I asked, "How's Soukup doing? Over."

"He seems okay for now, I guess. He's scared but not in shock or anything. Speed is probably a good idea. Over." I discovered later that Wilson dragged Soukup through a muddy paddy bottom to the safety of the Koreans. While he did this, NVA soldiers shot at him and his crew. (Wilson was awarded a Bronze Star for actions that day.)

"Medevac, Dash two copies. Let me know if Soukup needs out ASAP. We'll come in with a gunbird. Otherwise Base is launching another medevac package. How about the wounded Korean; is he okay? Over."

"Dash two, wait one." Then, " Dash two, the Korean has a flesh wound in the leg. He's not in immediate danger. We're all together here with the command element at the LZ. Over."

"Roger, Steve. Dash two is switching squadron common. I'll be back up your freq with updates. Call me on Base if something develops. Over."

"Roger, Dash two. Out."

"Klondike six dash six, go squadron common. Over." Major Dodds clicked, but not until he tried his transmitter again.

"Roger . . . switch . . . on . . . ver," he radioed.

Tom dialed in our squadron again. I waited for Major Dodds to check in. Once he did, I radioed. "Klondike Base, Klondike six dash six, Dash Two is with you. Over."

"Roger Dash two. Base is readin' you loud and clear. Over," Walker responded.

Thank God for the "twidgets," I thought. Here I am flopping around thirty miles away from the squadron but talking to people who are piecing together a plan. Although Major Dodds' FM had gone on the blink, by and large, the UHF and the FM radios worked when you keyed the mic. The TACAN, IFF/SIF (Identification Friend or Foe/Selective Identification Feature), and RADALT usually worked also. It was not magic, it was a specific group of smart as hell Marines in the Avionics shop that made sure we could navigate and communicate. Our lives would have been much more difficult without them.

"Klondike, Dash two, Base. Over."

"Dash two. Go ahead," I answered.

"Roger, Dash two. We're still bringing it together, but it looks like we'll have a gun section relieve you on station in thirty minutes or so. Buffalo City (HMM-165) is sending a Medevac section. They'll get the wounded and the crew. Check with Red Dragon to see if they can provide security on the downed Huey. We'll send a maintenance crew out in the morning to rig it. Buff City will external it out tomorrow. Over," Walker said.

"Roger, Base," I answered. "Dash two copies. We got a gun section and Buff City headin' out in thirty minutes. Our Huey needs security until it's rigged and pulled out tomorrow. If approved, we'll return to Red Dragon, provide updates, and make attacks until relieved. We'll return this freq for updates in fifteen minutes or you can contact us on Red Dragon freq. Over."

"Dash two, Base. Roger. Approved. Oh, and get Soukup if you have to. Out."

"Roger, Base. Break. Klondike six dash six, let's go Red Dragon. Over."

Two clicks. I contacted Steve again and briefed him, then made sure the front trace of the Koreans had not changed. We dropped into gun and rocket attacks and waited for developments. I'd been hogging the stick so Peckham flew these attacks. I felt tension in my shoulders and thighs. It was nice to have relief at the controls.

My intention was to be nearly out of ammo when our relief arrived. After the third pass on the target area, I told Steve I was leaving his freq to check progress with Base. I switched the flight back to Klondike common.

After we'd checked in, Ops provided the following: "Roger, Klondike six dash six, Dash two. The gunbirds are turning. They'll be Klondike eight dash six and wingman. Buffalo City Medevac is spinning also. They'll be airborne shortly. We've told 'em to call you on the Red Dragon frequency. Over."

Here came the cavalry. "Roger Base. Understand a gun section, Klondike eight dash six, and a Buff City section are turnin'. There's no news here. Wilson's not called us with more on Soukup. We're just keepin' the gun and rocket attacks goin'. Unless you have something else, we'll switch back to Red Dragon, provide updates, and continue our runs. Over."

Base had nothing more. We switched to Red Dragon and briefed Wilson. We'd used twenty-five of the fifty minutes we had. Fuel would soon be the driver. This would work, but it would be tight. We made more attacks, but conserved ammo.

In fifteen minutes we heard, "Klondike six dash six, Dash two, this is Klondike eight dash six. Over." It was Capt. John Arick, the assistant maintenance officer, under Waters. Arick was a super guy, smart, industrious, with an easy sense of humor, a Naval Academy man. I've always stood in wonder at men who had the preparation and self-discipline at eighteen for a military academy. I could not have done it, nor was I qualified. I discovered over time that Academy guys are intelligent. They may not all be great officers or great pilots, but they're smart. Arick was all three: intelligent, a super officer, and a solid pilot. Not surprisingly, he became a general.

"Roger, Klondike eight dash six. Klondike six dash six, Dash two's readin' you five by five. What's your ETA? Over."

"Dash two. We're fifteen miles two two zero Chu Lai TACAN, estimating ten minutes. Buffalo City Medevac is with us for the pickup. Any updates? Over."

"This is Dash two. No change. When you get on station, we'll make one last attack to show where we've been shootin' an' I'll point out where Medevac Chase is down, but you can't miss it. It's just short of the intended LZ. The Korean Marines have been tryin' to run off the bad guys near the command element where Wilson is, but we can't know how effective they've been. I guess Buff City will know when they go in. Also, if you want we can probably get Red Dragon to mark their front trace again with smoke so you won't be hammerin' the wrong guys. Over."

So it was that Arick and his wingman, Capt. Charlie Swinbun, arrived with a fresh section of gunbirds and two CH-46s from HMM-165. Major Dodds and I made one last pass at the trees and brush north of the LZ. The newly arrived aircrews watched. Before climbing out, I made another low pass directly over Wilson's downed helo to point it out, but Arick and Buff City Medevac already had it in sight and were in good radio contact with Red Dragon. The Korean Marines' front trace was again marked with yellow smoke.

Major Dodds and I were close to bingo fuel. We were also down to some 7.62 machine-gun ammo. We'd done all we could

"Klondike eight dash six, Klondike six dash six, Dash two. Anything else we can do? Over."

"No, Dash two. We've got it. See you later. Over," Arick responded.

"You've got it. We're headin' home, but we'll stay up your Fox Mike for a while. Over."

"Roger, Dash two," Arick answered, but he had other considerations, like suppressing bad guys while the Buffalo City lift bubbas pulled some chestnuts out of the fire.

Tom turned our helo to a northeasterly heading. Dodds flew loose formation. We began the thirty-mile drive to Ky Ha.

After a few minutes of drilling, I called Arick one last time, "Klondike eight dash six this is six dash six, Dash two. We'll be switchin' to squadron common. Anything you want us to relay? Over."

"Dash two, we're workin' over the area. Buff City will be going down for the pickup in two minutes. We'll call base with updates when we have them. See you later. Out."

"Roger, eight dash six. Break. Klondike six dash six, let's go Landshark Alpha and Klondike Base. Over."

Two clicks. Then, "Klondike . . . Rog . . . Over." Dodds tried his radio again.

"Klondike six dash six. You're still breaking up. Over." I called Base, briefed them that Arick's flight had arrived and that Buff City was about to pick up the crew and the wounded Korean. I also gave our ETA. Base acknowledged but their interest was now shifted to Arick. Ops would be awaiting word from them.

We made the obligatory calls to Landshark Alpha, the DASC, Chu Lai Tower for clearance through their space, and Ky Ha Tower for landing. We taxied to our line, picked up our taxi directors, set down, and shut down. Sergeant Corning and I did a quick postflight walk around the bird, looking for holes and leaks. My suspicion that a round had activated our audio warning system was unfounded. Our bird was not damaged. Tom and I met Major Dodds and the XO walking to the line shack. We quickly signed off the birds; I wrote up the audio horn and the Major wrote up his FM radio, then we headed for the ready room.

Many were assembled, including the CO. Major Dodds and I answered all the questions we could. Plans to retrieve the downed Huey were already in motion. A CH-46 was laid on to external the bird. Our maintenance crew would first remove the main rotor blades, and a grunt platoon had been requested in case the Koreans could not provide security.

Thirty minutes after we landed, Arick came up on squadron common frequency, "Klondike Base, Klondike eight dash six. Over."

"Roger, eight dash six. This is Base. Go ahead. Over," Garner answered.

"Roger, Base. Buffalo City has our crew and the wounded Korean and is headin' home. We'll remain on station until our ammo's gone. The zone is still hot and Red Dragon requests another section of gunbirds to relieve us. They're also going through channels for some fast movers. They even want diverts from Landshark. Over." (A divert is the redirecting of aircraft from some other intended missions.)

"Roger, Klondike eight dash six. We'll relay to Group. What's your read on the need for guns and jets? Over." Walker asked. He'd been standing next to Garner, and took the handheld mic from him for this exchange. We stood listening.

"Base, Klondike eight dash six. The NVA is not going away out here. If we can support this, I recommend we do. Over," Arick answered.

With raised eyebrows and furrowed brow, Major Walker looked at Lieutenant Colonel Maloney. Walker's expression transmitted the question to the CO.

Maloney was brief. "Get Group approval. Then do it."

He, like other more senior guys, saw a bigger picture. If we had some assholes located, we should bring as much harm to them as possible. That way they'd be unable or less inclined to give our side future grief. Getting your ass kicked good is both debilitating and disheartening. It is instructional for the kickee. Nope, if you have Nguyen, you don't cut and run, half step, fart around, and have a beer. You wade in. We'd gotten the wounded and made plans to get our bird, but we had bad guys located and a means to make their day miserable. The CO meant to get on with it.

"Round up relief crews and birds," Walker instructed Garner. "I'll call Group."

I figured they'd simply send Major Dodds and me out again; we were handy and already familiar with the situation. To my surprise, Ops called maintenance for K. D. Waters. The mission was going on into the evening, but Dodds and I were done. Waters and Mike Bartley, plus their copilots, and different crewchiefs and gunners were put on notice. They would take up the slack and press the fight.

In fifteen minutes, the Buffalo City Frogs landed across our ramp at Charlie Med. They discharged the wounded Korean and Lance Corporal Soukup. Next they taxied into our parking area, and paused just long enough to let our Klondike crew out. Then they continued to their own squadron area. Wilson, Andrews, and Corporal Parsons, the gunner, hopped out and disappeared into the line shack, after which the pilots came to the ready room. They were warmly greeted.

"Well, Boss, we messed up one of the birds," Wilson said to CO.

"We're just happy to see you guys, Steve," Lieutenant Colonel Maloney responded.

Following his inquiries about Soukup's condition, he asked, "Where'd you take the hits?"

"It was in the engine, sir. Hell, I saw the guy shoot us. He was to our front left, no more than thirty yards away. He hosed us on final with his AK. We heard a loud slam, the nose swung, and the horn sounded. We'd just come out of our flare. All I had time to do was level the bird and feed in collective. We probably had ten knots or so when we slammed in. The ground's not level there. The bird's sort of cocked up on its right side. We unstrapped and crawled out. Soukup was hit about the time we landed. Kimo got the first-aid kit from the helo to help him, but we were pretty much in the open. So we crawled and dragged Soukup over a dike to the Koreans, about forty yards from us. The bad guys were pingin' at us while we moved." Steve and Kimo were relieved and it showed.

"Well, we're glad you're okay and that Soukup's being tended to. This thing is developing even further. John just radioed. They want another section of guns and some CAS. We're seeing if Group'll approve it now. Looks like Captain Waters will take another section out."

And so it went. Waters and Mike Bartley launched with another section to relieve Arick and Swinburn. Later we heard that Waters ran several sections of fixed-wing A-4s into the ground attack mix as well as the ordnance he and Bartley delivered. The NVA broke contact and melted away under the pressure.

After our maintenance crew rigged Wilson's bird the next morning, a CH-46 from HMM-165 lifted the Huey back to the VMO-6 parking apron. The Koreans had provided security so our grunt platoon was off the hook. Another section of our gunships escorted the recovery of the downed bird. I was not involved.

Lance Corporal Soukup was out of the squadron for six weeks, but the medical folks did what they were paid to do. He came back, pale and a bit less smiley, but back. The round he'd taken hit in his abdomen but traveled down into his leg. After some "limited duty" time in the squadron while his body and maybe his mind mended a bit more, he returned to the business of flying, back to doing what crewchiefs do.

This episode stands out because it was unusual. The shootdown, the injury, the lead transfer, the audio warning horn, and the demonstration of power the squadron and the Group were able to bring were all memorable.

The original call to our squadron caused two unscheduled birds to be manned and launched in short order. Two more followed these, then two more. Buffalo City contributed to extract Wilson, his crew, and the wounded Korean. The next day, another gun section with Buffalo City guys retrieved our Huey. Added to these were CAS jets Waters controlled that evening. The machine at work was inspiring, made me proud of its efficiency, its competence. I was pleased to be part of something that great.

CHAPTER 11

Retrieving the Ontos Crew

Sometimes add-on tasks were requested of us by the DASC once we'd completed an originally assigned mission. Such was the case for me after I'd led a section of guns in support of an uneventful troop insertion. The CH-34s put the Marines on the ground; we stood by to help in case of trouble. There was none so we headed home. On our way back to Ky Ha, the call came.

"Powerglide (HMM-263) thirteen dash six. This is Landshark Alpha. Over."

"Landshark, Powerglide thirteen dash six. Go ahead," responded the HAC in the lead lift helo.

"Powerglide thirteen dash six, can you accept a divert to pick up two KIAs? It's near your route of flight. Over." After a pause, "Landshark, Powerglide thirteen dash six. We'd be hard-pressed. These birds are scheduled close on the heels of our landing. Over."

"Roger, Powerglide thirteen dash six. Break. Klondike four dash twelve, Landshark Alpha."

Here it came. "Roger, Landshark. This is four dash twelve. We copied your chat with Powerglide. Let me call Base and see if we can stay out longer. Over," I responded.

"Roger Klondike. Landshark Alpha, Out."

Then to my wingman, "Dash Two, stay up this freq. We'll be back in a minute. Over."

"Roger, Lead."

"Ted, let's dial in Base," I said over the ICS to First Lt. Ted Almida, my copilot. Without answering, he turned knobs and produced a different FM frequency.

"You're up, Dave."

"Klondike Base, this is Klondike four dash twelve. Over."

After a short pause while the ODO stopped "reading" *Playboy* and focused on my transmission, a response came. "This is Base. Go ahead."

"Roger Base, Landshark wants us to divert for a KIA pickup. Our insert mission is done; we're headin' for the barn. But the zone is on our way. We'd be out twenty to thirty minutes longer. We have enough gas. Can we accept the divert? Over."

"Roger, four dash twelve. Wait one. I'll check. Over."

Headed southeast, we drilled along at 1,200 feet, a half of a mile behind the Powerglide birds, and offset to the left. The day was bright, the country beautiful, and wind whipped through the doorless cabin of our gunbird evaporating sweat, keeping us cool. Shortly the ODO radioed. "Klondike four dash twelve, this is Base. We don't need the birds soon. You're cleared for the divert. Over."

"Roger, Base. Four dash twelve is cleared to divert. We're switchin' back to mission freq. Over."

"Roger, four dash twelve. See ya later. Base, Out."

I checked back in with my flight, called Landshark Alpha, accepted the mission, and received the ground unit's call sign, grid coordinates, and FM frequency. I bid adieu to the Powerglide CH-34s, which continued the trek to Ky Ha, then altered course for our gun section to the grid coordinates given.

I contacted the ground unit, they popped a smoke, and I headed down. My wingman stayed high, partly to deter any assholes who'd be tempted to shoot at us, and partly because we had room in our bird for both bodies that needed the evac.

I shot an approach to a wide section in a red clay road. As I closed on the landing site, the cause of the casualties was apparent. An Ontos was on its side, charred and badly mauled. One of its tracks was blown off and a crater was in the road adjacent to the Ontos. Land mine.

Ontos means "thing" in Greek. I've been told the Army didn't want it, so guess who gets a shit-pot full? It was a lightly armored, tracked vehicle, and mounted six 106-mm recoilless rifles. These beauties were nine feet wide and twelve feet long with a crew of three. A single-shot, 50 caliber, co-axial gun was used for spotting. The ballistics of the 106 and the .50 were apparently either identical or so close it didn't matter. Once the gunner put a .50-caliber tracer round on the target, he could slam away with the 106s, one, some, or all. The Ontos, vulnerable though it was, could blow the shit out of about anything. But this Ontos' working days were over.

My eyes shifted from the wreckage to two figures lying on the ground. They were not in the standard gray-green body bags. Instead, ponchos covered them, or had until my rotorwash sent them flying. Charred and protruding lower stumps jutted toward the sky at 90 degrees from the torsos. The Marines were obviously in a seated position when the catastrophe occurred. Nothing was below the knees, and the waist down was blackened. A stretcher was produced, on which both bodies were placed end to end. The ponchos were retrieved and once again placed over them. A grunt and our crewchief, Lance Corporal Pope, who'd unplugged his helmet to go help, brought the stretcher to our helo. They slid it in on the cabin floor between the rear seats and the ammo cans behind the pilots.

After Pope was satisfied, "Okay, Lieutenant. We're ready back here," came over the ICS.

I called my wingman to let him know we were coming out and executed a thoughtless hand, eye, foot coordination maneuver, then nosed the bird off into the wind. On the ground and predictably, the grunts turned their backs to avoid the inevitable sandblast.

The smell of burnt human flesh is distinct. Even with the passage of years, I am confident I would recognize it immediately. It is sweet and heavy, unlike any other odor. Although the wind whipped through our doorless cabin from both rotorwash and our forward airspeed, the smell was not blown away fast enough. It pervaded our helo and kept me focused on our cargo. It was like flying the helo was the distraction, rather than the dead Marines we carried.

Unable to resist, I glanced back from my pilot's position in the right front. Wind had displaced the poncho from the head of the dead Marine behind the copilot. He looked peaceful, asleep, no reflection of surprise or suffering, just rest. He was young. I was barely twenty-six, but this Marine was younger, probably around twenty. Wind played in his hair, almost suggesting life. He had a little stubble, a strong chin, was lean and blond, and sunburned from the Vietnam weather, from off saving our nation from perceived threat.

I thought about these two deaths as we flew home and have even more since. Some mothers, some fathers would suffer intensity of grief in the short run and a dull, empty aching for the rest of their days. In this life they would never again experience pure joy. Perhaps they'd even look forward to their own deaths as an opportunity to see and again be with their little man. One more woman, now well into her middle years, would occasionally stare out a window into nothing, wondering how life might have been had the Marine returned as he'd promised. Some letters heading for Vietnam would remain unread. A few possessions would be inventoried and sent home.

In a couple of weeks groups would gather at cemeteries; words would be said but not heard by the central figures, not understood by minds numbed in bereavement. Other clean, strong, young Marines would fire volleys. A flag would be folded with precision by white-gloved hands and presented to the unwilling. Some lives, including my own in a small way, would simply never be the same. The Ontos crew has been with me these many years and shall remain so.

We delivered the corpses to the Charlie Med helo pad at Ky Ha where a graves registration unit was conveniently colocated. They took charge of the ladened stretcher. I taxied back to our flight line and shut the gunbird down. Little was said among the crew, only the necessary. Body bags are bad, ponchos partially covering young, dead, and burned Marines are much worse.

CHAPTER 12

Army Parts

Captain Waters and the SNCOs in maintenance were like many Marines; they were inventive. Since our Echo model Hueys were a helluva lot like Army B and D models, our SNCOs worked with Army people at Pleiku for "hand-me-downs."

"Hey, Dave, you're not on the flight schedule. Let's take a slick down to Pleiku an' visit the Army. We might scrounge some parts they're tossing." It was my boss, Waters, talking.

"Sir?" At first I was baffled, but before he went into his explanation I recovered. "When do we leave?" We were outside the aircraft maintenance office, adjacent to the flight line. At the time I was chatting with Sergeant Storms, one of the check crew leaders, about testing a bird coming out of scheduled maintenance the next day.

"We'll shove off in about an hour, ten or so."

"Okay, I'll be ready." I broke off my discussion with Storms, went to the intel hooch, and picked up a new 1:50,000-meter map, one that showed Pleiku, which was southwest of Ky Ha and off the local map.

I killed time with some of the guys in the ready room, and at 0930 took my helmet bag and flak jacket to the line shack, checked which slick we'd be using, and went to the helo. After I'd emptied my helmet bag into the copilot's seat, I performed my usual preflight. I was satisfied the helo was in good shape; I plugged my helmet into the radio/ICS system and tossed my kneeboard and the new map on top of the glare shield.

The shield is vital; it kept the sun and bright reflections off the instrument panel so the dials and gauges were easier to read. I fished my gloves from inside my lower right flight suit pocket. They were the new kind, made of green fire-retardant fabric with gray leather on the palms and gripping surfaces of the fingers. The older gloves were pale gold-yellow and completely leather. When new, these were beauties, but it didn't take long for them to look like hell from preflights and just being around the fluids of helos. I folded the new map to the best vantage for navigation and looked it over until Waters showed up.

"How's she look?"

"It's okay, sir. I'd take it, no problem."

"Let's go then." He opened the pilot's door, stepped through with his helmet bag, sat down, dug out his stuff, plugged in, and strapped in. I opened my NATOPS checklist to the start sequence in anticipation of the challenge and response we'd go through. Waters had just paid me a huge compliment, trusting my preflight rather than looking the aircraft over himself. He'd also violated rules, but I guess he knew me well enough by then. The crewchief for the flight was Corporal Collum; he stationed himself in front of the helo for the start. The Maintenance Chief, Master Sergeant Lochbeiler, and the Aviation Supply SNCO showed up as we began the start sequence. They strapped in on the nylon-web seats in the cabin rear.

We started, taxied, took off, and headed south. I navigated; he flew. Then I flew and Waters navigated.

"These guys have so much stuff, sometimes they throw out good parts. You know how the guys can sometimes troubleshoot by changing parts? Well, sometimes we keep parts we remove unless we know they're bad. The Army guys have a bigger inventory and sometimes perfectly good parts are tossed or sent back to depot level maintenance for repair. We'd like to get some of that stuff. Top Lochbeiler and Staff Sergeant Farmer have already coordinated this a little with 'em. We're not just showin' up cold, but it ain't a done deal either. We don't have a damn thing to trade. We're just after a chance to reuse discards."

"Sounds like a good idea. Might reduce the cannibalism," I answered, aware that when no parts were available, sometimes a down helo became a parts bin to keep others flying. This can be a shitty deal for the maintenance guys, since more manhours are required to swap parts around than to replace a bad part with a new good one.

We flew to Pleiku single bird and crossed large swaths of South Vietnam to get there. Had we gone down, we might have been in trouble, but we routinely went to and from Marble Mountain alone. No one thought much about it on these "admin" runs. This was in stark contrast to mission flying. Virtually anytime we were on a "mission," tasked to us from higher headquarters, we went in twos. Someone was usually there to save your ass if you went down. Not this day, we were alone and unafraid in search of handouts.

The flight was uneventful; we eased into casual conversation and plopped along at 115 knots and 1,000 feet AGL. Vietnam slid beneath us and provided views low-level flyers rarely tire of, even though it was our routine.

Later in my career, I logged a hundred or so hours in a TA-4J, a small two-seater jet used primarily to train A-4 pilots. I liked the speed; you could get there in a hurry. And the G-forces were kickass. But I enjoyed the helos more. Low and slow, looking at mother earth and a crew to chat with was better for this farm boy. Maybe I'd been conditioned by then, but high and fast wasn't for me.

Although in flight school when I was told I'd be heading for helo training, I was crushed, in retrospect I was where I was supposed to be. I've never believed the sour grapes sayings about the jet pilots: "Sports car, sunglasses, big watch, small pecker," or "Mark Twain never met a fighter pilot." The truth is most of us went to Pensacola to become jet pilots. We all wanted afterburner, thunder in the left hand, G-forces in the seat of our pants. But the Corps had a spectrum of needs; it does what it wants with and to you. I got drunk after I received word that Phantoms were not in my future, but I never looked back.

We flew out of I Corps, the northernmost military division of South Vietnam, the one assigned to the Marine Corps, and into II Corps, the northernmost of the Army's Area of Operations. First we went south along Route 1, the only north-south highway in Vietnam, then inland to the country's high central plateau.

When we arrived at Pleiku, I was provided a lesson: The Army is huge. This truth screamed at me. They had zillions of helos, row after row, mostly UH-1Ds, the troop transporters, but great numbers of B model gunbirds also. Others were there as well and in magnitude beyond my experience. Helos out the ass!

We landed and hung around the transient parking area. I just shadowed Waters as he chatted with a couple of Army pilots. Our maintenance and aviation supply chiefs disappeared after a few minutes but soon returned.

"Captain Waters, we'll be back in thirty minutes or so. Meet you here?" Master Sargeant Lochbeiler said.

"Yeah, we'll see you guys back here. Take your time. We probably ought to grab some chow while we're here. So, if Lieutenant Ballentine and I are not here, we'll be eating," Waters answered.

Off they went with a couple of senior Army SNCOs. After a bit longer at the line, we hitched a jeep ride to the chow hall. Their food was about like the Corps', mass-produced, "sufficient in quantity and quality," a box I checked when I was the Command Duty Officer (CDO) at MAG-26 in my VMO-1, New River days.

The CDO spent the night in the Group Headquarters, oversaw the raising and lowering of the flag, ate in the chow hall, commented on the chow, and stood phone watch with a senior SNCO. We were there in case the shit hit the fan, first responders and trip-wires in the after-hours chain of command. Fire, murder, crashes, whatever, the CDO was called and initiated response, which usually meant he called some senior officer and got his more experienced ass out of the sack.

The CDO kept a logbook, in which a record was made of overnight actions or inaction (I liked that best). The log was briefed and given to the XO or CO in the morning. Sleeping on the CDO cot was never quite okay, but the whole experience trained lieutenants to increased responsibility and provided useful service to the command.

Waters and I stood out, since our flight suits were tan coveralls and the Army guys wore green. Just as we finished chow, the Klondike SNCOs arrived with the Army guys we'd seen earlier.

"How'd it go?" Waters asked.

"It went well, Captain. I think we mighta helped ourselves some. The Army has been kind." He smiled with a hint of slyness and looked at the Army SNCOs. They too smiled in conspiracy.

One of them offered, "We're all in this shit together, I guess. If we can help, we oughta." And so we were. The green-side military bubbas were "in this shit together" for sure.

They walked the chow line and wolfed their food. In ten minutes we piled into a jeep with the Army guys and headed to the flight line.

Before checking the bird over on preflight, I noticed two wooden boxes on the floor of the cabin. The haul included instruments, airspeed indicators, altimeters, clocks, and various small parts I didn't recognize, some of which appeared to be engine- or fuel-control related. The SNCOs were smiling like cats after a canary snack.

K. D. ran up the slick; we taxied, took off, and retraced our path to Ky Ha. The parts disappeared into maintenance, no doubt into various shops for expert sifting and assessment. I never asked, I had other activities on my mind, but I have confidence some of those parts kept our Hueys flying rather than awaiting the response of an aviation supply line that ran to the States.

What I learned from this outing was a lesson in dimension: The Corps was small compared to the Army. I was buried in the Marine Corps, so I had little appreciation for this truth. In my world, everywhere I turned there were Marines doing Marine things, the Marine way, with Marine stuff, and Marine equipment. I hadn't looked outside my backyard.

Size is mostly a product of function. The primary job of the Marine Corps is to assault the land from the sea, wedge out some turf, and achieve some limited objectives. The Army is designed to prosecute the nation's land wars. Since mission drives manpower, equipment, tactics, and structure, the profile of each service is different. Although the Corps can serve as a force in land warfare—Korea, Vietnam, and Iraq are examples—it is not heavied up like the Army.

A person can learn from reading, but sometimes there is no lesson like a sensory one. At Pleiku, I had a visual example of Army size, at least in their helo community. It was *big*. I was not staggered, but impressed. They could come at you in numbers.

CHAPTER 13

Flying Miss World and Vic Damone

VMO-2, our sister gunbird squadron at Marble Mountain near Danang, didn't have enough slicks to ferry Bob Hope and his entourage from Danang Airbase to and from the stage location of the 1966 Christmas show. The task came into MAG-36 from Wing and on down to VMO-6. First Lt. Barney Ross and I were each given a slick and told to go help the "Deadlock" guys at VMO-2. Not that it would have mattered, but Barney and I didn't mind at all. Helping with the lift meant we would see the show, unlike other Marines at Chu Lai, Ky Ha, and countless other locations. In writing this, I am not picking on Bob Hope and his troupe; they did all they could. But the military was scattered all over hell and back; not everyone could attend. To me, Hope and his gang remain heroes and heroines.

Barney and I leaped off early one morning in December and headed north along the coast to Marble Mountain and a brief by the VMO-2 bubbas on who, what, where, when, and how. Following our VMO-2 brief, six slicks (Barney and I were last two), flew to Danang Airbase, landed near the tower, and waited for the entertainers.

In short order a transport aircraft landed, taxied in, and shut down. Out they came. After a brief pow-wow between a liaison officer and the Hope people, they sorted themselves into small groups, each escorted by a Marine and each group headed for a different helo. I was way down on the pecking order; I can't remember whether Barney was dead-assed last or I was. We did not get Bob Hope or Joey Heatherton. But, a tall, striking, young woman from India, Miss World as it turned out, and Vic Damone were assigned to me. We greeted each other, they smiled, and, under the care of Sergeant

Corning, they hopped in back. He got them strapped in and gave them head-sets. After turn up, Corning got into the copilot's seat and we took off in sequence for the five-mile flight to the already erected stage. Thousands waited from all military branches, but mostly they were Marines. We shut down behind and to the left of the stage; the passengers smiled again, thanked us, and moved off to make spectacles of themselves. We found seats on some rising ground to the left front of the stage.

Soon the band began to play and here came Mr. Hope. He was phenomenal, truly funny, better in life than on television, a clever man of droll, risqué humor, performing for people who deserved distraction. For the next couple of hours they cycled through the cast of singers, dancers, and beautiful people. Miss World fit in this last category. She came out and was sort of interviewed by Bob, who made puns and double entendre remarks as they went along. She was entertaining to look at and generous, as they all were. As near as I could tell her talent was beauty. It has little purpose, but we would not be without it.

My favorite nonfunny person was Joey Heatherton. She'd come without her San Diego Charger pass-catching hubby (Lance Allworth), which was fine with us. She was exceptionally well put together, a freak of sorts because she actually approached the ideal; one of those favored at one end of the spectrum, as others might be pitied at the opposite. She cavorted and danced, kicking high, to the delight of the assembled. Hope asked her questions designed to demonstrate her lack of intelligence. My suspicion is that she was not just a knockout body and face, but a bright person as well. But I suppose you need a shtick in showbiz. Hers was the beautiful airhead. She did great with it for about a decade. My guess is she retired years ago in Palm Springs to comfort with her cats and garden, although without Lance I'm told.

At the end of a memorable afternoon, the entertainers bid their audience farewell, and, after a few patriotic and religious songs from Anita Bryant (I think), we were done. We headed for the helos, turned up, and waited for the performers. When they arrived, Corning invited either of our passengers to fly in the copilot's seat. Miss World accepted and, smiling broadly, she let Corning strap her in, which is a little more complicated in front, since shoulder harness and lap belts are used. In the rear it's seat belts only. He gave her a headset, then showed her the ICS button on the floor.

"Can you hear me?" I said over the ICS. "If you can, just step on that plunger and you can answer." I reinforced what Corning had said.

She looked at the floor and stepped on the switch. "Yes. This is exciting for me," she responded in that distinct and melodic, sing-song and clipped Indian accent.

"I expect this is kinda new," I responded lamely. What the hell does the son of farmers say to Miss World?

We took off in lazy sequence for the short flight back to Danang. "Ever fly a helo?" I asked.

"No," she laughed. "I don't think I could." Her teeth were beautiful, small, white, even. She had a nice dusky complexion; her hair shone and was pulled back tightly in a bun. To my tastes she was too thin, too "Twiggy" and willowy, but her features were even and flawless, dark eyes, a full mouth. Shit, she was Miss World! Not just your average garden-variety woman. I could see how a guy might vote for her.

"It's a piece of cake," I lied. "Get on the control with me and I'll talk you along."

She said nothing, but kept smiling and she latched on to the cyclic and collective and placed her feet on the rudders. Since she was tall, probably five eight or so, she had no trouble reaching the pedals.

"The stick controls the nose position and tilts the main rotor." I began telling her a few rudiments. We plodded along with her on the controls at seventy to eighty knots first above then below five hundred feet. The ball, which indicates balanced flight, swung back and forth as the helo crabbed first one direction then the other and the nose oscillated slowly above and below the horizon.

As we approached our landing site, I talked her into a mild descent and the beginnings of our speed reduction. As we passed below 250 feet and 60 knots however, she stopped receiving, computing, and responding to my tutoring. She stiffly held the controls and looked straight ahead. Her thighs inched together until they closed on the stick.

"I have the aircraft," I said into the ICS and got on the controls. No response, no slacking of pressures, she stared at the approaching tarmac near the Danang tower. I took a firm grip on both the cyclic and collective. I moved the stick abruptly two inches laterally in each direction, firmly contacting and opening her sari-covered thighs.

In my peripheral vision I could see her eyes open widely as she turned to me with a slightly startled look and let go of the controls. Then she smiled broadly again.

"You're not ready for landing yet. We need a few more hops." I said and began the muscle memory sequence of nose up, collective down, right rudder; then nose level, collective up, and left rudder. The Huey came into a hover. I pushed through ground effect and set the helo down.

Vic and Miss World deplaned with smiles and thank-yous. We told them how great it was they'd come. Corning secured the cabin again and jumped into the copilot's seat. Within a few minutes Hope and company disappeared into vehicles and headed, no doubt, for food, some well-deserved rest, maybe a chat about the performance, a night's sleep, and on to entertain again.

Ross and I had plenty of fuel for our return to Ky Ha. Once our flight took off, we said good-bye to the VMO-2 guys over the Fox Mike radio, peeled away, climbed to fifteen hundred feet, and headed south on our fifty-mile flight to Ky Ha.

Bob Hope, who started these troop entertainment outings in World War II, will always be a favorite of mine. He's been dead a while, but others are stepping up to entertain deployed military folks at Christmas. But Hope was special. His spontaneous comic wit and stage presence were probably unique. He was a giant; he took us away from our place and time, if only for a couple of hours. The audience roared at his tongue-in-cheek observations about our lovely vacation spot near the South China Sea. The grunts especially hooted when he talked about our well-appointed accommodations, our exquisite cuisine, and the chance many of us had to observe nature while on pleasant hikes in the hills.

Hope may have been one of a kind; he had both World War II and Korea under his belt and was probably at the top of his game for the Vietnam War. Still he was remarkable and bighearted, a great American. Those who came with him were super also, but he was the genius.

Tapping the inner thighs of Miss World with the stick makes my lip curl even today. I wonder where she is and if she remembers. I doubt it, but this Kansas man does.

CHAPTER 14

Downed by Fire

We were hanging out in the ready room. First Lt. John Boden and I had our noses buried in paperbacks. As usual it was hot. Jerry Garner had his ass nailed again to the ODO chair; he ran the flight schedule, handled minor fireballs that came in, and generally wafered the easy stuff away from the Ops Officer.

The green field phone rang at Garner's desk. Boden and I looked up as Jerry pulled the handset from its cradle. His eyes concentrated; his brow knit. From where it hung behind his desk, he grabbed a clipboard with mimeographed forms on it and began filling in blocs. While writing, he glanced at us and nodded, then reached for a button on the wall and pushed it. A horn sounded throughout the squadron area. The medevac was being launched. That was me; Boden was my copilot. That day we crewed the unarmed medevac slick.

I stood and headed for the screen door to the ready room, the flight line, and the already preflighted Huey parked near the line shack. Boden went to the ODO desk and, hovering over Garner, began to absorb information: location, call sign, unit, frequency, number of casualties, enemy in the area, nature of wounds, and whatever else was known and useful.

Second Lt. Francis Kinkelaar III hastened into the ready room, knee-board in hand, and joined Boden at the ODO desk. Francis was the copilot of the gunbird chase. He'd absorb the same info Boden copied.

As I approached the medevac slick, the crewchief, Corporal Nickerson, and a Navy Corpsman walked briskly from the line shack. We met at the bird. John Arick, pilot in command of the gunbird chase, came striding from the aircraft maintenance hooch. Boden and Kinkelaar would show up at the birds with the briefing details, while Arick and I ran up the Hueys.

"Looks like we got some business," I said to Arick as he went by en route to his helo; it was parked one line up the ramp from mine.

"Yeah, and just when I was making a little progress on some ball-juggling. Murphy's Law, I guess." John was the assistant aircraft maintenance officer, right under Waters, senior to me a year in the Corps, but my peer as an aviator.

Nickerson unhooked the main rotor blade from where it was secured by a cord to the tail stinger. I put on my flak vest, climbed into the cockpit and strapped in, then pulled on my helmet and gloves, and attached my kneeboard. Next I threw switches, rolled the throttle to the flight idle detent, got a "thumbs-up" from Nickerson, and pulled the start trigger. The nickel-cadmium battery spun the starter, which spun the Lycoming turbine. Igniters snapped, the main rotor began its left swing, and I heard the engine light. The exhaust gas temperature needle eased off its peg.

Both Boden and Kinkelaar came trotting from the ready room to our helos. John put on his flak jacket, slid in, strapped in, and donned his flight gear.

"Single guy wounded, about sixteen miles two nine zero degrees. Unit's still in contact," Boden offered into the ICS. We were near engine and rotor operating rpm and our temperatures and pressures were in the green.

"Okay, John. I'll get us headin' in that direction and you can fill me in as we go."

"Chase is up and ready," Arick called on the squadron Fox Mic. Shit, that was fast. I was at my bird the same time he was, but he beat me. Using a small spring-loaded switch under my left thumb, I ran the power turbine to 6,600 RPM.

"Roger, Chase. We'll be with you in a heartbeat." I scanned the panel for instrument readings and checked the radios for proper setup. All looked good.

"You guys ready?" I asked the crew.

"Yes, sir," came parrot responses from Nickerson and the doc. Boden looked at me, nodded, and held his thumb up.

"Ky Ha Ground, Klondike Medevac. Taxi for two," I called over the UHF radio. We didn't need to tell the ground controllers or the tower from which mat we were lifting. Although Ky Ha had two large helo parking mats, one north and one south, the controllers knew which call signs went to which squadrons and where those squadrons were located in our complex. We were on the south mat.

"Klondike Medevac and Chase is cleared to taxi, switch to tower approved at pilot's discretion. Runway three in service," came the answer.

This last part was not news; runway three was virtually always "in service." It faced the ocean and typically an onshore breeze.

I nodded at our taxi director and, on his signal, pulled the helo into a hover, and checked the gauges; all was okay. The director motioned us forward out of our spot, gave us a right turn signal, and we headed down a taxi lane toward the runway. In my peripheral vision, I noted Arick had pulled the gunbird out of its spot and into his taxi lane. He taxied parallel to us, one taxi lane up the ramp.

"Chase, go Tower," I called on the Fox Mike as we approached the runway.

"Chase switchin'." Then, once Arick was on the new frequency, "Chase is up."

"Roger, Chase. Break. Ky Ha Tower, Klondike Medevac and Chase ready for takeoff three south," I called.

"Medevac and Chase are cleared onto runway three south and cleared for takeoff. No reported traffic."

"Roger. Medevac cleared for takeoff." I kept the slick moving, turned left on the runway, lined up with the centerline, and checked my gauges again. Then I added power, fed in left rudder to hold heading, and dipped the Huey's nose. We gathered speed and flew off the Ky Ha cliff. I turned left, rolled out on a 290-degree heading, and kept the power up, but not at max. I climbed to 1,200 feet MSL.

"Chase coming?" I said into the ICS.

"He's back there, sir. Probably a hundred and fifty yards or so," Nickerson responded.

"Thanks." Then over the Fox Mike, "Chase, can ya stay up?" Gunbirds lugged rocket pods, machine guns, and feeder shoots, all exposed to the wind. Also, unlike the slick, the cabin doors were off, which produced even more drag. Slicks could easily slide through the air ten knots faster than gunbirds.

"We're hanging on, but don't pull in anymore," Arick answered.

"Roger, Chase." I kept the power where it was.

"Dave, we'll be calling Fearsome on 41.4. They're right here." Boden held up a map, showing me a point.

"They're still in light contact. This heading should do us fine for a few more minutes. They're just on the front of a low hill mass about twelve o'clock, fourteen miles or so. You can't make it out from here. But we're trackin' okay," Boden said.

"Okay, John. Thanks, just keep us headin' right," I answered.

"Chase, let's go Landshark," I called on FM.

"Roger, Chase switchin' Landshark," answered Arick. Then, after he'd adjusted his UHF frequency, "Chase is up."

"Roger, Chase. Break. Landshark Alpha, Klondike Medevac and Chase are with you. We're twelve hundred feet, four miles, three two zero radial Chu Lai. We're headin' to sixteen miles two niner zero radial, Chu Lai. We're on medevac mission 4122 dash two. Over." (Dash two in this case meant we were on the second sortie that day under the same medevac mission number.)

"Klondike Medevac, Landshark Alpha. Roger mission 4122 dash two. No savaplanes in effect for that quadrant. Over."

"Roger, Landshark." We drilled along for a couple of minutes in silence. John followed our track on his 1:50,000-meter map.

"Chase, let's go Fearsome Fox Mike. Over," I radioed on squadron common FM frequency.

"Chase, Roger. Switchin'," John responded. Boden dialed in the Fearsome FM frequency and Arick checked in, "Chase is up." Arick and I had been in country about eight months. Most was routine, no fiddle-farting around, trying to figure out anything. The learning curve was behind us.

"Roger, Chase," I answered. After another minute I called the ground unit. "Fearsome, this is Klondike Medevac. Over."

Nothing. I waited a minute or so and closed on the briefed grid coordinates. Then again, "Fearsome, Klondike Medevac. Over."

"Roger, Medevac. This is Fearsome Bravo. Over."

Apparently I was in contact with Bravo Company, thus the call sign Fearsome Bravo, rather than just Fearsome. "Fearsome Bravo, Klondike Medevac. We're estimating your position in five minutes. Can you mark with smoke on-call and are you still in contact? Over."

"Medevac, Fearsome Bravo. We can pop a smoke. It'll be yellow. We've had no fire for about fifteen minutes. But Charlie's still in the area. Last contact was west, on the outskirts of the vil. Over."

"Roger, Fearsome. Medevac will call for smoke and make our approach from the east, away from the vil and your last contact. Over."

"Roger, Klondike. We'll hold the smoke for your call. Our wounded can't walk. We'll bring him to the chopper. Our Marines are in the eastern half of the vil. None of our people are in the western part. Over."

Boden gave me corrections and we tracked closer to the briefed grids. We eased over a ridge and there it was. "That's it, Dave. These guys should be in that vil and just to the east and southeast of it," Boden offered and he pointed to an approaching hamlet cradled on the front side of a ridge. Rice paddies fronted the vil from our direction.

"Okay, John." I could see the village plainly and visualized the disposition of friendly troops.

"Medevac Chase, you got a fix on our potential problem areas? Over," I called to Arick.

"Roger, Medevac. We'll set up to cover the western area of the vil. Over."

"Okay, John. Break. Fearsome Bravo, let's have your smoke. And, if we need to, are we cleared to fire in the western part of the vil? Over."

"Roger, Medevac, smoke coming, and you're cleared to fire in the western half. Over."

Out came the predictable billow. I looped right over smoke and vil, noted wind direction and velocity from the yellow drift. I selected a suitable landing site nearest the smoke and began a descent. Several small rice paddies separated the zone from the hamlet. The wind was light. I had plenty of power, since I was just lugging around four people, unlike the chase, which had four people plus ammo, rockets, pods, racks, and guns.

I lowered the collective, fed in right rudder, eased the nose up to slow the bird and began an approach to my selected LZ.

"Fearsome Bravo, Medevac will land just southeast of the rice paddy. We're comin' in now. Over."

"Roger, Medevac. We'll start in that direction with the wounded. Over."

Near the ground I inched the slick's nose up even higher and reducing the collective more to kill off the last of our airspeed. Then I rocked the nose forward and pulled in power to cushion the landing.

Arick came up on the FM. "Chase is in on a dummy run. Over."

Shortly after we were on the ground, he passed on the left. He pulled up at one hundred feet. John posed a threat, a warning. Often this worked.

Three Marines came toward our helo carrying a fourth in a poncho. They waded out into the muck of the rice paddy. Just behind me our Corpsman opened his cabin door and stepped onto the skid tube. The Marines made only slow progress through the unsure footing of the wet rice paddy. Just as the doc said, "I'm gonna go help," it happened.

Small water geysers kicked up in the rice paddy, not where the Marines were crossing with the wounded man, but to our two o'clock. The geysers marched across the paddy toward us.

"We're takin' fire," I said into the ICS. "Doc, stay put." Then into the FM, "Chase, we're takin' fire. We're liftin'."

"Roger, Medevac, we'll be in position for a run shortly. Over," Arick answered. He was climbing and turning, not yet ready to attack.

As I rapidly pulled in power and started the helo moving, I heard the cabin door slam shut. Then I released some of the left pedal pressure, allowing the Huey's nose to swing right. We climbed and turned.

From a quick scan of the instruments, I noticed the engine torquemeter reading first sag, then go to zero. But the power held. I flew over the Marines in the eastern half of the vil.

Shortly after Arick called. "Chase is in with guns." He started an attack and danced red-orange 7.62 balls into the western extremes of the hamlet.

John had no specific target; he was just blazing away, which was often enough to keep heads down. And you might get lucky and hurt or kill folks who were trying to hurt or kill you.

As I pulled up and curled right, I noticed the look of surprise on the faces of the Marines bringing their wounded buddy. I will always remember it. But I could not stay, could not sit at risk in the open, hoping the bird would be flyable after a peppering and that we'd not become casualties ourselves. One round in the engine and it's lunched; then no one's going anywhere.

I didn't realize it at the time, but I'd just made a decision that would haunt me all my days. I was faced with two mutually exclusive obligations: One was to rescue the wounded Marine; the other was to keep my crew, the aircraft, and myself from injury. I couldn't do both. Although squadron policy was to avoid sitting in a hot zone and prudence dictated that I not risk four for one, I am troubled by this experience. I have been for forty years, and will be until they close my lid. I think of that injured Marine almost daily, in dreams and waking hours.

Someone needed me and I walked. In doing my job, I failed to do another job. My helo was damaged temporarily, its pilot permanently. I will always remember, always feel pain, remorse, and guilt, and always be saddened as I replay the episode on its continuous loop in my mind. *Se la guerre.* Who goes unpunished?

Our Huey had trouble; my gauges were telling me something. After I'd gained five hundred feet and departed east from the vil, I said into the ICS, "Corporal Nickerson, can you check out back on both sides of the bird. See if you can notice anything. My torque's at zero."

"Sir, I'll look." He opened the door behind Boden and leaned out into the slipstream. "Nothing there, Lieutenant." He repeated this on my side.

"Shit, sir, we got a big slick of something comin' out over here. It's all over the bird and running back in the wind. I don't think it's hyd fluid. It don't seem red."

I keyed the Fox Mike. "Fearsome Bravo, Klondike Medevac. The helo's taken some hits and I need to see what's wrong. We have to abort this evac. We'll let our higher know that your Marine still needs pickup. Over."

"Roger, Klondike. We'll call battalion too. Over."

We'd been hurt. It was not just an instrument malfunction. If it had been a hydraulic leak, I could muscle the bird home and land it with a complete system failure. It was just a hell of a lot more difficult to horse a Huey around without hydraulics. But Nickerson knew hyd fluid from engine or transmission oil. Losing lubricating oil was a different matter; without oil, surfaces get hot and over time moving parts seize. I needed to put the bird down and take a look.

I leveled at one thousand feet heading east in the general direction of Ky Ha, but I was not going to chance driving that far. We'd have to find some place closer.

"John, anything out there in the direction of home? A grunt or arty compound you know of?" I said into the ICS. The engine and transmission oil temps and pressures were holding.

Then to Arick, "Chase, we have oil streaming from the starboard side. We oughta set her down out here, scope the problem, and make a decision. We're looking for a grunt or artillery base camp or compound. Over."

"Roger, Medevac. We have you in sight and are following. At your two o'clock and about three miles is a base camp. It's on a hill out there. The top is pretty much chewed up with fighting holes and bunkers. You might be able to make it out. It looks light orangish from all the diggin'. I flew over it yesterday escorting a resupply and we passed it to our left a while ago. Over."

Life might become less troublesome. I glanced out the front right as Arick talked and made out orange scarring on a hilltop.

"Roger, Chase. We see the hilltop and are headin' there. Over." As I spoke and adjusted the slick's heading, I glanced at the oil temperatures and pressures. They were still holding, but since we were venting oil, that could not last. We had a couple miles to go.

"Fearsome Bravo. We're leavin' your freq. Break. Medevac Chase, let's go squadron common Fox Mike. Over," I radioed.

"Switchin'," came Arick's reply.

"Klondike, Fearsome Bravo copies. Out."

"Chase is up," John checked in. Boden had switched our FM frequency to Klondike common. Arick and I could now talk not only to each other, but to Garner at his desk in our ready room. I called and described our situation.

"Base, Medevac's taken some hits in the pickup zone. We're leakin' oil and headin' for a grunt base camp to check it over. The wounded Marine from our mission has not, repeat, not been evacuated. Over."

"Roger, Medevac. What grids will you be landing at? Over," Garner responded. Good question.

"Wait, over." I answered. Boden was already going through the "read right, up" sequence to produce the six-digit grid. But Arick and Kinkelaar were ahead of me.

"Base, this is Medevac Chase. They'll be going in to BS279342. Over."

"Roger, Chase. Understand BS279342. Over," Garner answered.

"Base, read back correct," Arick answered.

"Chase, you've got the radios. You probably oughta let Landshark know too. Over." I called to Arick. What the hell, he could do that and leave me to select an LZ and get the slick on the ground. The engine oil pressure had dropped a little. Not a good sign, though not a surprise.

"John," I said to Boden on the ICS, "I'm not gonna shoot a steep approach to any tight hilltop pad. I just want inside their wire. Let's look for a spot on the flats."

"Okay, I'm searching," Boden answered.

We closed on the base camp. I reduced power and altitude. Arick made necessary contacts and maintained banter with Garner. They arranged to have maintenance people in the ready room to help assess the helo damage once Nickerson had taken a look. I saw a likely LZ at the same time Boden did.

"There's a spot, Dave. Just to the north and at the base of the hill. That grassy area. It's gotta be inside the wire."

"I see it." I reduced power and set up for a landing to the east, the direction of the daily onshore breezes. It would be a near straight-in approach. Collective down a bit, nose up, a little right rudder. We were a quarter mile out and dropping through three hundred feet at seventy-five knots. The temperature was holding, but the engine oil pressure had descended further.

I began the final flare. We crossed the concertina wire; I brought the Huey over a grassy spot and dropped it to the ground and, as Nickerson exited the helo, rolled the throttle to flight idle. John and I threw the necessary switches while at flight idle, and, after depressing the flight idle detent button, I rolled the throttle off. Rotor brake, fuel pump, radios. I guided the main rotor blades to a stop, then turned off the battery.

Boden and I unstrapped and took off our helmets, gloves, and kneeboards. I swung open the pilot's door. Corporal Nickerson was already beginning his inspection.

"Look here, Lieutenant Ballentine." He pointed to two dime-sized holes about six feet high in the pilot's side engine-transmission access cowling. The holes were about ten inches apart. Oil seeped out at the seam where the engine cowling and fuselage joined. From there aft, much of the helo was slick with oil.

Three Marines approached, but they were not yet near enough to talk with, so I watched Nickerson as he climbed up the helo's side, undid fasteners, and opened the cowl, exposing fluid lines, reservoirs, pumps, and electrical wire bundles and one side of the engine and transmission.

"Look at this shit," he said pointing to slender tubes, which supplied oil to the engine and returned it to a reservoir. The feeder line was nicked, but the return line was shot through.

"Probably did right in settin' her down," Nickerson mused.

"Looks like it; we'd a' run out for sure. Can't fly long with an oil-starved engine," I agreed.

"What next?" Boden wondered out loud.

"I guess we chat with these guys, get on their FM or our own, tell Arick what's up, then wait and see what Arick and Base arrange. If it were up to me, I'd fly out parts and an engine man, flush the system, reattach everything, ground run it, check for leaks, and fly her home."

As I said this a second lieutenant, a sergeant, and a lance corporal walked up.

I turned to them, smiled, and took a couple steps to meet them. "Gents, I'm Lieutenant Ballentine. This is Lieutenant Boden. That's Corporal Nickerson, the crewchief." I motioned to Nickerson who was still up on the side of the bird. "And that's Doc Madden, our Corpsman today. We were out on a medevac west of here and got shot a bit. We needed temporary sanctuary. So we set her down here."

We shook hands; they commiserated. I showed them our problem and asked if they had an FM radio I could use. They did, of course.

Nickerson was making a schematic drawing of the injured hardware so the information, if not translatable over the radio, could at least be taken back with Arick in the gunbird.

"Lance Corporal Srodes, how about fetching Corporal Hensley and his radio," the infantry sergeant said to the junior Marine with them.

"Got it, Sarg," and Lance Corporal Srodes turned and retraced the path he'd just made. Before he'd gone more that seventy-five feet, he shouted through cupped hands, "Fannin, Fannin, get Corporal Hensley and his PRC-25 down here in a hurry."

"Okay," someone named Fannin called from higher up the hill.

Nickerson continued sketching and labeling, and Boden and I shot the breeze with the grunt lieutenant, a platoon leader, and one of his squad leaders. Within a few minutes, Corporal Hensley showed up with his PRC-25 radio.

"Here you go, Sarg," he said to the squad leader and handed over the radio, which the Sarg gave to me. I was about to switch its freq to Klondike common and call Arick, but saw he was making an approach to our LZ. Rather than starting a conversation, I waited for him to land.

When he landed, he made no move to shut his Huey down, but motioned me instead to his gunbird. When I arrived, he shouted to me through his open window and above the engine and rotor noise, "What's wrong with it?"

"We had an engine oil line shot through and another one nicked. We can replace 'em here and fly it home, no problem. We'll need some oil, the lines, and the tools," I answered.

"Does Nickerson have a handle on what's needed?" he shouted.

"Yep. He's making a diagram of the lines so there'll be no confusion."

"Okay, good. You guys are all coming with us. A maintenance crew will come back, maybe with Nickerson, later today. We'll fix it and fly it home later," John offered.

"Am I supposed to stay to bring the bird back? That makes sense to me," I asked.

"No, they want you and the crew home. Make sure the grunts can give it security for a few hours. Then get your stuff and let's get out of here."

"Okay. Whatever they want," I responded and wheeled around, returning to the slick about eighty feet away.

"Okay, gents, huddle up," I said. Everyone gathered in, including the infantry lieutenant. I looked at the lieutenant, "Can you guys provide a few hours of security? We're gonna fix it and fly it home today, but we're leavin' for now."

"Sure, we'll watch it, no problem," he answered.

"Okay, good. Thanks." Then to Corporal Nickerson, "You got all you need to make sure the right parts get back here?"

"Yes, sir. It's just two lines and I have a drawing."

"Okay, guys, all of us are going home in Captain Arick's gunbird. I don't know who comes back for repair and to fly the slick out. Probably me and you." I looked at Nickerson and he nodded.

"But we have our orders. Let's collect our stuff, close up the bird, tie down the rotor, and we're outta here."

So we did. We strapped into the web seats along the rear of Arick's gunbird. His crewchief, Lance Corporal Phelps, checked that we were secure and let Arick know we were. John pulled the gunbird into a hover, checked the gauges, noted the power, lifted the Huey over concertina wire, and took off. We gathered speed and altitude and headed east.

It was a short, pleasant trip of twelve miles or so. It felt strange riding in the rear with nothing to do but look at the ground slide by and, out of habit, glance at the flight instruments. After landing, Arick was directed to a parking spot near the line shack. He shut down and we all headed for the shack.

"I wonder what happened to the wounded Marine," I said on our way in. Of course no one knew.

"I think they'll need to get the zone a little cooler to try again. Maybe a section of guns could keep Charlie duckin' long enough to get in and out," Boden offered.

I went into the line shack and told the maintenance bosses what had happened. Corporal Nickerson was more the center of attention, since he could provide precise fix-it information. My services were not needed; I headed for the ready room.

"How we doin' this?" I asked Jerry Garner.

"You and Boden are done for the day," he answered straight-faced.

I was surprised. "Don't they want me to retrieve the bird? I can go back out with the maintenance guys."

"Nope. It's been decided by the Ops O. You guys are done. Take your pack off, read a book, fuck around, whatever."

I was a little baffled, at the edge of annoyance. I was forming a response, but was interrupted before it came out.

"It's done, so quit, end of discussion. I guess they figure if you're down from fire and we can spare you, you are spared, at least for the day. You ain't going." I could tell from Garner's words and tone that no matter what, I'd not be going back to recover the slick.

"We've already called in a replacement medevac crew. Another slick is designated. Even Arick is off the hook as chase. We'll get the wounded Marine as soon as they relay word to us to launch again."

"Okay, but it's not a problem." I put my flight gear, helmet bag, and flak jacket under the bench seat in the ready room where I kept them. I sat down, chatted with the guys, and reviewed the day's events in my mind. Then I considered my options for the afternoon. Maybe a test hop, otherwise I was a guy with zero leaning on him, a book, a letter, maybe a nap. I guess that would work. But what about the wounded Marine?

"Guess I'll ease by maintenance and see what's shakin'," I said after a while. I opened the ready room screen door and eased out into the sun.

I saw the quality control chief, SSgt. Red Hillmandollar. We talked a bit and then I chatted with my boss, Captain Waters in the maintenance office. No test hops were available.

Shit, I was a free man.

Over the course of the next twenty-four hours, I had many opportunities to explain what happened. Everyone wanted to know details. My story was simple: I sat in a zone and here it came. I lifted, got some instrument panel indication of oil malfunction, which was confirmed by the crewchief. I sat her down in a safe place, Corporal Nickerson troubleshot the problem, and Arick brought us home. The pilots were especially interested in the cockpit indications, something to store away for future reference if they got holed in the engine oil lines. Torque, the twisting moment the engine applies through the transmission to the rotor head, is somehow measured through the engine oil system. If torque goes to zero, you need to take a look.

I discovered later that Arick, also a test pilot, flew out as a passenger with maintenance guys that day. They fixed my wounded helo, and he flew it home. I read a book on my rack, wrote a letter, reread a couple of old ones, and napped.

In retrospect, I am touched by the squadron's effort to give us a little slack after an unusual outing. I don't think I needed it, but it's the sort of beau geste that makes sense. My crew and I had been forced down by small-arms fire. It didn't bother us, but the older guys were giving us a little slack just in case.

There is no end to this episode in my life. I asked around the next day to see if anyone knew if the wounded Marine had been retrieved. Garner said he'd not launched the medevac again for that purpose. I can never know what happened, but I feel badly about it. If I need forgiveness, I hope I have it. But it's always most difficult to forgive yourself.

CHAPTER 15

Tactical Air Controller (Airborne) and Adjusting Arty and Naval Gunfire

A Huey pilot's designations started with Pilot Qualified in Model (PQM). After that a number could follow, section leader, division leader, carrier qualified (CQ), post-maintenance inspection pilot (PMIP), and Tactical Air Controller (Airborne), (TAC(A)). Except for occasional visitors who flew with us, everybody was PQM. They'd achieved that designation in the States. And apart from PMIP, which was largely driven by whether or not you were assigned to maintenance, most VMO pilots acquired the other qualifications as a function of squadron longevity.

The TAC(A) designation was a little bigger deal than the others. As the title may suggest, it meant a pilot was qualified to coordinate the overall conduct of flights involving various units and types of aircraft in tactical situations. What it usually meant in 'Nam was he could direct and control "fast-movers" (jets) in their attack on ground targets. And anytime you controlled jets in the TAC(A) role, your call sign automatically shifted to "Klondike Playboy," although you might have launched, for instance, as Klondike fourteen dash seven.

We didn't practice this much in the States. When we did get some jets to control the more experienced guys usually did it. Maybe the squadron didn't want to show its ass with a rookie on the radio. This left second lieutenants, even inordinately gifted ones, to watch, listen, and learn. I absorbed what I could in this "training," but was far from competent or confident in this on arrival "in country."

Because controlling jet attacks on ground targets was routine for VMOs, becoming a TAC(A) was important. Early in my tour I sat in the copilot's seat and listened to the old hands running the jets in. The Marine A-4 Skyhawks, from the airstrip next door at Chu Lai, usually performed this mission. Their call sign was Oxwood and they routinely nailed whatever target we identified. This competence was not surprising; the A-4 was designed for ground attack, and the primary mission and training of its pilots concentrated there. I came to expect that when jets checked in on the UHF radio with the Oxwood call sign, the target would be hit.

As my tour rolled along, the F-4 Phantom, primarily a fighter, was increasingly used in South Vietnam for ground attack. I suppose earlier they were mostly sent north. Their call sign was Condole; initially they were not as good as Oxwood, but they improved. Near the end of my tour, the bad guys were in serious trouble if either showed up to help.

Once a section of Navy F-8 Crusaders was sent to us. These guys flew the most beautiful jet in the history of Naval and Marine Corps aviation, and it was a pure fighter. The pilots must have been the last of a dying breed, since most Navy fighter pilots were flying Phantoms. F-8s were probably great against MiGs, but these, at least, were not so great in air to ground. I remember once one of them got target fixation, pulled out too late, and took his F-8 through treetops. We could see the slight swath he created in the trees. He immediately called, "Galloper Dash two is off target. I may have hit some limbs."

"May have" my ass, I thought. The section of F-8s skedaddled back to either a trap aboard some offshore carrier or a divert to land at either Danang or Chu Lai. I assumed he made it home but knew he'd sustained metal damage. He'd get to chat with his CO and the safety officer. Some metalsmiths would be disappointed as well.

The ordnance load for Skyhawks (A-4), "Scooters" they were called, and Phantoms (F-4) was typically 250-pound bombs, napalm, and 20-mm (mike-mike) cannon. These last were machine guns; they make .50-caliber rounds look small. The bombs and napalm were hung on racks, and the 20-mike-mike was internal on the A-4 and external in a wing pod on the F-4.

Missions in proximity of our units, CAS as they were called, required a controller. If a VMO TAC(A) was on station the task fell to him. When no TAC(A) was overhead, the job went to an FAC, assigned to the grunts, or to a Forward Air Controller (Airborne) (FAC(A)) who usually flew in a light fixed-wing aircraft. For obvious reasons, a controller was vital whenever ground Marines were in the vicinity of the target.

Jets, like the helos, typically flew in twos or sections; when they checked in on the radio you'd hear, "Klondike Playboy, Oxwood six dash ten is with you. Flight of two alpha fours. Over." We'd get their ordnance load, give them a TACAN radial and distance to get them in our area. Once they were overhead, we'd get them down to an altitude so we could eyeball them and they could see us. We'd describe the situation, where our Marines were, where the enemy was, and where our helos would hold. Then we'd give them a run-in heading, what ordnance to drop on each pass, mark the target, and get the hell out of the way.

We usually asked for bombs in pairs, although you might ask for a "stick," in which case a whole rack of bombs was rippled into the target, sprinkling along the run-in axis. This did a fine job of making the day unpleasant for any bad guys on or near the target. As soon as the first jet pulled up, the second was cleared in either to the same target or one adjusted to another area from the visible impacts of the first jet's ordnance.

Napalm was a witch's brew of jet fuel (JF) and chemical ingredients. A jelly-like substance resulted. The bomb exploded in fire on impact and spread along the release axis; flames billowed and oxygen was sucked from the air. People near a napalm attack had trouble breathing. It was less effective in rough terrain and in heavy foliage, where it could not spread. But we used it in all terrain. I always felt sorry for anyone in or near the red, fiery smear of napalm. It was both spectacularly beautiful and lethal. It could not have been a good way to die.

The 20-mm cannon might be used to chew up a tree or brush line, a riverbank, a vil, trenchwork, or any other area or object that warranted chewing up. Generally we never sent the jets away without using all they had, but the 20-mm was the last we called for. Fifty-caliber is big, but 20-mm is huge. The earth danced, foliage was chopped up, and huts splintered and collapsed from these rounds. Twenty-millimeter was impressive, though less spectacular than napalm.

To mark the target, our first choice was a 2.75-inch white phosphorus rocket, "willie-peter" as it was commonly called. Often some of our tubes were loaded with these, and sometimes a whole pod. It exploded in a vivid white plume, often spewing tendrils, and was clearly visible to anyone airborne. Another onboard option was high explosive (HE) 2.75-inch rockets. These exploded with a gray-brown cloud and were less apparent on impact, but if the fast-movers were low and watching the target area, they could see it.

The last onboard possibility was a red smoke grenade. Jim Jaeger, one of the original VMO guys, taught me early on how to mark from altitude. First you established the helo at one thousand feet AGL and one hundred knots. Then, flying over the target, you'd ask the crewchief to toss out a grenade as the target passed between your rudder pedals. (You could see the ground forward and beneath the rudder pedals through a plexiglas chin bubble.) The smoke would land close to the target and you adjusted the jets from that mark.

The final possibility was to ask the ground unit to mark the target with a 3.5-inch willie-peter rocket. The 3.5-inch replaced the World War II–era "bazooka" sometime before the Vietnam War. The grunts often had these and, if they had willie-peter rounds, they came in handy for marking. The grunts knew best where they wanted the ordnance delivered. So, if they could mark, you could just ask the jets to role in on the willie-peter plume.

Once the jets had a "visual" on the mark, they could be moved any direction, using clock positions and distances. "Oxwood four dash seven, this is Klondike Playboy. Move your hits fifty meters, two o'clock from the mark. Use zero three zero degrees for your run-in heading and pull out to the right. Let's start with a pair of snakes. Over." This, for instance, would adjust the jets relative to the impact of the marking device or previous hits. "Snakes" were snake-eye bombs, named for the painted circle ringing their tips. They normally had speedbrake contraptions attached to their tails, high-drag, as they were called. Once a bomb separated from its rack, these brakes deployed and slowed the bomb so the jet could fly away and not through the exploding bomb's frag and debris pattern.

About halfway through my tour, I received the TAC(A) designation and was awarded, as others were, a special squadron patch. That patch is still on the front of my battered and bruised leather flight jacket. It's a black patch on which is a white Hugh Hefner Playboy rabbit. Around the bottom edge are the words, Klondike Playboy—TAC(A). The patch means nothing to anyone except to those who wore it. In thirty years it will mean nothing to anyone. But Klondike controlled a bunch of jets; it was part of the mission, part of the experience of a VMO pilot.

■ ■ ■

The grunts had Forward Observers (FOs) to bring artillery and Naval Gun Fire on target. VMOs did it also, but less frequently than TAC(A) missions. We received no patches or designations for this. Youngsters like myself became proficient from watching and listening to the old hands, and Marine artillery was pretty easy to work with.

Once radio communication was established, we'd get them to fire one round at a target, usually from a 105-mm artillery tube. After they radioed, "On the way," we'd watch the ground. When we saw the impact, we gave the firing battery adjustments in meters, left or right and up or down, until the impact was on the target area. Then we'd simply radio, "Fire for effect with eighteen rounds." (Or some other number.) All six of the battery's howitzers were adjusted to match the "dope" on the tube used to get the first round on target. Then all six fired three times each. Eighteen 105-mm rounds plowed the target.

Once artillery was on the target, it could usually make short work of a problem. The good thing about "arty" was it could hammer away over time, unlike with the jets, which ran out of bombs and got low on fuel. The downside of arty was that it took a bunch of 105-mm rounds to equal the effects of racks of well-placed 250-pound bombs, two canisters of napalm, and four hundred rounds of 20-mm. Each had strengths; I'm pleased we had both.

Finally, we controlled Naval Gunfire; not often, but we did. My only experiences were with five-inch guns from a frigate or destroyer. I could bring them on the target line okay, but they often struck short or long. Also, they typically had only one gun to fire, so were less impressive in volume of fire. I'd like to have controlled a battleship's main guns or even a World War II heavy cruiser. One battleship was deployed, maybe two, but it was not in play on any of my missions. We had the smaller caliber, 5-inch stuff. The Navy was ready and eager. I could hear it in their voices, but one round at a time does not bring as much to the fight. A Marine 105-mm howitzer battery, on the other hand, was designed, trained, and equipped for the mission and did a hell of a job. But the TAC(A)-CAS activity was much more our bread and butter.

CHAPTER 16

First Lt. Lyle Motley Gets
His Sinus Cavity Crushed

TECHNICAL DISCOURSE ON TAIL ROTOR
SEPARATION OR FAILURE

One of the many concerns in flying the Huey is the loss of a tail rotor. Engine failure can be troublesome, but you can practice for that by shooting many, many autorotations. Practice "autos," as we called them, were maneuvers in which you simply lower the collective (that lever under the pilot's left hand) and roll the twist-grip throttle to idle RPM. The throttle is also under the left hand. To shut the engine off completely, one had to push a detent button; then continue rolling the throttle. Viola! No turbine whine. Anyway, we practiced autorotations ad nauseam during training. If you can't do these, you can't save your ass nor the asses of your crew. And engines quit; I lost two.

We could practice for many emergency eventualities, but not the loss of a tail rotor. We could read about it, memorize the procedures, and try to envision what would happen in the cockpit, nothing more.

The Huey's tail rotor is designed to counteract the tendency of the airframe to rotate in the opposite direction of the spinning main rotor blades. The main rotor rotates left, counter-clockwise when viewed from above; the fuselage wants to go the other way, to the right. To compensate, the helo engineers put a small rotor on the end of a tail boom. Pilots controlled the pitch, and thus lift, on those tail rotor blades through floor pedals. Varying tail rotor blade pitch compensates for the varying twisting moments imparted to the fuselage by the pilot as he increases or decreases pitch on the main rotor blades.

When pilots added power, the left pedal was required to hold heading; when they reduced power, the right pedal was needed. Otherwise the helo's nose would simply swing back and forth with power setting adjustments.

One more piece of tedious information is warranted to assure confusion: Without the tail rotor, the Huey fuselage is supposed to streamline in the wind at speeds above forty knots, but it does not. It counter-rotates about its vertical axis. (Bob Whaley, Marine Huey pilot, affirms this and he ought to know. He lost his tail rotor up around Phu Bai, and, even though Bob was above 40 knots, he counter-rotated to a crash from 1,100 feet. According to Bob, in the Echo model streamlining takes place at maybe seventy, not forty. He thinks the forty-knot rule might have worked on the Army's Delta model, since it has a longer tail boom, but not the UH-1E. Even though Bob entered autorotation, his bird counter-rotated all the way to mother earth. He and his crew survived, but all were seriously injured and the bird was destroyed.)

The fuselage will streamline in a crab at some speed. Flying in a crab means the nose of the aircraft is pointed in a different direction than the course the aircraft is making over the ground. You can't carry a high-speed crab to landing. Imagine running a Huey onto the ground at highway speed with the helo's nose 30 degrees to the right of centerline. With that combination of speed and crab you'd be lucky to live.

So, even though a pilot might crab the bird along for some time without its tail rotor, streamlining the fuselage in the wind, eventually he's gotta slow down to land. Once he decelerates below some magic airspeed, the fuselage begins its inevitable swing to the right, its counter-rotation around the main rotor mast.

Such rotation has to induce vertigo out the ass; the pilot doesn't know up from down, right from left, his ass from third base. He is in huge, huge trouble.

Before impact the pilot is supposed to shut the engine down and enter a full autorotation. This reduces, but does not stop, the right rotation. Imagine rotating to the right and as you near the ground, trying to initiate a flare to kill off forward airspeed. It's a nightmare. The notion of flaring a rotating helo is mind-boggling. While the world turns through the Plexiglas of your cockpit windscreen, you close the throttle and flare!

The Huey will crash at the end of this maneuver, if maneuver is the correct term. Maneuver suggests some willful act. A tail rotor separation allows for some willful activity and a whole bunch of being along for the ride.

I only had one tail rotor problem in all my Huey flying. It was nothing like a loss, but it was an attention-getter. At the end of a test flight after a tail rotor re-rig, I brought the helo into a hover. I had the left rudder jammed to the stops and the nose began swinging to the right. True to my training, I rolled off the throttle, did a hover autorotation, and cushioned the landing. The crewchief and I just looked at each other. I shut her down. The guys put on the ground handling wheels and towed the bird to the hangar. They fixed it, and off we went again. But this was a rig problem; I still had a tail rotor and it was still producing some thrust. It worked, just not well.

LYLE MOTLEY'S SINUS

First Lt. Lyle Motley was flying up north somewhere west of Phu Bai. He and his crew were taking heavy fire and were giving it back. He pulled out of a gun run and heard some tearing sounds from the rear of his helo. Almost immediately, his bird yawed to the right. No amount of left rudder brought the nose back. In fact, the rudder pedals were unresponsive in either direction. He slowed the helo and the yaw developed into fuselage rotation. Since he was climbing off target at a high power setting, the rotation picked up speed. Lyle experimented for only a couple seconds with various control inputs to solve the problem. Nothing worked. The world was spinning.

With some resignation, Lyle lowered the collective. The twisting moment reduced, the rotation slowed. But now Lyle was headed for the ground in bad guy country. Reality sunk in; with little choice, he rolled off the throttle and entered full autorotation. His spinning slowed further, but did not cease. As he neared the ground, Lyle tried to flare, tried to add collective and cushion his landing like NATOPS instructs. He crashed with great force on the lip of a huge bomb crater. These large circular divots were all over the place west and northwest of Phu Bai.

The helo ate itself. In a flail of main rotor blades, the tail boom smacked down and broke off, the skid tubes first spread then tore from the helo, and, after some slams, rolls, and tearing, the Huey finally stopped almost upside down. Although the cabin of the Huey is "crashworthy" and has saved many lives, it was not strong enough to withstand all forces. Lyle's head, helmet and all, received a mighty blow. The upper right of the cabin bore down, his helmet broke, and the sinus cavity above his right eye was crushed. Everyone lived; all were hurt. Lyle was battered the worst. He and the other crewmembers limped and crawled away from the wreckage and were aided by the grunt Marines they were supporting. Lyle's wingman picked them up and medevaced them to Phu Bai.

They all returned to Ky Ha except Motley. He simply disappeared into the Naval Hospital system: Japan, Okinawa, aboard ship, or Hawaii. We were down a pilot, everyone else took in his belt just a hair and Klondike pressed on.

Eventually, at least a month later, Lyle came back. He flew as copilot for a week and was back in the saddle. But his return created a stir. Everyone wanted to hear about the crash, his injury, and how he'd been fixed. We all knew his head was somehow squished; I was surprised to see him at all. We cornered him. "Alright, Motley, let's have it, and don't leave anything out." And after his discourse on the tail rotor failure, he launched into the medical side. "Well, guys," he offered in his smiling southern drawl, "this sinus cavity above my right eye was caved in." Lyle pointed to his skull around his eye. "The bones were just broken and pushed in." He paused to let that sink in.

"So, once they got my ass to the hospital, they drilled a small hole above my eye, into what had been the cavity. Then, are you shittin' me, they pushed a little balloon in the hole and pumped it up. They left the balloon in place under a dressing. The damned thing held the cavity in the right position, from the inside. It healed that way. About three weeks later, they let the air out of the balloon and pulled it out. They told me not to bang it for a while. They hemmed and hawed and x-rayed me from time to time, but it's all okay now. I looked like hell, all black and blue, then purple, green, and yellowish. But after a bit, I got back to lookin' like my handsome self."

"Did it hurt like hell?" Swinburn asked.

"At first when they didn't give me any or enough painkillers, and even after they started me on 'em, sometimes they didn't get to me in time. But they pretty much kept me on pills, so it wasn't too bad. Truth is, except for air conditioning, clean linen, and some nice-looking Navy nurses, I got bored with it. Ready to get on with my life. Hanging around a hospital ward can be slow motion. Books and TV get old and they wouldn't let me go anywhere."

"You're a lucky man," Ross piped up. "Tail rotor trouble scares the hell outta me, scares the hell outta everyone."

"It's no fun. But it all happened so fast I didn't have much time to think it over. We were low when we took the hits, so we were down almost before we knew it. But you can bet your ass you'll be rotatin' on impact. I don't give a shit what you do in the cockpit. We hit hard." He paused then finished. "It's nice to be breathin' and not permanently screwed up."

Something was not quite the same though. Maybe Lyle was wiser, a little altered by horrific experience. He still smiled, still had his sunny disposition, and joked, but something more serious lay beneath the surface. He was not quite as spring-loaded to a smile as before his slam-down. It might be like a professional football player who breaks a leg, but goes on playing once it heals because football playing is what he does. But something had changed.

Lyle had a secret only those who'd lost a tail rotor knew. He looked the same and flew just like the rest of us, but some innocence was gone. Maybe he'd discovered his vulnerability. That can change a man. Young men often believe they are impervious. No one is and this is nowhere more apparent than in war.

CHAPTER 17

Alcohol and Abuse

DRIVING UNDER THE INFLUENCE

One night at the club, Capt. Brooke Shadburne came in looking for pilots. Five of us were huddled at a table, hands wrapped around some euphoria-inducing libations. We entertained each other with the usual, our flights that day, somebody's success, any recent demonstration of "balls" or "aw shits," and stuff from home. The "aw shits" were rare because the squadron, like all squadrons, was populated with competent guys. Even the FNGs, who bore a little watching, were an able lot. The screening process was good for aviators; only about half who started with me made it through to wings. So the shittiest guy was still pretty good, and after some training the difference between the best helo jock and the worst was reduced. Solid Stateside training helped.

That night Shadburne was a man on a mission; he was scouting for Huey drivers. "Hey, guys," when he spotted us. "We need four pilots to disperse aircraft," he said as he closed to our table's edge.

"We might get mortars tonight and we're scattering the birds. The crew-chiefs are already standin' by."

Captain Mike Bartley looked up and became our spokesman. "Shit, Brooke, what happened to eight hours bottle to throttle? We're suckin' down suds here and now you're askin' us to strap on a Huey and leap off *at night?*" The sun had been down for at least a half hour.

"Yeah," Brook answered, "the Ops O knows, but he said as long as you're not drunk, you'd have to do."

"None of us is drunk, but we've sure as hell had a round," Swinburn added.

I looked at my empty shot glass and reached out to test the heft of my beer can. It was about half full. I felt the effects of alcohol, but I was not drunk. My tongue had not thickened. That would come later with an increase in IQ, wisdom, the expanse of my knowledge base, and an enhanced ability to articulate even the most complex and subtle ideas. And this is a no-shitter; everyone agreed and was aware of my near miraculous mental improvement with drink. Of course everybody else got smarter too, and it was hard to get a word in edgewise with all the smart bastards sitting around waxing eloquent.

We glanced at each other, eyebrows raised.

"What the fuck, I guess I'll be okay," Bartley piped.

"I suppose," from Swinburn.

"I probably ought to hang back on this one, if I can. I started earlier than you guys," offered Jack Chiaramonte.

"I guess I'm in," I heard myself say.

"Shit, me too. I'll just toss this one down and we're off," Ross offered. We laughed but knew he'd not be packing in more booze if we were off to fly, especially at night.

They needed four; Shadburne had his "volunteers." We scooted back our chairs and headed out, leaving Chiaramonte alone at the table. He'd slide over to join the lift bubbas or they'd join him. He'd not be alone long. (Jack transitioned to jets after his tour with VMO. Later I heard he disappeared over the Pacific on a flight to Japan.)

We walked the four city blocks down a gentle hill to the VMO-6 ready room and flight line.

"Okay, gents, here are your bird assignments and where you're to take 'em. The call signs and freqs are also here for those of you goin' outside the wire to grunt bases in the area," the ODO offered. We jotted down needed info on kneeboards, checked coordinates on our personal maps and the ready room map board, and estimated TACAN radials and distances to LZs. Then we headed to the line shack to sign for the birds and meet our crewchiefs.

I caught a break this time; at least I thought I did. My helo dispersal site was inside the Ky Ha–Chu Lai perimeter, on a point of land only three-quarters of a mile south of our runway. I'd flown by it on every mission that took me south. It was a tight little prepared LZ near a cluster of hooches, above a fifty-foot drop to the coastal rocks and the surf line below. Who knows what purpose that LZ served? The hooch cluster was "inside the wire," and a road led in. Shit, you could drive there in complete safety from our runway. But they had a helo pad anyway. Some bored Gunny or officer probably thought it would be a good idea and put Marines to work.

I was glad I didn't have far to go and could get back to my rack for the night. The other guys were headed outside the wire and would probably have to call for illum to get into their assigned LZs. I was fine with a short ride and a landing. A squadron jeep was to pick up me and the crewchief and return us to our hooches for the night, but we'd have to get the bird at first morning light and bring it home.

I had no one to call on the radio and no distance to go. My job was to find the unmarked LZ with my searchlight. I'd stay up Ky Ha tower freq during the whole thing.

The crewchief was waiting for me at the line shack with other crewchiefs. "Sergeant Corning, how's she look?" I asked as I grabbed the yellow sheets for the gunbird I'd been assigned and started thumbing through yellow sheets. Since Corning had signed the bird off, I knew the answer to my question. The helo "looked good," otherwise he'd not have signed it off.

"Nothing recent, Lieutenant Ballentine; some stuff a couple weeks ago. She looks good to me," Corning answered.

Crewchiefs preflight and sign off birds before they are released to the pilots. A crewchief's signature meant he was willing to leap off in the aircraft. It might be the same idea as with parachute packers. Every once in a while somebody in authority goes to the paraloft and says, "Grab one of your chutes. Let's go for a jump." Except the crewchief "jumps his chute" every day his helo flies. God bless the helo crewchiefs. I can't guess how many pilots would not be here if not for them.

I glanced through the book of yellow sheets, which reflected the recent history of flights and any maintenance performed. As Corning reported, it had a clean recent past. I signed for the bird and grabbed my helmet bag from where I'd dropped it on the line shack floor. Corning and I headed out into the night and the dark flight line. I threw on my red-lensed flashlight for the preflight.

"Sergeant Corning, I've had a drink. Ops knows, but watch me. This might be a little abnormal. I keep hearin' alcohol and flying don't mix. Tonight I'll know," I said as we walked.

"You'll be fine, sir. I'll keep an eye out."

"I expect we'll soon see if I'm fine or not."

I tossed my gear on the pilot's seat, preflighted with my flashlight, and told Corning we were headed down the beach a short distance. Then I went through the start sequence and ran her up.

The Huey has a landing light and a searchlight. The landing light swings out from the belly and stops at a fixed angle for a normal approach; the searchlight is stowed just beneath the helo's nose and can be swiveled and pointed anywhere by a multi-directional "coolie-hat" toggle under the pilot's left thumb. After turn up, I turned on the searchlight, but left it stowed. It bounced light straight down from the nose of the helo and lit up the ground area around my bird. I left it on and got clearance to taxi and take off. We headed south. I stayed low and kept the speed down to fifty knots. As I flew, I moved the searchlight to shine out in front of the helo and threw on my landing light, which swung from the Huey's belly at its fixed angle.

Ky Ha tower was still launching helos on runway three, but a light breeze had already shifted to offshore. That was good; I could make my approach from over the water into a light breeze. I'd not have to come in over a built-up area.

I had some help from moonlight, from lights in the Ky Ha complex, and from the compound where the LZ was located. And, after I'd drilled along for a minute and farted around with my searchlight, I found the LZ no problem.

But after that, the whole thing was an embarrassing demonstration of incompetence: too steep, too fast, over-shooting, too high, lost sight of the zone on final, can't find the zone for re-attack. You name it, I screwed it up. I plumbed around like I didn't have over a thousand hours in model. I made a dick of myself in the skies of Southeast Asia. If anyone near the LZ was a spectator, I indicted at least the Huey community and probably the whole of Marine helicopter aviation. At least I had the presence to wave off my shitty attempts and take her out for another try. I salvaged the third pass, and got on the pad, but it took a massive effort of concentration and it wasn't pretty.

After I was on the deck, "Shit, Sarg, don't tell anyone. Okay? That was horrible." I laughed and so did he.

"You got my promise, Lieutenant," he answered. The crewchiefs knew who was good, who was better, and who was best. They flew with us all. Corning probably had a good time of it with the guys, but I'd done my best. My best was just woefully inadequate that night. The approach and landing should have been a one-time thing, not a series of flawed efforts.

Flying under any influence of booze was and is a huge mistake; what they preached was true. I was now a believer. Closure rates, angles, nose positions, power anticipations, rudder, nimbleness of thumb in searchlight control, shit, everything was off. I reacted rather than anticipated. I was simply "behind the aircraft" in all categories.

A jeep arrived shortly and took us to the squadron. I was ready to share my story with hooch-mates, but they were mostly gone to outlying camps for a night in their helos, sleeping on inflatable rubber ladies.

After another jeep ride at 0730, Corning and I picked up the Huey.

Drinking might make you smarter, but it sure as hell doesn't improve your aviating skills.

Late one morning in the ready room, Second Lt. Jerry Buerger came through the screen door. He was smiling large. "Guess what I just heard?" he offered as bait.

From behind his ODO desk, Garner broke first, though we were all curious. "We're waiting, Buerger. Out with it."

"You gotta hear this." He was barely able to suppress a laugh. "I was just jaw-jacking with one of the Millpoint (HMM-363) guys. He told me they caught a messman beating off in that little building behind the mess hall. I think they keep the potatoes there."

Snickers first, then laughter. I suppose masturbating, sore subject though it is, is not uncommon among humans. I considered it once myself. What *is* uncommon and sad is to get caught.

Whenever this rare subject surfaces, I'm reminded of a trip I once made with a young woman to the primate exhibit at the San Diego Zoo. They should have warned us, changed the sign, made an announcement over a bullhorn; perhaps a handout at the entrance would have served.

In the largest of the cages, one that housed at least twenty monkeys, a few adolescent males (wouldn't ya know!) had "discovered" themselves. One especially perverse and flexible little scamp was engaged in the unthinkable. I noticed and, though I tried to suppress it, a smile turned into a chortle.

I looked at my partner, a southern gal, but, as women often are, she was way ahead of me. She stared straight to the front and she was not smiling, not smiling at all.

"I think I've had enough of the monkeys," she offered. "Can we go?" It was not a question, but a demand. She moved out; I followed along, trying but failing to feign indignation. On the way out I overheard young mothers trying to herd out protesting children.

"Sarah, Timmy, don't you want to see the red and purple behind of the baboon? He's just around the corner?" or "Kids, I'd like an ice cream. Ummm, yummy. Wouldn't you?" Yes, the young moms were wanting out of the monkey exhibit. Some of the guys, on the other hand, were enjoying the hell out of it, pointing, nodding, smiling, and laughing. If they were with women though, like me, they were heading for the door.

I've wondered about those monkeys a time or two in my life. I'm told monkeys are smart and I've supposed the little farts, in protest of their incarceration, may have waited to perform until the families arrived. So much for a mellow Sunday at the zoo.

But a messman *caught* was just the sort of base event to break the monotony for a group of junior pilots. We enjoyed it immensely for a while, wondering out loud how the Marine would ever live it down and supposing a story that rich and demeaning would haunt him all his days in the Corps, ending mercifully only at discharge. (Maybe I should say separation from service.)

After a time the conversation branched out. I was called away for a test flight and the day progressed.

At day's end, I headed up the hill to my hooch. I was hailed on the parking apron by First Lt. Pete Lepo, a Ridgerunner (HMM-163) pilot down from Phu Bai for who knows what. I knew Pete well; we'd roamed and scouted together a little in our Pensacola years.

"Ballentine, wait up," he shouted as he and another young officer walked my way. I stopped; they closed. Then, "What kinda messhall are you guys runnin' down here?" he challenged good-naturedly. His companion and he both grinned.

I responded almost immediately, "Is this about masturbatin'?" By then we were all smiling big time.

"Yes, hell it is. We heard they caught some Marine beating off in the mashed potatoes." Pete was laughing now.

It was infectious; I started laughing too, but my laugh was especially hard. When in control, I responded, "Pete, this story has changed over the last six hours."

"Buerger told us they caught a guy pounding off in the potato shed and now it's into the mashed potatoes! What next? This fuckin' thing has a life of its own." We laughed for a while and had a good time with the rumor and its growth. Then we split, each heading to his separate purpose.

That evening I went to chow with Motley, Ross, and Swinburn. There they were on the steam table, lovely, heaped trays of white mashed potatoes. Large metal serving spoons protruded from slightly mounded tops. But only a few divots had been made in the surfaces.

Rumor spread quickly at Ky Ha. Most had lost their appetite for potatoes, at least for that night. A man can't be too careful about some things.

CHAPTER 18

Ky Ha Miscellany II

OBSERVATIONS ON THE PECKING ORDER

When I think about the ordering of the civilian world compared with the military, a difference leaps out. In the military, the warrior class is at the top, those who go in harm's way and get shot at. In the helo community it was the aircrews, pilots, crewchiefs, and gunners, those who hung their asses out, if not daily, at least regularly. This was the inner circle, and even though ball size varied, the starting size was not small. We took it to Charlie and the NVA, and they took it to us in the great international muscle-flexing gambit called war.

Flying is not for everyone. It's demanding and inherently dangerous. Aircraft break while airborne, and, when you add to that reality, the efforts of folks to kill and injure you or the machine you're flying, the situation creates a distinct culture. Helo aircrewmen had slightly longer strides. (My guess is that infantrymen had and have giant ones.)

In the civilian world, doctors and lawyers are respected, usually well rewarded for their effort and position. They typically live good lives of responsibility and are at least moderately affluent. But in the squadrons, the Flight Surgeon, though he might be a hell of a guy and of immense value, was not an aviator, not a warrior, and therefore somehow beneath. This brutal truth, and I feel guilty in saying it, makes perfect logic to me.

I always felt at ease, at home, among guys who were helo aviators, pilots, crewchiefs, and gunners. There was an undercurrent of understanding, an unspoken common experience that transcended. I knew I could rely on these men when the shit hit the fan. I was not so sure about the untested rest of the world. So, there was for me an ordering that had nothing to do with emblems on collars or stripes on sleeves.

Door gunners were an impressive lot. These guys volunteered and they ran the gamut of squadron jobs from administration to ordnance, from intel to hydraulics. They were hidden tigers. I was amazed by the spectrum of guys who flew as door gunners. After signing for the bird, I'd head out to preflight and there was the crewchief, the man who flew daily, took care of his helo, and was well known to me and to all the pilots. With him was a door gunner, a trained volunteer from some other, nonflight-related job in the squadron. He might be a limited duty officer, ex–gunnery sergeant named Willis from admin, First Sergeant Fenton, our most senior SNCO, Corporal McDevitt, the unit diary clerk, also from admin, or Sgt. Rod Croft from ordnance. These are only some examples.

I'd brief them on what we were up to and any useful specifics. We'd strap the gunbird to our asses and leap off the Ky Ha cliff. These gunners, and of course the crewchiefs, manned swivel-mounted M-60s in the cabin just behind the pilots. They dished it out the helo's sides and saved my ass on more occasions than I will ever know. They stood in the rear doors, gunner's belt securing them to the helo, slightly crouched over their guns, and hammered away. God bless 'em!

When the mission was over, especially if it'd been a hot one, we'd all smile, maybe chat a little. Most of it was left unsaid or maybe there was nothing to say. It was all captured in a glance. I'd thank them and we'd go back to our other work. But these men were the bubbas, the *fuckin' guys*, the inner circle. Everybody else, well, was everybody else.

I read in some book about Marine helos in 'Nam, that the squadron Sergeant Major sustained a serious wound while serving as a gunner. This came as no surprise to me. He was out doing the do, just like our First Sergeant Fenton often was. He was one of the *fuckin' guys*.

I think I always respected a man and his rank, believing he had a birthright to some respect and had earned some more from his achievement. Yet, even though I know every job in the Corps was essential in some way to the overall function, my special unspoken respect was held, maybe wrongly, for the aircrews, without regard to rank. These were my own, my brothers. They were at the top of my cultural microcosm.

PICKLING A LOAD

"Pickle" is an innocent word. Women, maybe some men, pickle cucumbers. I remember this from my early farm days. Some people do it to herring; the Scandinavians are wild about this one. You can also, as I discovered one bright morning on a test hop, pickle a CH-34D helicopter. This last kind of pickle is an aviator term, entirely different from what one might do to cucumbers and herring.

Recently promoted Corporal Ault and I were out on a routine test hop.; We were working through a checklist of maneuvers. The day was nice, a great aviator day, visibility forever, gentle breeze off the ocean, and vivid color contrasts from the blue-green sea, to tan beach, to inland green. I was happy going about squadron business.

We were at 1,200 feet above the Ky Ha airfield; I liked to stay within autorotation distance of the runway on test hops, especially during the early phases. The helo might have a surprise or two in store the first time it'd flown in a while, especially if it had undergone major surgery such as engine, fuel control, or lift surface changes.

"Lieutenant Ballentine, look at that. A Frog's externaling a 34," Ault said into the ICS as he pointed left front through the windshield. Sure enough, a CH-46A (Frog) was just airborne off the north Ky Ha runway. Forty-sixes were called "Frogs." They received this nickname since they were wide and low at the rear and narrow and high in front. When on the deck, they resembled, in a half-assed way, the amphibian. Beneath the 46, dangling from a nylon pendant was a CH-34D, often called a "Dog" from the model number "D" at the end of its designation.

"That's gotta be a load," I answered. "Guess they're taking it north." I was not so preoccupied with the tests that I could not watch. The Frog climbed left and turned out over the water just off the Ky Ha north runway. The combination looked strange, like two dissimilar helos flying in unusual formation. The one beneath flew without a rotor head. The Dog's rotor blades had been removed; it streamlined in the air, blunt nose forward. Aside from the appearance, all seemed right. The Frog started leveling at 1,200 feet, what I supposed would be his cruise altitude. His northern course suggested Danang as the destination. No doubt he was delivering the 34 to have major maintenance performed, the kind not practical at Ky Ha.

As the Frog leveled, the 34 beneath began swinging slowly fore and aft. After watching a couple of swings, "Shit, that don't look too good," Ault observed.

I took a closer look. "Yeah, he needs to get that beauty stable," I answered. We continued to watch, postponing the test procedure, distracted by developments.

After fifteen or twenty more seconds and a couple swings, Corporal Ault offered in a matter of fact tone, "Lieutenant, that ain't gettin' any better."

"Yep, could be gettin' into load oscillation," I countered. The CH-46 executed a gentle turn and, from the belching of darker turbine exhaust smoke, I guessed the pilot was adding power, trying to put a little G-force on the load. This is typical NATOPS procedure for stabilizing an external load.

Sometimes G-forces would dampen out the swing. But G-force was not working; the Dog swung in ever-increasing amplitude.

"They're not gonna make it," Ault said almost absentmindedly and with a tinge of resignation. He was right. After four more swings of the dangling CH-34, the Frog HAC had had enough. He pulled the handle or hit the switch, releasing the nylon load-pendant from the belly of the bird. He "pickled" the load.

It was almost slow motion. The CH-34D descended, rolling slightly right around its longitudinal axis as it fell. It made a terrific splash in the South China Sea just northeast of Ky Ha. The impact caused its left tire to pop off its wheel and fly high in the air. It made a separate, smaller splash a few seconds later. The dropped helo stayed on the surface for only seconds, then disappeared beneath the blue-green surface.

"Ky Ha Tower, Northbrook (HMM-164) three dash twelve. Did you see that?" From the tone of the pilot's voice I could tell he was not happy, but I liked his style. If the tower had watched it all, no need going through a bunch of explanation and bullshit, no need in broadcasting to the world that you'd just jettisoned some valuable Marine Corps property.

"Northbrook three dash twelve, Tower was watching. You're cleared to land runway three north. The only reported traffic is a Huey on a test hop over the field."

"Roger, Tower. Northbrook is cleared to land three north," the pilot responded, and he did.

Ault and I continued our tests, but we'd had a break in the routine, a subject for ready room, hooch, bar, and safety officer discussions, an opportunity for all pilots to do an inventory of what to do when an external load starts misbehaving. We had some juicy, useful deviation.

The Northbrook pilots could not have been pleased. The HAC would have a number of opportunities to explain what happened, first to squadron senior people and the safety officer, then to the rank and file of curious pilots. And some CH-34D squadron was down a helo. They'd be curious too, though not in an investigative way. That was Northbrook business. Yep, the HAC would be doing the "dancing bear" routine for a day or two.

Not that evening but the next, again out of boredom and a need for socializing, I headed for the club. The Northbrook HAC was there and, anxious for the story, he had a cluster of pilots around him. Most of them were not Northbrook guys; they'd already heard it. The account was straightforward.

"That sonofabitch started swayin' a little as we leveled off. I tried the NATOPS stuff with slight turns and power, but the swings just got worse. Just before I pickled that bastard, it was swingin' so far forward I could see it through my chin bubble. And, shit, when it swung aft, my airspeed dropped twenty-five knots. It was too damn dangerous to keep fighting. A couple

more forward swings at that rate and it might have hit my bird. I let her go."
We all listened in rapt fascination.

"They tryin' to fry your ass or anything?" someone asked.

"No. Hell, we did it by the book. But the book don't always work. We're clean. They still gotta go through the investigation goat-rope though." The conversation and question-answer session continued.

He was right about "the book" and its standardized procedures. NATOPS has saved a lot of asses, but as great as it was, it was not a panacea. Judgment and a pilot's inventive headwork had to be relied on as well.

To preclude or at least reduce the possibility of load oscillation, eventually the helo communities began experimenting with small drogue chutes and other load-stabilizing innovations. We all had training in lifting, carrying, and setting down external loads. Usually practice was with a large concrete block, since no helo carcass was lying about on which to train. But a helo carcass behaves differently than concrete, so pilots trained procedurally and got used to the weight, but couldn't train to the aerodynamic affects of load shapes. Lifting another aircraft was always new.

Hueys, of course and mercifully, were not in the helo-lifting business. We didn't have the lift capacity.

MOUSTACHE GROWING

I first experimented with moustache growing in VMO-6. It was late in my tour, eight months into a thirteen-month stay. More as an experimental curiosity than anything, and since change helps keep life interesting, I stopped shaving my upper lip. Maybe I'd concluded that being shot at allowed a guy to take a bit of liberty with this sort of small change. Back in the States such independence from Marine Corps regulations would have ruined me but in a war zone, some of the small stuff fell away.

Between-flight boredom was probably the cause. In this regard, Vietnam was a combination of experiences. Time was absorbed in a routine of work at the squadron, flying missions or test hops, a little socializing at the club or in someone's hooch, chow, showering, reading books, writing letters, and boredom. Most of the flying was interesting (except convoy escort), and some of it was too damned interesting. But boredom was a component of life.

My moustache would be whatever it turned out to be; I simply let it grow. Although Marine Corps regulations held moustaches to the width of the mouth with hairs clipped short, and none overhanging the upper lip, mine exceeded that. It was full, bushy, and wide.

A gunnery sergeant named Remp started growing one about the same time. He was a shit-hot guy, one of the folks who worked in aircraft maintenance. He sported a handlebar. It wasn't the kind that curls up at the end; his went straight out. We kidded each other with comments like. "I think mine's longer than yours, Lieutenant." Or "Yours is not very big around but it sure is short, Guns."

We were competing, at least we told everyone we were. That way, if anyone said anything, I could blame Remp and he could blame me. We weren't really competing, though I was interested in his progress and he in mine.

Though I've never been good with causality, I don't think I was challenging the Marine Corps system. Still, I had a moustache, so did Remp, and it was okay.

Of course I had to endure comments from the guys like, "Ballentine's cultivating on his upper lip what I grow wild on my ass." Over time the hasslers tired of hassling. If I'd been more senior, I'd have heard none of this. It would still have been said, just not to me.

No senior officer said a word, not in the VMO-6 chain of command, nor outside it. But before I came home, off came the face hair.

I've had a moustache since my retirement from the Corps. It's now laced with gray, but what the hell. . . . I wonder if it has anything to do with 'Nam. I don't think so, but as I've said, I'm no good with causality.

LOYALTY AND A BAR SCUFFLE

We were loyal to the Marine Corps. Oh, sometimes it was referred to as "The Crotch," "This Green Mother-Fucker," or "The Green Machine," but I was pleased to be part of it, as were my associates. Some of the pride came from mythic traditions well known in our nation The Corps trained us in its history and tradition; knowledge and attitude were built into us. As an example, John Musgrave, poet and 'Nam vet, gave me a small vial of sand from Iwo Jima. I respect the men who walked on it and I cherish it because I know something about the sacrifice, the cost in death and injury of that battle.

Part of the pride likely came from the Marine Corps' approach: We did it the hard way, with less, made do, innovated, and worked around an issue, needed a dollar and got sixty-seven cents, that sort of stuff. Marine Corps "work arounds" are apparent from our use of discarded Army Huey parts and from our squadron metal shop fashioning gun sight reticules for our birds. Nobody issued instructions on either of these; someone saw a hole and filled it. Need is a mother.

Internal to the Corps was pride in and loyalty to specific units as well. In this respect, Klondike was no different than hundreds of other organizations. It produced, for instance, great intramural sport activities. And I even saw one bar fight over a slight to VMO-6. It was between First Lt. Seth Horten (fictitious name; true story) from one of the lift squadrons and Capt. Mike Bartley. I knew Horten a little from flight training days. He'd come through the pipeline the same time I had. We were acquaintances, but not tight.

Seth came into the bar one night hot, tired, and pissed off over who knows what, but he was chippy and spoiling for release. He'd grown into a sizable and strong young man, about 200 pounds and 6'1". Seth said something unkind about VMO-6 within earshot of several of us. We turned. I thought he was joking; he was not.

Bartley said, "Who's gonna say something about VMO?"

"I am," came a quick response. Seth pushed himself away from the bar and faced Mike. "Fuck VMO!" He offered with volume and emphasis.

Mike, not a small man though shorter and lighter than Seth, closed on him in a heartbeat. He ducked under a roundhouse right from Horten, grabbed him around the midsection, and slammed him back-first on the barroom floor. They tussled, but Mike was clearly in command. The rest of us from both squadrons jumped in to separate the two, and a major from Seth's unit used his authority to get the two settled down. Things sort of returned to normal. It was all about loyalty. Not institutional, they were both Marines, but unit.

Two notions remain with me from this episode. The first is lingering amazement at Horten's willingness to cross some unseen but ever-present line and denigrate another organization in the presence of its members. Something must have happened to cause it. The second is Mike Bartley's ability in a bar fight. Later I discovered he wrestled through college. Only another wrestler might have been his equal. When Seth missed with his fist, he was going down. He probably didn't know anything about what was happening to him. He just knew he was on the floor, maybe out of wind, and his ass was on the bottom of a two-man pile.

Several lessons leap out at me. Loyalty is one, estimating an opponent a second, and mouths overloading asses a third, but it's closely tied to the second. Others exist I sure; I'm glad I can learn some lessons from simply observing.

NERVES AND CIGARETTES

Anytime I got the shit scared out of me I wanted a smoke. If I was out doing the serious business of VMO against guys who wanted me and my friends dead or hurt, and to prove it they were shooting, when my cheeks were back on the ground, I was bummin'.

Why is that? Docs likely have an answer, or maybe a series of them. I just know when we were in the ready room debriefing an exciting hop, any smoker around was likely to get hit up. I didn't buy cigarettes, since I *didn't* smoke. At least usually I didn't. But get the adrenaline pump going and when the shit was over, I needed a smoke or two to get me down. Cigarettes had a tranquilizing effect, settled me so I could talk at a normal pace. Otherwise my mind spun away at a fast as hell rate and my mouth tried to keep up. I had to hold myself in check or words would have tumbled out of me like water through a sieve. A couple of smokes later and things were back to regular; a somewhat reasonable man returned.

Adrenaline is a powerful chemical; it creates or releases a different person. At least that's my take. I've been involved in experimentation on this one.

HOOCHES AND HOOCH RATS

Most buildings were "Southeast Asia Huts," hooches as we called them. We also had larger metal "Butler" buildings here and there; these were used for maintenance hangars when the work could not be done on the flight line. Although other specialized constructions were scattered about, the chow hall for instance, by and large it was hooches.

These wood-frame buildings were used for the ready room, squadron offices, line shack, intel, logistics, and sleeping quarters. They were identical in construction; life was simpler that way for the Navy Construction Battalion guys who erected them. Without the disturbance of folks farting around with blueprints, wanting alterations at whim or even from the dictates of need, the builders could build away. And they did.

The hooches were roughly eighteen by thirty-six feet, with a screen door at each end and a swath of screen three feet wide running around the building halfway up from the bottom. Hinged, wooden flop-down covers could be lowered to block the screened area during the cooler months and when rain was driven nearly horizontal by heavy winds in monsoon seasons. Roofs were corrugated metal and the buildings were raised slightly above the ground on footings.

Electrical wire, strung in exposed rafters, ran the hooch's length and switches at each end of the building controlled bare-bulb lights overhead. In our living hooches, electrical outlets were spaced along each interior sidewall, which allowed bedside lights, radios, tape players, and even refrigerators. Usually each hooch had a fridge. This worked great unless one or more of the noisy diesel generators that provided electrical power to the compound failed. Then we had to shut stuff off. We could tell when loss was impending; the overhead lights dimmed. When this happened, we reached for switches and plugs.

The hooches we lived in were clustered by rank. The junior enlisted and NCOs (corporals and sergeants) and the SNCOs (enlisted ranks above sergeant) stayed in the squadron work area, but in separate buildings. Captains and lieutenants lived up a slight hill, about three city blocks away from the squadron workspaces and the flight line. The senior captains were assigned together, as were rookie captains and lieutenants. Majors lived still farther up the hill, as did the CO. They used jeeps for travel to and from the squadron, partly because rank hath its privilege and partly because they lived farther away.

Hooch Rats I

In the rainy season, rats, not the small timid, candy-ass sort, but big, bold bastards, came in from the wet and cold. They usually visited in the middle of the night and transited our hooches on the exposed electrical wires running the building's length in the rafters. Every once in a dark as hell while, a normally sure-footed rat would misstep. Then he or she squealed on the eight-foot drop to the floor below. The squeal from a knowing rat (they must have understood that this was gonna hurt) rousted and annoyed most of us, though we had some heavy sleepers, guys oblivious, short of some more major auditory event.

"What the fuck was that?" or "Fuckin' rats!" And back to sleep.

We all kept flashlights handy at the side of our racks. They came in handy, not only as navigational aids in after-hours trips to the pisstube, but they served in rat-fall investigation as well. On a couple of these occasions I fumbled, found mine, and threw around a beam of light. I never saw more than a splat on our wooden floor, the kind made by an en route to terminal-velocity wet rat experiencing sudden stoppage. I hoped one would be lying there whimpering, waiting for a lieutenant-administered coup de grace. But such was never the case. One could hope they were at least injured and had learned not to make further sorties into hooches. I doubt if they reached this conclusion; it was wet and cold outside. I'd try to sneak in too.

In the warmer seasons this was less of a problem. Outside was generally okay for the rat population, at least usually.

Hooch Rats II

Early in my tour I managed to commandeer a waist-high bookshelf from a departing officer. I used it as a divider; it marked off my turf from my neighbor's and allowed us a hint of waist-down privacy. It also served as a repository for books and provided useful storage for clean laundry and my seven-eighty-two gear, steel-pot helmet, poncho, web-belt (pistol attached), and combat boots.

Keeping the helmet and pistol handy was a good idea. If we came under mortar attack, we were to don our helmets, grab our pistols, and head for one of the numerous sandbagged bunkers that decorated the area. If bad guys came through the wire, all bets were off. You'd certainly want your gun and steel pot, but where you went, well, maybe a bunker would not be the best choice. One had to consider grenades. I thought under our hooch would do. That was my plan, though I never had to execute it.

One morning during the winter months I awoke, rolled my legs off the rack, came to a sitting position, yawned, stretched, scratched, pulled on my socks, and stood up. Then, while holding the gaze of Charlie Swinburn who sat on his rack across the aisle from me, I released a long, noisy methane embolism.

Swinburn shook his head. "Jesus, Ballentine, could you at least try?" Charlie wondered.

I told him I was and tried not to laugh, but failed. Since no wind stirred our hooch, I suffered most. Poetic justice comes to mind. Then I pulled on my flight suit.

I sat down again and grabbed my flight boots. Something was amiss. On close inspection I noticed that some low-life bastard had cut off my bootlaces even with the eyelets. Just before I started raising hell with my hoochmates, I noticed my non-aviator combat boots, the ones I kept in my bookcase. The laces on those had suffered the same fate.

"Okay, which one of you turds is fuckin' with my bootlaces?" I paused. The guys looked in my direction. Nothing but blanks.

I tried again, "Some bastard cut off all my laces last night!" Still nothing. I looked from guy to guy, Swinburn, Bartley, Motley, and Kufeldt. From their responses you'd think they were innocent.

"What the fuck are you talkin' about?" Bartley asked.

"Look at this shit," I held up a flight boot by its sole, pointing to the cleanly cropped laces.

"Beats the dog shit outta me. But I got better things to do than low crawl my ass over there in the middle of the night to trim your bootlaces," Motley rejoined. He smiled in his genial way.

A ray of logic shined. Why indeed? I vowed to continue my inquiry and increase my vigilance. I replaced the laces from the PX later that day. In the meantime, I dropped down three eyelets in my flight boots so I had enough lace to tie and got on with my day.

Over the course of the next few days others in the hooch joined me in complaint and accusation. Some perverse bastard was cutting off bootlaces. But who? The question hung in the air at the hooch and even got bandied about in the ready room.

Straightening up my stuff was a rare action for me. I am untidy. How I survived in the Corps, with its preoccupation for orderliness, is a mystery. But shortly after the bootlace incident was one of those rare occasions when I felt compelled to do some housecleaning. Who knows what drove me, need, boredom, or maybe something unkind was said about my living conditions. Anyway, I went to work. During my straightening up, I pulled my steel helmet from the bookcase shelf. When I did, all sorts of string, scraps of cloth, bits of fuzz, and this and that, including eight or ten bootlace ends tumbled to the floor. For a moment I struggled, like the proverbial pig staring at a stopwatch. Then epiphany! The rat bastard responsible for clipping bootlaces really was a rat bastard.

Apparently one had been laboring away at home-building under my helmet. I made the find known to my hooch-mates, who looked, marveled, and learned. I collected and tossed the nest materials into a shit-can outside. I set the helmet back on the shelf, this time crown-side down, so I could more easily monitor the previous construction site.

I imagine the rat returned a few times in the middle of the night to search for her home, got pissed at lost effort, and found an alternative elsewhere. I watched my stuff and moved it around with some regularity for days thereafter, looking for signs of rat action. No more occurred during the winter of 1966–1967. Next year I was gone; another lieutenant was in my digs. I suspect he had visitors.

CAPTAIN MIKE BARTLEY, HERO

I think I did my share, went when I was called, stood in the rotation line like everybody, and trusted the ops guys to spread the mission load. I did not pester the ops scheduler by insisting that I do anything. I didn't need to. There was plenty to go around, and the flight schedule pretty much reflected mission parity for the crews.

But Mike Bartley, in the late stage of his tour, lobbied to fly daily (which we generally did anyway) and, when our squadron was tasked with medevac pickup, he was especially keen on flying the missions. As I've suggested elsewhere, medevac pickup, flown in a slick, was the most dangerous and the most rewarding mission. You might save a life, but wounded Marines usually meant the enemy was present at or near the LZ. And helos are noisy, so you can't sneak up; they are also big, relatively slow, and, during pickup, they are stationary and easy to hit.

Maybe Mike was bored. If, for instance, he had one or two staff noncommissioned officers working with him, life could have been pretty simple. By the time Marines are NCOs (corporals or sergeants) they know what's going on and how to do things; by the time they are SNCOs (staff sergeants and above) they are truly professionals. Much of what junior officers do, especially pilots, is get the hell out of the way and stay informed so they can answer questions of those more senior. So Mike may have been freed up in this way and bored as a result. Whatever his nonflying work circumstance, he spent a bunch of time in the cockpit. Squadron Operations was happy to accommodate him, and he racked up more missions than anyone in the squadron on my thirteen-month tour.

"What the hell are you doing, Bartley? You know it's dangerous out there. Small men with big guns shoot at you. It's fuckin' Indian country," I ragged him, but I was curious.

"Yeah, but it beats the shit out of hanging out here. Time goes quicker. And, what the hell, I'm trained; I'm here; I kinda like the action, and there's a chance I might save an ass or two."

"Yeah, but shit, if it's not your turn in the barrel, someone else will save the ass or two," I pondered out loud.

"I guess, but who's better at it than the old guys?" he countered.

He had a point there. By then Bartley and I and others were the "old guys." Less experienced pilots were more apt to do something wrong, either too dangerous or not dangerous enough. In some respects the best warriors are the experienced. The Greeks knew that 2,500 years ago and arranged their phalanx to reflect it.

I stared at him, "I suppose so."

I never got the impression Bartley was the risk-taker, daredevil sort, though I'm convinced aviation attracts a type with some of that built in. Nor did I believe he tried to outshine the herd with mission count. No, he just would rather fly, especially medevac where you sit in a zone that typically has bad guys around and wait for Marines to bring wounded to the helo. These missions had a higher purpose than the routine.

He may have also known that in the long haul the Marine Corps was not his home (Mike's an attorney in New York); that he was passing through. Such knowledge might cause a person to do all he can while he's there, maybe so he would always be able to look in the mirror and be okay with himself.

Whatever the reasons, Mike Bartley flew his ass off in the late stages of his tour and often it was as medevac. And though I'm not one to dredge up corny expressions, I've come to believe he was noble. Without fanfare or braggadocio, he performed a series of selfless deeds, which reflect the best of what it is to be human. I would stand aside for Bartley any day, not simply because I try to be polite, but because he's earned the nod.

REST AND RELAXATION

Five days in a Far-Eastern city, long, hot showers, dim bars, cold beer, a hotsie bath or three, exotic foods, people, and sites. I, who was about to die, saluted Fumiko and a couple others. Mea maxima culpa. Then back to Ky Ha.

Cpl. Pete Greene, crewchief, at his station in his bird. *(Courtesy Peter Greene)*

Cpl. Pete Greene, crewchief, next to his Huey. *(Courtesy Peter Greene)*

Armed Huey on takeoff at Ky Ha. *(Courtesy Peter Greene)*

Lt. Col. W. R. Maloney, CO, VMO-6.
(Squadron cruisebook)

Capt. Steve Shoemaker, "Rocketman."
(Squadron cruisebook)

Capt. Jim Perryman. *(Squadron cruisebook)*

Capt. K. D. Waters, my boss in aircraft maintenance. *(Squadron cruisebook)*

Ky Ha O'Club, on the perimeter and the skyline! At least it was sandbagged.
(Squadron cruisebook)

Squadron-area shitter. *(Squadron cruisebook)*

LCpl. Rick Ault, crewchief.
(Squadron cruisebook)

Maj. Bill Dodds, section leader when
Wilson was shot down. *(Squadron
cruisebook)*

From left to right: the author, Captain Cho, Maj. Ed Sample, and Capt. K. D. Waters.
We were midstride in a shit sandwich. Waters was the section leader. The XO, Major
Sample, was his copilot. I flew as Waters' wingman, and Captain Cho, a one-day
visitor and jet pilot from the Korean air force, was my copilot. We were at Ky Ha
refueling and rearming to return to a fight. Notice I'm smoking, a sure sign of recent
engagement. Also note that the three VMO pilots are a sober lot; only Cho is smiling.
He just didn't understand. *(Squadron cruisebook)*

First Lt. Jerry Garner, sometimes operations duty officer. *(Squadron cruisebook)*

First Lt. Tom Peckham, my copilot when Wilson was shot down. *(Squadron cruisebook)*

First Lt. Steve Wilson, shot down trying to medevac a Korean Marine with his gunbird. *(Squadron cruisebook)*

LCpl. R. Soukup, gut-shot when Wilson was shot down. *(Squadron cruisebook)*

GySgt R. Remp, fellow moustache grower. *(Squadron cruisebook)*

The author and his 'stache. *(Squadron cruisebook)*

First Lt. John Boden. May have been my copilot when I was forced down. *(Squadron cruisebook)*

Capt. John Arick, the gunbird chase pilot on my medevac mission when I was forced down. *(Squadron cruisebook)*

Three crewchief studs: Sgt. R. Hockenbury, LCpl. J. Phelps, and Sgt. A. Storms.
(Squadron cruisebook)

Capt. Mike Bartley, O'club brawler and hero. *(Squadron cruisebook)*

Sgt. A. Corning, my crewchief while I flew "under the influence." *(Squadron cruisebook)*

First Lt. Barney Ross. Barney and I flew slicks in support of the Bob Hope show. *(Squadron cruisebook)*

First Lt. Lyle Motley, the man with the caved-in sinus cavity. *(Squadron cruisebook)*

Capt. Glen "Andy" Olsen, flight leader for the SOG mission. *(Squadron cruisebook)*

First Lt. Dick Boston, copilot on the SOG mission. *(Courtesy Dick Boston)*

Sgt. A. Storms, crewchief on the SOG mission. *(Squadron cruisebook)*

Cpl. W. McDevitt, door gunner on the SOG mission. *(Squadron cruisebook)*

Gunbird and crewchief at Phu Bai. *(Courtesy Peter Greene)*

PART 4

Studies and Observation Group (SOG)

CHAPTER 19

A Few Words on SOG

Some Army guys have balls the size of grapefruit; they are courageous men who seek lives exposed to danger. All service branches have heroes: people who act or react situationally in selfless ways for the sake of others or maybe for the sake of the mission. Smothering a grenade, exposing oneself to certain danger to rescue another, are examples. But not everybody volunteers for the steady-state, no-shit dangerous work. This requires a different sort, a magnitude beyond the norm. In these jobs, every day might offer opportunity for heroism; indeed life itself is heroic. Army SOG guys qualify.

Most of these courageous and adventuresome men go unnoticed, blend in; everybody looks alike, two arm, two legs, a torso, and head. But after that, men sort themselves by qualities: character, drive, intellect, courage, and the like.

I'm not one who believes the military is a cross-section of society, that it's just America in uniform. I think the military is a distillation of sorts, especially in the combat units. This stuff is not for everybody. And the SOG guys were a distillation from the combat units, another refinement, a skimming for the occasional and rare are-you-shitting-me warrior. Here's where the grapefruit ball-size idea comes into play. SOG field-operations guys represent the antithesis to survival instincts. A little danger can be exciting, even addicting. A lot of danger is too exciting, threatening beyond the okay for most of us, but not for SOG.

I eased into a gym for a workout at Ft. Bragg in the late 1990s and there were two such men, Delta for sure, one a staff sergeant, the other a sergeant first class—both tanned, maybe from jungle work against drug cartels, both in shape, both with confident carriage, men who could hold a gaze, dominators. I was comforted by them. America at its finest in some respects, maybe humanity at its finest, tools for policy, credits to our nation, standing in a line as long as human history, at once different but still part of the great stream. SOG guys were of this stripe.

SOG missions, though all classified, involved going to the weeds in small units to gather information about the enemy. These paint-faced survivalists, skilled in ways most of us prefer only to read about, were not the hyperbolic "Rambos" of Hollywood. No hyberbole was needed. They were to go it alone, live off the land, watch the enemy, collect, intervene, destroy, and be the stealthy well away from friendly units. Shiny Brass was the code name for those working along the Laotian border.

All their ops were secret, as I noted when I looked at after-action reports for the missions I write about below. The grid coordinates, for instance, were not recorded in the reports. Indeed, initially they refused to tell us much about what we were up to, that is until our flight leader, Capt. Andy Olson, countered with his own refusal: He would not launch without a complete brief. They checked with their headquarters and relented. We got to know something about their activity in the late winter of '67.

GETTING THERE AND THE BRIEF

It began innocently enough. I appeared on the flight schedule as the wingman to Capt. Glenn "Andy" Olson. Andy was a senior captain selected for major; I was still a first lieutenant. He was to lead a division of gunbirds to Phu Bai in support of a mission. We'd be gone two days, maybe three, doing the stuff we did as a routine: Fly there, get a brief, provide gun cover to lift birds for an insert, and fly home. The line up was Olson, me on his wing, and two lieutenants, Bob Todt and Lyle Motley, as pilots in command of the other two helos in our division. Todt led that second section.

My copilot was First Lt. Dick Boston, the crewchief was Sergeant Storms, and our door gunner was Corporal McDevitt from squadron administration. Dick was reasonably new to country and still learning the ropes, but was the solid sort, quick thinking, and able to handle the Huey. Sergeant Storms and Corporal McDevitt were old, reliable hands. I'd flown with them often. I was pleased with the crew I was assigned.

The evening prior to launch we all threw some stuff in a bag for the trip. In the morning we met with Captain Olson and were briefed for the hop to Phu Bai. It didn't include much, stay up my freq, let me know you hear me when I call to change freqs, loose formation, beach route north, Hai Van Pass, gas at Phu Bai before parking, then meet in the local squadron's ready room.

We grabbed our flight gear and flak jackets, signed off the birds, threw our bags in the helo's cabin, told Storms and McDevitt what we knew, pre-flighted, turned up, and checked in on the radios. Andy led us first to the runway, then on takeoff and the ensuing flight north along the coast. We flew over the Danang complex, through the Hai Van Pass, and, after another fifteen minutes, into the Phu Bai area.

The flight was uneventful, and, although the weather was okay, Andy directed us to shoot individual practice Ground Control Approaches (GCAs) to the strip at Phu Bai. As it turned out this practice was rehearsal. We hot refueled in the Phu Bai pits, then parked near the CH-34s of the HMM-163 Ridgerunners, the lone squadron permanently assigned there.

We secured the birds, grabbed our stuff, and went into a strong-back tent the Ridgerunners used as a ready room. Strong-backs had wooden floors, rather than just mother earth. We were assigned to nearby hooches for our temporary quarters and told to meet back at 1530 for a brief. It was late morning, gray and dreary, the sky was overcast, a little rain fell, but the ceiling was high, probably eight thousand to ten thousand feet.

I farted around in my assigned hooch, chose a rack, stored my gear, and shot the shit with the other pilots. Then I heard the Frogs arrive. After a while you can't mistake the different sounds of engine and rotor combinations. I didn't have to look. My ears told me whether it was a CH-34, CH-46, CH-53, or Huey. These were CH-46s and, from the sound, they were arriving in number.

I looked through the screen that ran around the hooch. Nine birds. From tall, bold initials on their tails, I knew they were Bonnie Sue helos from HMM-265, stationed at Marble Mountain. They were here to provide lift for the mission we were supporting. Good, I thought. I'd know some of their lieutenants; they'd come through flight training with me. Some were friends, others acquaintances.

Nine. That's a bunch of Frogs. This lift was going to be pretty big. They could put in over one hundred guys in one trip. They all taxied to the fuel pits, then repositioned as we had to the parking apron. In they came.

I kicked back to give them time to receive their marching orders about where they'd sleep, the 1530 brief, get to their hooches, and put up their stuff. None of them were assigned to my hooch, even though we had two unoccupied racks. To chat with the lift bubbas I'd have to get off my lazy ass. I sighed. Life was hard. It was the old "if the mountain won't come to Mohammed, Mohammed must go to the mountain" routine. I rousted myself, grabbed my utility cover, and headed for the door.

"Captain Olson, I'm gonna go chat with the Frogmen," I offered on my way out.

"Okay, Dave, see ya' later."

Finding them was easy. They were just two buildings away and I'd listened to them tromp in while I stretched on my rack. I opened the Bonnie Sue hooch screen door and spied Jim Hodgson and Jack Exum.

"How they hangin'?" I asked as I strolled in.

"Hey, Ballentine. Same shit, different day," Exum answered.

"Yep, just another day in the Bonnie Sue business," piped Hodgson.

"I guess you guys are here for the shindig tomorrow?" I inquired.

"Yeah. You guys too I s'pose," Hodgson offered. But, before I could answer, he added, "I thought this was Deadlock country."

Deadlock, the call sign for VMO-2, did range the north when they had birds available, but they were often heavily engaged around Danang or elsewhere up north. When their plate was full, northern missions fell to MAG-36. If it was gun work, VMO-6 was pressed into service. We were farther away, but helos are mobile.

"Yep," I answered. "We're here in support. I guess Deadlock is up to its ass in gators, so we got called. This must be a kinda big lift. You guys are here in some strength." It was a question as well as a comment.

"I think so, but we don't have any details. They told us to bring an extra helo. That's about all I know. That, and we're not lifting Marines. Army SOG guys, I think," Exum offered.

"That's sorta what I heard, too. I'm confused. What the hell is the Army doing in I Corps? Ain't this Marine territory?" I usually didn't think above the sparrow's-eye view, but I was puzzled.

"Some stuff the Army does, the Marine Corp don't. Some kinds of recon, special forces shit, I don't know. But I can't imagine nine Frogs full of recon or special forces guys. If you're recon, aren't you supposed to sneak around, be quiet, hide? If they go in anywhere near whoever's out there, wherever the hell 'out there' is, they'll know we're comin' and about where we land," Exum countered.

We mused, chatted, swapped lies, and got caught up a little. Then we went to noon chow where I branched off and joined Boston and the Klondike guys. I thought, since we were putting in the number of troops that eight or nine Frogs can lift, maybe no bad guys would fuck with us. Or maybe we'd offer such a large and tantalizing target, they'd be unable to resist.

At 1525, five minutes early but perfectly on Chesty Puller time, I went to the ready-room tent with the other pilots. At the front were two officers, a captain in a flight suit, whom I presumed led the Bonnie Sue helos, and an Army major. Sister service interlopers are always interesting. I checked over his uniform, how he handled himself, and noted the small differences in comportment and language. The Bonnie Sue captain, a guy named Carver, welcomed us, told us we were here to support an Army SOG mission, introduced the Army major, a man named Spencer, and took a seat. Here came the nuts and bolts.

"Afternoon, gents," Major Spencer began. "I'll keep this short, but tomorrow fifteen Army SOG soldiers and ninety-four Nungs, these are Chinese mercenaries, will show up on our ramp at 0730. They'll break down into sticks of fourteen and load on your lift helos at 0800. At 0815, we'll take off and go to DX724146. It's just south and east of the Ashau Valley." He pointed to the map as pilots jotted down grid coordinates on their kneeboards. We'd locate and note the LZ grids on our personal 1:50,000-meter maps later, after the brief.

"The LZ is a relatively treeless ridgeline that should fit four helicopters at one time. We'll bow, of course, to your decisions on how many will fit and how you'll land. We'd like to get as many troops as possible on the ground as soon as possible, in case there's enemy units in the immediate area."

"Our mission is recon in force. We've known for some time that routes from the north run around and through the Ashau Valley, but we need more precision. Is it a trickle or a full-on fire hose? Is it supplies only or combat units or both? If it's both, what's the mix? We're going out in numbers this time so we can't be easily run off if detected. Our plan is to stay in the area for eight to twelve days, then be lifted out, but likely from a different LZ."

"We know the NVA might be in the area. We've tried to go somewhere they're not, but our landing may receive a warm welcome. Once on the ground, we'll move and, hopefully, start gathering intel. Our call sign is Nightrider and we'll be up 42.6 Fox Mike, at least for the first twenty-four hours. After that we'll switch, but that won't affect what we're up to tomorrow."

"The time en route to the LZ is twenty-five minutes at 100 knots. We're traveling light and the Nungs are small, so we've calculated fourteen men per bird and eight helos. Let us know if we need to change that. There will be no LZ prep, except what you may get from your gunship escorts, but no arty, no fast movers. We're just going in. Marine recon and patrols from Khe Sanh north of the LZ report NVA unit movement regularly. And we've scattered a bunch of ground sensors out there which also detect movement. We just need to get a better feel for what's happening."

He paused. "I think that about does it. We'll meet here again at 0645 tomorrow for last-minute tweaks. The chow hall opens at 0600. So we can eat before our 0645 meeting. Any questions?"

"What's the average weight of a man and his gear?" Bonnie Sue's Captain Carver asked.

"We'll be 185 pounds per guy, average. That puts the troop weight around 2,600 pounds per bird."

"What's the elevation of the zone?"

"We'll be at 2,100 feet MSL," the Army major responded. "Oh, and the temperature will be about 65 degrees." He'd done his homework; the lift guys needed this info to bounce against performance charts.

"Okay," Carver said as he stood. "Anyone else have something for Major Spencer?" Silence.

"Okay, that LZ is approximately twenty-seven miles on the two six five radial of Phu Bai's TACAN. Bonnie Sue flight will maintain the same crews and formation we flew up in. Like the Major said, report here at 0645 for updates. We'll preflight and be turned up by 0800 and load. We'll take off at 0815. We'll use squadron common, 41.2, for turn up and switch to Nightrider on my call en route. I'll make all the calls for the flight, beginning to end. If my radios head south, Captain Trask, who's leading the second division, will lead the flight. My division will follow."

"Acknowledge and check in on each frequency change. We'll fly out loose at three thousand feet, check the zone size, and ask Klondike to snoop around a bit. If it will fit all eight, we'll all go in; otherwise a division at a time; mine first, unless Trask has the lead."

Carver turned to Andy with raised eyebrows, "Captain Olson, your guys okay with checking the LZ?"

"Yeah, we'll locate and recon the zone. We'll stay with you on all frequency shifts and have a section of guns on each side of your formation on the insert. We can smoke the zone if you want," Andy answered.

"I'll hold off on the smoke decision," Captain Carver countered. "I'd rather not. I'll let you know when we're in the area, if that's okay."

"No problem. It's your call," Olson responded.

We all listened intently; no one was distracted. It had to fit together. This was the business end of Bonnie Sue and of Klondike.

"You want us to shoot up the area as you guys go in or wait and see if you take fire?" Andy asked.

Captain Carver didn't have to ponder, "Don't wait, just start shooting on our approach. By the time we're landing any NVA for miles around will be alert anyway. We want suppression on landing, while we're in the zone, and on lift. Nobody out there's on our side. Am I right Major Spencer?"

"That's affirm. We have no recon around there, nor do the Marines at present. Anyone you see is almost certainly NVA, not VC, but NVA."

"Okay, Andy. Shoot 'em up, by all means." He paused again. I liked this guy. He was direct, experienced, professional, strong, and had the respect of the bubbas. He'd do; Bonnie Sue had a good one.

"The weather is supposed to be high, thin overcast. At that time of day, winds will likely be calm or light. We'll know by takeoff. If we smoke the zone, we'll know for sure. The ridgeline runs generally northwest to southeast. We'll land perpendicular to that, either to the east or the west. The slope of the ridge is gentle near the top, but drops off pretty damn steep after that. We gotta land on the crest," continued Captain Carver.

He paused, "Who has a question?" It was silent.

"Okay, one last thought. We have a ninth Frog as backup. If someone goes down in the chocks, just have the troops unload and go to Dash nine; it's Exum's helo. He's last in our line and he'll be turnin' like everyone else. If no one goes down on turn up and Jack's not pressed into service, he'll bring his empty bird along anyway for SAR (Search and Rescue). If anybody goes down in, Jack's job is to get you."

Carver looked at the tent ceiling a moment, scouring his mind for what he might have left out. Then, "That's about it, I think." He looked at Andy, "You got anything Captain Olson?"

"No, at least not for the crowd," Andy answered. "You Klondike pilots stick around a minute after we break."

"Okay, if no one has questions, we're done until 0645. We'll meet here for last-minute stuff," Carver concluded. Eyes broke lock from the front of the briefing tent; metal chairs started scooting back on plywood decking, pilots stood. Seven Klondike pilots clustered around Captain Olson.

"We'll maintain the section integrity we did on the way up this morning. On the troop insertion, Dave and I will take the north side for suppressive fire. Bob, you and Lyle, stay on the south. Use guns but conserve ammo a little in case someone goes down someplace and we need to help. We'll maintain the radio discipline briefed by Bonnie Sue. Turn up on their freq and ripple check in as Klondike Dash two, three, and four. This is an Army–Bonnie Sue show; we'll do whatever we can to help."

"Dave," he said to me, "ease over to the crews and give them our pre-flight, turn-up time, and a general idea of what's up tomorrow. We'll give the crews individual mission briefs at the helos in the morning."

"Yes, sir," I answered.

Then Andy turned back to the group, "You all need to do a map recon of the terrain from here to there and around the LZ this evening. Any questions?"

We had none. We broke up; most headed back to the hooch or to the chow hall. I had a task.

"Dick, I'm headed to the crews. No need you comin'. I'll see ya at chow or later. I can't think of a damn thing in addition to what Major Spencer and the captains offered. I know it's bad guy territory out there; maybe that says it all."

"Okay, Dave. See you," Dick responded. We each headed our separate ways. I was off to chat with the crewchiefs and gunners or as many as I could find. They'd be in their hooch or hanging around the helos. As it turned out the split was about even. I gave them an overview at both locations. When I left they knew the mission and our preflight and launch times. The birds would be ready.

At the time and often since, I've thought about these men, most were in their late teens or early twenties. They were some of the best people I have known, committed, hardworking, courageous, and trusting. My crewchief, Sergeant Storms, was probably twenty-three or twenty-four; the gunner, Corporal McDevitt, a New York City man, was about twenty. They were good Marines. Maybe nothing else needs to be said. Both were products of the national psychology of the late 1950s and early 1960s, each convinced we were doing what was necessary and proud of his contribution. They had just a hair of swagger. Operating a machine gun from the door of a helo can give you that. These guys were a credit to our nation and to whomever raised them.

The evening passed in a forgettable, uneventful way, chow, a shower, a drink, a chat, a book in the rack, and oblivion.

Someone from the duty section came to the hooch around 0600; he threw on our lights and got us moving. We left our personal gear in the hooch; we planned to retrieve it on our way back through Phu Bai for fuel en route to Ky Ha. Fat chance. I shaved with cold water as usual, using the ten-dip Ballentine mantra, brushed my teeth, and threw in some black coffee and SOS at breakfast.

Like everyone, I was early for the 0645 brief, which was mercifully short since nothing had changed. After we were in place, "Okay guys listen up," Carver began. "The whiskey–x-ray (weather) is no factor; high, thin, broken to scattered, wind light until around 1000; then easterly increasing to ten to twelve knots by 1400. We can probably land any direction we want."

"The Army tells me the SOG guys will be here any minute to break into sticks for loading. The charts say we can hack a 2,100-foot zone. We'll do division takeoffs, me first, and just head for the LZ. I'll go slow so tail-end Charlie and the Klondike birds can catch up."

"The Bonnie Sue helos will drill out at 3,000. When we get in the area, Klondike will take a look at the zone, but we won't smoke it." Carver got eye contact from Andy when he said this.

"The gunbirds will provide suppressive fire during approach, landing, and takeoff. We'll land, I'm guessing, a division at a time, unless this zone is huge. I'll let you know when I see the place, but plan on division landings unless I say otherwise. Turn up on squadron common Fox Mike and check in when you're ready. Like I said yesterday, stay with me on each frequency shift. If you get helo problems in the chocks, contact me and, if necessary, move the troops to Exum's Frog. He's our backup and our SAR. We'll turn as briefed yesterday. Be loaded and turning by 0800. We'll take off by 0815. Any questions?"

Silence met his inquiry.

"Any comments from Klondike?" Carver eyed Andy.

He shook his head sideways, "No, we got it; no smoke and cover with guns. We'll have a section working each side."

There were few, if any, new guys in HMM-265. The whole squadron had been in country at least six months. VMO-6, on the other hand, was experiencing some aircrew shuffle each month; replacements for the original squadron guys were already in. I was one of them, but now guys were showing up to replace those of us who'd replaced the original crews. Dick Boston was one of these.

Klondike was changing, yet the same. Aircrews learned the missions, the terrain, the radio procedures, and, after a bit of practice, took over, only to be replaced later by others. It was March 1967. I'd be heading back to the States the following month. I was the most in-country experienced VMO pilot on this outing, though not the most experienced aviator and not senior in rank. That was Andy.

It was reasonable that few, if any, questions were asked. The HMM bubbas were experienced; their Captain covered the bases. Each pilot knew what to do and what was expected. The copilots in our Klondike birds were coming up on the power curve, learning by observing, and by doing. The departure of guys like me would have little to no effect. Although I liked to think my absence would have a huge negative consequence, it wouldn't. Klondike rolled along.

After the brief, we broke up. Most of us hit the head; it wouldn't do to have to piss like a racehorse or to shit real bad while engaging the enemy. We then moved to the helos to brief crews and preflight.

CHAPTER 20

Insertion

"Sergeant Storms," I greeted our crewchief as Dick and I approached the gunbird. "How's it goin'?" Storms was sitting in the Huey's cabin on the red nylon web seat near his swivel-mount M-60, the position he occupied during flight.

"It's goin' okay, Lieutenant. The helo looks good and is all signed off. McDevitt's in the shitter; nope, here he comes now." Storms nodded in the direction of a slender figure approaching the Huey from the hooch area about sixty yards away.

"Well, we're off to make the world safe from the specter of communism," I offered as I opened the pilot's door and threw my flight bag on the seat. My comments were partly tongue-in-cheek and partly what we believed in 1967. Dick threw his stuff in on the copilot's side. We were already wearing our flak vests. I tossed my utility cover on the glare shield, which hooded the instrument panel. I'd put it under my seat with my helmet bag after preflight.

"Yep, that's what we do, sir," Storms responded to my comment about communism.

"I'll give you and McDevitt a quick and dirty when he's here. Nothin's changed though." I grabbed an aluminum folder, crafted by our metalsmiths, from the pilot's seat. The helo's "yellow sheets" were inside. I already knew the bird's history, I'd flown it yesterday. I just found the signature bloc and signed, accepting the Huey.

Dick and I began our preflights. We checked fluids, tensions, bearing tolerances in the rotor head, and stabilizer bar dampener functions. All seemed right, and safety-wired or cotter-pinned where required. Corporal McDevitt was at the bird well before we were done. He took the aluminum folder to the Ridgerunner's line shack where it would be kept during our flight. Then he and Storms chatted while Dick and I climbed around on the bird. When we were satisfied the Huey was still airworthy, we joined Storms and McDevitt.

"Okay, guys, here's the deal," I began. "The Army's puttin' in about one hundred folks, mostly Chinese mercenaries, though there's a sprinklin' of incharge Army SOG guys goin' along. We're supportin' two divisions from Bonnie Sue. They've got an extra helo with 'em just in case they need to rescue anyone or as a backup if someone goes down in the chocks. The zone may be hot; nobody knows. We'll be providin' suppressive fire on the insertion. They'll probably go in one division at a time. As usual, cover our asses when we're coming off target, but if you see anything that's a target on our runs, hammer away. Ain't no friendlies out there. Only assholes and they're NVA, not VC."

They both shook their heads slightly. "Yes, sir. We got it."

It was nice to be with experienced guys; both knew what to expect, what to look for, and how to react. There'd be no hesitation and little need to ask me for instructions in the heat of activity. They'd simply get crackin'.

"We're still Captain Olson's wingmen and we're takin' off right after the lift birds. We'll cover the north side at the LZ. Lieutenant Todt's section will be on the south. Keep your eyes and ears open. Let me know if you see anything, muzzle flashes, people moving around, or guys trying to shoot at anyone. You know the drill."

"Unless you hear from me, you are cleared to fire, period. The zone is almost due west, close to the Laotian border and near the southern end of the Ashau Valley. You know how the valley usually is bad guy country."

I paused trying to think if I'd overlooked anything. Nothing occurred to me. "That's about it. You guys got any questions?"

"I'm okay, Lieutenant," Sergeant Storms offered.

"Me too, sir," McDevitt responded. Then he asked, "Oh, we headin' back to Ky Ha later, Lieutenant?"

"I expect. It's up to Captain O, but our job is to escort an insertion, not to stick around for the eventual extraction or whatever. Shit, who knows when these guys will be comin' out? The briefer said it'd be more than a week."

I motioned to the groups of men with their field packs near each CH-46. "Looks like they're carryin' enough for a while." Although the packs were not huge, they were large enough to suggest this was not an overnighter.

The Frogs were beginning the start sequence. First the onboard Aux power units came to life with their high-pitched whine, then the engines, then the release of rotor brakes. The troops would load shortly. I glanced at my watch. It was 0755, time to get the Huey turning.

"Okay, no more questions?" I paused. "Let's get her spooled up."

Dick and I strapped in, slipped on helmets, gloves, and kneeboards. We ran through the start checklist using the challenge and response method. He'd read an item; I'd do it and tell him it was done. Both of us could recite this in our sleep and find the switches blindfolded, but it was the best way to preclude oversight. Within five minutes, we were at 6,600 turbine RPM, the rotors were swinging at operating speed, and our radios were crackling.

I started hearing Bonnie Sue checking with their flight leader. After all nine Frogs were up and talking, Olson called. "Klondike Flight, check in."

I keyed the mic, "Klondike Dash two's up."

"Roger, Two," the sequence was followed with Bob Todt in Dash three and Lyle Motley in Dash four.

Then, "Bonnie Sue Lead, Klondike flight is up and ready. Over," Andy radioed. I looked across the helo mat; all birds were turning, all the SOG guys had disappeared, swallowed by the Frogs. Nine Frogs and four gunbirds were ready.

"Phu Bai Tower, Bonnie Sue twelve dash one, flight of nine CH-46s for taxi and takeoff. We're on mission 1326. Over." Phu Bai had no ground control. They had only one resident squadron, HMM-163, and the Tower could easily manage traffic for the parking ramp, the taxiways, and the single runway.

"This is Phu Bai Tower, Bonnie Sue. Your flight is cleared onto runway three three and for northwesternly takeoff. Turn out at pilot's discretion. No reported traffic. Understand mission 1326. Over."

The flight leader acknowledged and confirmed our mission number; nine 46s taxied in sequence onto runway 33 and organized themselves for takeoff. Bonnie Sue Lead made one last FM call to his flight to assure all were ready, after which Carver pulled his helo into a hover. He added takeoff power, lowered his nose, and headed down the runway. Eight Frogs followed. They accelerated and climbed left to a westerly heading.

"Phu Bai Tower, Klondike fourteen dash one, four Hueys for taxi and takeoff. Same mission as Bonnie Sue. Over," Olson called.

We were cleared. We had taxi directors at Ky Ha, but not here. I checked outside the helo, saw nothing in my vicinity, and pulled the Huey into a hover. After a quick check of the gauges, I moved off our parking spot, following Andy onto the runway. Todt and Motley came behind.

Once in position, Andy radioed again, "Klondike fourteen dash one is lifting." I watched his Huey respond to power demands and cyclic and rudder positions. I replicated his maneuver and took off behind him, but to avoid being kicked around in his rotorwash turbulence, I stayed offset to the right. He climbed left and kept his power up to overtake the Frogs still easily visible through our windscreen. We followed.

I flew very loose on Olson's right. My Huey was performing just like it was supposed to. I accelerated to one hundred knots and held a shallow climb.

The morning was not brilliant like many were. As Carver had briefed, it was cool, in the '60s. Engines and lift surfaces like cool air; we had plenty of power. I knew the Frog drivers were liking the temperature. It's always good to have extra power when you're going into a zone, especially a high one. "A little something for the wife and kids," as they said.

Since I didn't need to go into a zone, I didn't have these concerns, but extra power available was nice. A helo guy always wants fuel, power, and large, large places to land. It doesn't always work that way.

The landforms were clear, but visibility was not perfect; a slight morning haze still softened the landscape. It would burn off within the hour, but for now it hung, making the ground features slightly less distinct than would soon be the case.

The flight out was uneventful. Dick followed our progress on his map and I flew; then he flew and I followed our map trace. The Bonnie Sue flight stayed slow so we caught up and ran a little ahead as planned. Andy kept us beneath and to the right of the lift birds, which had climbed to three thousand feet.

Dick and I trailed along, and fifteen minutes after takeoff we were near the LZ. Andy located the zone first. I noticed he'd changed course slightly and followed with my eyes the direction he flew. The zone was unmistakable. Just as Major Spencer had indicated, it was a ridgeline oriented generally northwest to southeast. Along its axis, the ridge was clear of trees for about fifty yards, with a gentle east-west slope from its summit. After fifteen yards of gentle slope however, the land fell away precipitously. The Frog driver would not have a nice level place, but they made their living landing in tight spots. It would do.

At the time, Dick was on the controls. "That's gotta be it, Dick," I said into the ICS, and pointed forward and down to the left.

Since he was busy with the helo, he could only acknowledge, "Okay, I see the ridge about a mile or so ahead; kind of bald with trees at both ends, right?"

"Yep, that's it." No sooner had I finished than Olson came up on the Fox Mike radio.

"Bonnie Sue Lead, Klondike Lead. We have the zone about twelve o'clock, less than a mile. Over." The 46s were above and three-quarters of a mile behind.

"Klondike, Bonnie Sue Lead. We concur. That's it. TACAN's rollin' up on the right fix also. You goin' down for a look? Over."

"Roger, Bonnie Sue," Olson answered. "We'll take a peek. Break. Dash three, keep your section high. Dash two, take interval and follow me down. I'll look in the middle and right; you look middle and left. Over."

"Dash three's stayin' high," came Bob Todt's answer.

"I'll take it, Dick," I said into the ICS. As soon as he felt me on the controls, he responded, "You have the aircraft," and pulled his feet and hands from the controls.

I keyed the mic, juicing the Fox Mike. "Roger Klondike Lead. Dash two's takin' interval. We'll follow you and be lookin' mid and left. Over." I lowered the collective and raised the nose a few degrees. Holding altitude, the airspeed began bleeding. Andy pulled away.

"Klondike Lead is heading down. Want some smoke, Bonnie Sue? Over," Olson transmitted.

"Klondike Lead, that zone's prominent and winds are still light. We'll pass on the smoke. Break. Bonnie Sue Flight, we'll go in division at a time and land to the west. I'll take the leftmost part of the zone. Go right echelon for landing. Over."

The Bonnie Sue flight rippled in over the radio and maneuvered into right echelon for landing. The second Frog division would not start down until the first was in the zone.

Olson neared the LZ and slowed to get a good look.

Into my ICS I said, "Stormy, you and McDevitt keep your eyes peeled. Be ready, muzzle flashes, tracers, people. You know the drill. You see it; you shoot it. Dick, let's go guns and put us hot, just in case Olson takes some heat." Dick reached to the lower center console and made the necessary switch adjustments.

"You're hot, Dave," he responded. Andy was about to clear the zone. I nosed the gunbird over, ready, as was the crew. Airspeed increased a bit, but I held it in check; this was not a gun run. I was just snooping. The landform was folded and beautiful, lush and green, though scarred here and there from artillery or air strike impacts. It looked peaceful, nonthreatening.

Olson had cleared and started a right pull up, well to my front. "Klondike Lead is coming out. Looks okay center and right. Over."

We were close now, a hundred feet above the terrain, a football field away from the zone. Everyone keyed for the unusual and especially for a cracking sound or muzzle flashes against the dark green foliage. We flew over the left side of the zone with nothing but the sound of our rotors and the whine of our engine and transmission in our helmets. The LZ was covered by low growth, which obscured the ground beneath. The foliage was two to three feet high. When their wheels touched, Bonnie Sue would be belly down in the growth.

"Klondike Dash two is coming out. Nothing unusual. Over," I radioed. This might be a walk in the park, I thought.

"Roger, Dash two. Break. Bonnie Sue, Klondike Lead. We'll get in position and cover you with guns on your way in. Might take a minute. Over," Andy radioed.

"Roger, Klondike," Bonnie Sue Lead answered. "We're flyin' over the zone now. We'll let down in a left 360 to land. Over."

"Roger, Bonnie Sue. We'll be ready. Over," Olson responded. I climbed out to the right with full power, still alert. All was peaceful. I hooked back following Andy, but a quarter mile behind.

Dick threw a switch on the console. "Your guns're safe."

"Roger."

I watched outside but also glanced at the altimeter and the Vertical Speed Indicator arrows. We were separating from the ground at a nice clip. I leveled the wings heading opposite the direction of our recon run, but kept the climb coming to 2,800 feet MSL.

Bonnie Sue had crossed the LZ. Carver transmitted, "Bonnie Sue Lead is startin' down." The first four Frogs began a 360-degree descending left spiral. The other five remained high.

Todt's section of gunbirds was in position to support on the left, Olson and I on the right. The first division of Frogs was already slightly below my altitude, strung out to the right side and behind the lead Frog.

"Klondike Lead is in with guns," came Andy's call. Closely following his transmission, "Klondike Dash three in hot." Todt nosed over as Andy had. The Frogs rolled out of a spiral turn and set up for final approach, noses raised, bleeding airspeed.

The lead Hueys from each section began spraying the sides of Bonnie Sue's final approach course with 7.62 ammunition. The 46's touchdown would come in less than ten seconds. I turned to the right, ninety degrees from the run-in heading and slowed to sixty knots. The Huey's main rotor blades made the usual popping sound. I was near position to begin my run, but waited for Andy to pull up.

"Klondike Lead is off target." Within five seconds Todt in Klondike Dash three called off target also.

I turned to the target heading. Just as I nosed over came the call, "Bonnie Sue is taking fire left side." In the background of his transmission we could hear his crew slamming away with their automatic weapons. Carver was excited.

"Dash two, in hot, guns," I radioed. Dick threw my arming switches.

"Dash four in hot," came a call from Motley's bird. We started down in a routine that was all too familiar. In the absence of any specific target I raked the right side of the approach and LZ with 7.62-ball and tracer ammo. Red-orange balls shimmered and danced their way into foliage.

"Bonnie Sue Dash four is taking fire, right side of zone," came another call from the lift birds. They were being shot at from both sides. All Frogs were on the ground, ramps down, discharging troops, and they were taking heat left and right.

We continued our run, but wanting to relieve the heat on the Frogs, I pressed closer than usual. Storms and McDevitt opened up with noisy bursts.

"We're coming out and still taking fire, Klondike," Bonnie Sue Lead called. He and his copilot were no doubt leaning back in their armored seats, which provided side and rear protection. We could hear their crews still hammering behind the radio transmission. As I neared the bottom of my run, the first division of Frogs lifted. They flew straight ahead; lightened now, they gained altitude rapidly.

The second division of Bonnie Sue helos was well into its approach spiral. They rolled out of their turn and lined up with the zone for landing. These guys had puckered asses. Not knowing a zone is hot is different than knowing. They were flying into bullets. In that situation, an already high pulse rate goes into overdrive from a supershot of adrenaline. The helo gunner and crewchief would be cranking it out, the pilots well back in their seats. Everybody's heart would be pushing blood in a helluva hurry, but the guy at the controls still had to stick the landing. Even though he might want to add power and get the hell outta there, he had to land.

I finished my run at the time the second division of lift helos was flaring. "Klondike, Dash two is off target," I radioed. Motley made a similar call from the left side.

Dick threw my armament switches to safe and let me know. I added full power and pulled up and right. McDevitt and Storms kept squirting bursts into the trees and landforms below. Any area that looked like a hiding place became a target.

"Bonnie Sue Dash five is taking fire." Shit! We have a division of gunbirds shooting up the territory and the bastards down there aren't bothered, at least not enough. They just keep popping away. This was a good sign that there was a bunch of them; so many and so spread out that we can't keep them all under fire.

I gave a fleeting thought to the SOG guys. I was glad my ass was in the loud helo and not being unloaded for a recon mission. Indeed, maybe the recon was already a success. They'd discovered the exact location of a major NVA combat unit. It was at the LZ! Maybe the lead Frogs might have just made the landing, kept everybody aboard, and taken off. We could all just fly home, bring in some B-52 strikes, and go out later to count bodies. These thoughts were fleeting; I was still busy with the business of VMO.

Storms and McDevitt ceased their M-60 rattle as I turned downwind. It seemed quiet, with only the whine of our straining engine and the whop of blades. We flew opposite the direction on our run in and climbed again to 2,800 feet.

Olson started another run. The second group of Frogs settled for landing. Todt called from the left soon after.

"I think we were taking fire on that last pass, Lieutenant," McDevitt said into the ICS.

"You see anything, McDevitt?" I asked.

"No, sir, but I heard some snaps through all the noise, like near-miss rounds crackin' by."

"I ain't surprised. Bonnie Sue is sure takin' it. They're probably shootin' at all of us," I answered. We approached a point where we could turn back to the target area, though I'd be crowding it a little, and no doubt steep in my run. It was better to get back on the target than let Bonnie Sue come out of the zone without cover. I turned.

"Bonnie Sue Dash eight, blade strike. Over," came an excited call from the last 46 into the zone.

My mind went into mild shock. Blade strike is serious. Olson called off target; I lowered collective and aligned the target area through my sight reticule.

"Dash eight, Bonnie Sue Lead. Understand blade strike? Over," Carver voiced the question all were mulling.

"Dash eight, yeah. We caught a tree on the right. The front rotor's out of balance big time. Over." The pilot was almost shrill.

"Dash eight, can you fly the bird?" It was Carver again.

"No," came the answer. "We're rockin' to beat hell. We'd throw a blade or the transmission would come unhooked. Over."

"Bonnie Sue Lead, this is Dash five," interrupted Captain Trask, the division leader in the LZ. "We can bring the crew out. Over."

"Dash five, Bonnie Sue Lead, are you still takin' fire? Over."

"Yeah. We're takin' hits," Dash five answered.

"Dash eight, shut her down. Get away from the 46. Be ready to get in the SAR bird. Break. Dash five, get outta there. Copy?" Bonnie Sue leader radioed. Both eight and five acknowledged.

"Klondike Dash two in with guns," I called. Dick had thrown my armament switches and I was already in the run. I'd held my transmission while the Frogs developed a plan.

Down we went. I lined up the target area, centered the ball, leveled the wings, pulled the trigger, danced the red balls around in the area to the right side of the LZ, and listened to the M-60s racket. I glanced at the injured Frog near the end of my run. Its rotors were slowing to a stop. The downed 46 sat in the extreme right of the ridgeline LZ.

Three CH-46s pulled up, nosed over, and flew straight ahead out of the zone. A lonely Frog remained. I hammered away at the end of the run, as did the crewchief and gunner.

As we pulled up I heard, "Bonnie Sue Lead, this is Dash nine. Am I cleared in?" This was Exum, the SAR. He'd held in a three-thousand-foot orbit east of the LZ.

"Roger, Dash nine. This is Bonnie Sue Lead, you're cleared in. Break. Klondike Lead, cover nine. He's gonna get a helluva bunch of attention. Over."

"Roger, Bonnie Sue. We got him," answered Olson. But everyone knew Exum would be in great danger. Four targets had just been reduced to one.

I called off target, as did Motley in Klondike Dash four from south of the zone. We began our climb back to position.

"Dash nine is heading down."

I was at max power again. We separated from the terrain with as much haste as the engine and rotor could provide. I surrendered some airspeed to gain altitude more quickly so we'd get back in attack position. The magic numbers for a helo seemed to be eighty knots and eight hundred feet. Stay at or above both and your chances of being hit in the cabin area went way down. I climbed to the downwind leg for another run.

"You want this one, Dick?" I said into the ICS. I knew the answer before the words were out. Every pilot wants the stick and throttle.

"Sure." He got on the controls.

"You have the aircraft," I said from years of conditioning.

"I have the aircraft," he countered and he flew us down a course opposite our run-in heading, accelerating to 110 knots and settling at 2,800 feet again.

Andy called in hot again, as did Bob Todt from the left side. I imagined the CH-46 crew was out of the aircraft hugging the ground somewhere nearby. The SAR bird came down in a hurry. Exum was already turning through the ninety-degree position and heading in the direction of the LZ. Then came another surprise call.

"Bonnie Sue Dash nine to Lead, we've lost visual on the zone. Are we headin' okay? Over." Jesus! Jack and his crew had somehow lost the LZ. They were closing on the ground and going in the right direction, but in the search mode.

Dick had flown our Huey through the ninety-degree position and slowed to begin his run. I watched as Jack Exum's bird started fast taxiing at one hundred feet above the ground toward the landing site.

Olson and Todt called off target. Motley called in hot from south of the zone.

After a pause, Carver bailed Exum out: "Dash nine, this is Lead. You're headin' okay. The LZ is about one o'clock, three hundred meters. Over."

"Roger, Lead. We're lookin'," Exum answered. We could hear his crew's automatic weapons in background. He was in nearly the worst of situations, slow, close to the ground, a single target, and lots of assholes around with guns. The only way it could have been worse is if he were completely stopped, hovering.

"Klondike Dash two, in hot," Dick radioed and down he took us. Once again the Huey spewed tracers and ball ammo. Once again Storms and McDevitt fired out the sides.

"Dash nine is taking fire, but we have the zone," Exum radioed.

As Dick made his pass, Dash nine flared to kill airspeed and settled in the middle of the LZ. Then we passed him and he disappeared lower left. Dick added power and raised the Huey's nose. We started up and right again.

"Klondike Dash two. Off target," he radioed. Now was an especially bad time for Exum and his crew. No gunbird was heading down to provide fire support. Olson and Motley were not quite in position and we were just off target. As much as we tried to keep constant fire on a zone, it was usually not possible.

But shortly Andy called, "Klondike Lead, in with rockets." He was, as he suggested in the brief, conserving a little 7.62-ball ammo for eventualities. Following Andy's cue, Todt made a similar call from the south side of the target area.

"Dash nine has the pilots and gunner; the crewchief is missing. We're still taking fire. We'd better lift," he radioed. His voice was strained like that of Dash eight's pilot after the blade strike. Behind his transmission, we all heard the bark of his crew's automatic weapons.

"Roger Dash nine. Get out of there," Carver radioed. Dick had turned us ninety degrees to the right; through my door window I watched. Exum pulled in a bunch of power; first bushes and trees bent away from rotorwash then the Frog came out of the LZ. Andy and Todt were firing rocket pairs into the area north and south of the zone.

Dick put us back on altitude, flying again in the opposite direction of our attack heading.

"Bonnie Sue Lead to flight, let's go Nightrider Fox Mike. Over." Everyone acknowledged and switched to 42.6. Until that call, we'd all been on Bonnie Sue squadron common, 41.2.

Olson was off target. Dick called in hot with rockets as did Motley. Dick squirted pairs of 2.75-inch rockets, one from each pod, every time he pulled the trigger. I'd made the necessary switch changes on the lower center console.

Shit, I thought, maybe like everyone in the flight; we got a bird down, a crewmember on the ground, we landed a hundred plus guys in a hornet's nest, we're getting low on ball ammo, and Dick just squeezed off four pairs of rockets, over half our load, covering Exum. To make matters worse, we'd been out here a while and fuel was a concern. How we gonna save this day?

Carver made a call, "Nightrider, Bonnie Sue Lead. Over."

"Roger, Bonnie Sue, Nightrider reads you five square. Over," came an immediate answer.

"Nightrider, this is Bonnie Sue. We left a Marine down there. Is he with you? Over."

"Bonnie Sue, Nightrider. He's not right here but we have him. He's on the other side of the LZ with part of the team. He's okay. Over." Nightrider was almost whispering.

"Nightrider, Bonnie Sue. Roger. That's the crewchief of the downed bird. Are you guys in contact? Over."

"Bonnie Sue, Nightrider. Negative. They are close enough to shoot at the helos on approach and in the zone, but they're east of us. Over."

"Roger, Nightrider. You guys have any casualties we need to get out? Over."

"Negative, Bonnie Sue. But we have to move off the zone. Over."

"Roger, Nightrider. You got time for us to make another run for our Marine? Over."

"Negative, Bonnie Sue. We gotta move out. We'll keep him with us and our positions will be known through SOG channels. You'll have to get him later. Over."

"Roger, Nightrider. Keep him safe. We'll coordinate a pickup." After a pause, "I guess maintaining security around our 46 is out of the question? Over."

"We can't stay here, Bonnie Sue. We're movin' out. Sorry 'bout the helo. Over."

"Okay, Nightrider. We'll be in touch. Bonnie Sue Lead. Out."

There was a bit of finality in this transmission, partly because it likely meant the end of a CH-46. It would certainly be stripped of its automatic weapons and ammunition, and, if not destroyed, it would be booby-trapped. Retrieval would be a problem in simple circumstances; but with NVA units in the area, it might not be worth the cost in men and machines.

"Bonnie Sue Lead to flight. Check in with battle damage. Over." Here came a litany of woes. No aircraft experienced major system malfunction, but all helos except one had sustained punctures in the cabin area. Who knew what else might turn up on postflight inspection?

Andy asked the Klondike birds for a similar report. Nothing was registering on any of the instruments and at least there were no holes in our cockpit-cabin areas. Like Bonnie Sue however, we'd only know after landing.

"Bonnie Sue flight, this is Lead. Let's go to Phu Bai. We'll stay up Nightrider freq for now. Over." They rippled acknowledgement over the FM.

Andy called the Klondike birds. "Klondike flight, form up loose. Over." We had him in sight. Dick pulled in some power and moved in Andy's direction. We flew east, destination Phu Bai.

I energized the floor button ICS switch. "Well, guys, I doubt if we'll be goin' to Ky Ha today. There's a Marine out there, and a Frog, and I wonder if Nightrider can stay away from the bad guys. We'll see, but I bet we're comin' back."

Dick flew us to Phu Bai. We chatted a little, but a sense of foreboding descended. Yep, we'd be going back. We knew it without being told. After landing, refueling in the pits, and taxiing into our spots, we all looked the Huey over on postflight. The only round we'd taken was through a skid tube, near its front on the copilot's side. Sergeant Storms noticed it first.

"Lieutenant Boston, ya got a near miss, sir. Check out your skid tube when you dismount. Two feet closer to centerline and it woulda hit your seat," Storms said this just before unplugging his helmet. Then he went to the front of the Huey to catch a rotor blade on the shutdown sequence.

Later from ready room chatter, we learned only Motley and I among the Hueys had taken rounds. The Frogs had all been hit. Exum's bird had eighty-six wounds in the cabin area, forty-three holes coming in and forty-three going out. It was the worst hosing I knew about in my tour. We were all amazed that the crewchief and gunner were not hit. Lesson: Don't lose sight of the LZ, especially when you're close to the ground. Air taxiing in the search mode is a bad idea in Indian Country.

One of the lift pilots told Andy he'd seen so much shit coming at him, he was reminded of over-Germany flak from World War II films. The Frogs got most of the attention, as usual. Some of their birds were laced by big holes, the kind made by 12.7-mm. These are similar to U.S. 50-caliber in size and spew iridescent green tracers every third round, not every fifth like ours. That we escaped without any helos shot down was miraculous. Our only loss was self-inflicted.

Metalsmiths would be busy making skin patches and riveting them in place, but not until these helos returned to their home bases. The HMM-163 Ridgerunner metalsmiths at Phu Bai had enough to do just patching their own birds.

The "Runners" were permanently assigned to Phu Bai, and any helo action north of the Hai Van Pass went first to them, which meant they were busy bubbas, maybe overcommitted. Only if they couldn't provide did the work filter south to Marble Mountain and Ky Ha. The Ridgerunners and my buddy, First Lt. Pete Lepo, were so busy that eventually Provisional Marine Air Group 39 was formed and stationed north of Phu Bai at Quang Tri. That came later in 1967; VMO-6 became part of that group. But in March of that year the Ridgerunners were going at it by their lonesome-assed selves most of the time. They were busy, and, since the enemy was almost always NVA, it was especially dangerous.

Nightrider briefed the SOG headquarter folks on what happened and Captains Carver and Olson did the same up the Marine Corps chain of command: downed bird, crewchief in the weeds, SOG guys on the move, and many bad guys just east of the LZ. Predictably, we were all told to hang loose while they considered options; calling it a day and going back to Ky Ha was not among them.

"We just have to wait and see what's up," Olson said in a ready room pow-wow with the Klondike pilots.

"I've been told," he continued, "to have the crews ready, to rearm and preflight the birds for quick reaction to whatever. The ball-buster is we're supposed to get shitty weather later today. It might even be too shitty for helos. We'll see. That's all I have. Any questions?"

We all looked at each other; no one had any.

"Okay, stay handy. Hooches, here, chow hall, or at the birds. I'll keep you up to speed when I find out anything. Make sure the crews know what's up. Anybody needs me, I'll be here, at the hooch, or at chow." Andy was finished.

We broke up. "I'll go out and chat with Storms and McDevitt, Dick. No need of you coming along. I just want to make sure they know everything and see if anything more has turned up on the helo. See ya at the hooch or wherever."

"Okay, Dave. I'm headin' to the hooch. I'll be there unless I'm at chow." He glanced at his watch. "It's about 1100; it'll open soon."

"Alright. Later." We split. I headed for the flight line and our helo where it was squatting on the metal matting one hundred yards away. McDevitt and Storms were sitting inside the cabin shooting the shit.

"Lieutenant Ballentine," Sergeant Storms greeted me. "What's going on, sir?"

"It's a wait an' see scenario, Sarg. The heavies on the Army and the Marine side are cogitatin'. We ain't headin' for Ky Ha, but I guess you guys figured that. The Captain's stayin' on top of stuff and will pass the word when he gets it."

"Yes, sir." Storms paused, shifting gears. "The Huey looks fine except for that one ding. We ain't rearmed yet. The ordnance guy will be over shortly. We've gone over the guns and cleaned 'em. Corporal Croft is with us; he's the gunner on Lieutenant Todt's bird. He'll be coming 'round to make sure the pods and guns check out when we rearm. We want these damn things to bark when we pull the trigger." Sergeant Storms smiled a little. Like all experienced crewchiefs, he figured he could do about anything, but some stuff was left to the "experts" in specialties—Corporal Croft from ordnance, for instance.

"The helo though," he continued, "she's lookin' good, sir."

I glanced down at the skid tube. It had two holes at the top of the its curved part, near a flattened surface where the copilot placed his foot before swinging through the door into his seat. The hole under the tube was clean; the one coming out the top was blossomed, ragged, and angry. After a while in war, a person becomes a little matter of fact about being shot at. Though it was always exciting, we all lost the "are you shitting me" surprise response when a helo was damaged. Whenever someone was hurt or killed was an exception. Then we were sobered, each driven to private thoughts, reminded of the nature of our business; we mused about uncertainties and the eternal. But holes in helos happened with enough frequency that they lost some of their psychic impact. They became curiosities to be avoided when possible, but it was not always possible. Everybody got holed.

"Well," I said, "I'll let you guys know when we get news. I guess I'm sayin' the obvious, but one of you needs to be at the bird or hooch and that person needs to be able to get the other one ricky-tick. [USMC for quickly.] Who knows when decisions will be made, or what they'll be."

As I said this, I felt a little sheepish. They were way ahead of me. Both of these guys were great Marines, each with a keen sense of responsibility. I sorta knew they'd stay handy, but I didn't need to be searching the PX or barbershop if we got a decision to move.

"We got it, Lieutenant. One of us will be here or at the hooch." Storms paused. "Somebody said weather might be movin' in. You heard anything, sir?"

"Yeah, we may have to deal with weather. Could they make this a little more fuckin' interesting?" I drifted into sarcasm.

"We can usually get under the shit. It will have to be real crappy for us to be on a weather hold, but it could happen. It's another wait an' see thing."

We chatted a bit more; then I bid them good-bye and headed for the ready room. As I crossed the flight line, I glanced at the sky. We were high overcast. The sun was no longer peeking through, and it seemed colder.

I ducked through the flap of the ready room tent; a few guys were hanging around, Olson among them. "Anything yet, sir?"

"Naw, we're just waitin', Dave."

"I chatted with my crew, so they're spooled up and standin' by for whatever, whenever. They're rearmin' the birds, but it's a work in progress." I paused. "Unless you got somethin', guess I'll head for the hooch, maybe chow."

"Okay, I'll pass the word as soon as anything comes in. See ya later," he offered and turned back to join a small group of Bonnie Sue captains sitting nearby.

The day progressed in anticipation. The weather slowly closed in, the high clouds thickening. By 1600 we were solid overcast with the ceiling down to eight hundred feet and lowering. Light rain fell. At 1700, the pilots were gathered again in the ready room.

CHAPTER 21

Extraction I

Major Spencer started and he was to the point. "Our team is in contact and has been off and on since we put 'em in. It's not lookin' good. They've sustained casualties and they're compromised. They've asked to be extracted and headquarters agrees, but the crappy weather we have here is also out in the mountains. We probably can't get to 'em. We may be a little better off in the morning, so we'll go then. The team'll have to hang on a while and they know it."

"They've relocated northwest. They are now at DX718165 and will stay there, unless driven elsewhere by the NVA. They're still up 41.2 FM. We'll tell you if that changes, and it probably will. I'll let Captain Carver give you the aviation piece of the brief. Captain Carver." The SOG major nodded at the Bonnie Sue captain. He stood and faced the pilots.

"Okay, guys, here's the story. We have high overcast and low overcast. It's six hundred feet give or take now, but may lift a little by morning. Cloud thickness of this lower layer is about four thousand feet. We can fly up through this shit, break out on top in between layers, rendezvous, fly out to the area, and look for a hole. If there is one, we'll let down through it and try to get Nightrider. If there's no hole, well, we'll come home and shoot individual IFR [Instrument Flight Rules] approaches back into Phu Bai."

"We can either use the TACAN approach here or get a GCA, whatever approach control wants us to use, and it may be some of each. We're not going to try to fly formation in the clag. Once more," he paused for effect, "if the weather is shitty, and it's projected to be, we'll make individual takeoffs and climb outs. Phu Bai Departure Control will assign us climb-out headings and takeoff intervals. Once we break out between layers, head for the eight-mile fix on the two seven zero radial, Phu Bai TACAN. We'll form up there and head out as a flight of eight. Once our birds are off the deck, Klondike will follow. I've already coordinated this with Captain Olson." He nodded at our cluster of eight Huey pilots.

"Turn up and fly out on squadron common. I'll switch the flight to Nightrider freq when we get near their area. Our new mission number is 1623. Any questions?" The room was silent.

"Okay, here are copies of the approach plates for Phu Bai." A lieutenant stood on cue and passed out sheets of paper sized to fit a military kneeboard. Most of us already had these, but we all took a new one. Sometimes they made small changes; it was best to keep current.

"The Phu Bai freqs you'll need for getting back in here are on these approach plates. Departure Control is 261.4. Got it? 261.4. We'll turn up squadron common and Phu Bai Tower. They'll tell us when to shift to Departure Control for our individual takeoffs and climb outs. We'll be turned up and ready to taxi at 0800. We'll meet here again at 0700 for updates or adjustments. My guess is we'll be IFR in the morning just like they're forecasting." Once again he paused. "Questions?"

Silence. The pilots were letting it sink in. We all had new TACAN Number One and Number Two approach plates into Phu Bai. We had the Departure Control, Approach Control, squadron common, Tower, and Nightrider frequencies, and we had the mission: Get Nightrider.

"Okay, gentlemen." (I usually smiled a little inside when anyone referred to me as a "gentleman." Thanks to the badgering of Mom and my high school sweetheart, Jeannie Corlew, I managed with forks, elbows, and tooth-picks in public, but I was usually more comfortable eating over oil-cloth than linen. Though Carver'd used "gentlemen," I wasn't smiling that after-noon. I was all ears.) "That's it for now. If we can get out, we'll go. We'll hope the weather breaks up a bit here and especially inland."

Carver paused, but was not finished. "It will take us at least twenty-four minutes to get our twelve birds up through the clouds. That's once we're on the runway. Then we'll rendezvous and fly out together. We have enough fuel to get there, get them, get home, and shoot our approaches. But it'll be close; because of IFR sequencing, almost half our gas will be used just get-ting in and out of Phu Bai." Carver paused. "Okay. That's it. Unless you got questions, see you at 0700."

But before the pilots started scooting chairs, he raised his voice and said, "Oh, sorry. Captain Olson, you got anything from Klondike?" He looked at Andy.

Andy stood. "I do. My squadron tells me, not twenty minutes ago, that it needs to have Lieutenant Todt's section back at Ky Ha by COB tomorrow. That won't matter if we can get Nightrider out tomorrow; but if this thing gets drawn out, we'll be down to my section of guns. And a gun section is light for this job. Maybe you guys can weigh in and lever this thing better than I could. That's all I have." Olson eased back into his chair.

Carver, still standing from his previous speech, furrowed his brow. "We need to look into that," he said slowly. "We took a pretty good hosing on the insert with four gunbirds working the area and our own crews were hammering. Getting these guys out with only a section of guns will increase the danger. I'll go through my squadron and SOG to see if we can change that." Everyone murmured assent.

"Okay. We're done, gents. Make sure your crews know what's up." Chairs began to move; pilots stood and the typical hubbub ensued as it usually does after briefings and meetings.

Everyone understood; tomorrow we go into the clouds. Then out to get Nightrider and become targets for the NVA in so doing. It's what we did. There was little jocularity that evening.

For openers, most helo guys don't like IFR. We did it, but we're used to being under the clouds, not in them. Most of our IFR was simulated, using blinders on our helmets so we could only see cockpit instruments. We all knew how, but it was typically only practice. Jet pilots fly IFR all the time. It's how they get from one place to another. But helo jocks don't; we just flew under the clouds. At Andy's insistence, on arrival we'd all shot GCAs into Phu Bai. He must have been intuitive. Tomorrow we'd be brushing off our skills and launching into the clouds, an unsettling thought, though like the others, I was trained for it. This reaction to IFR flying was the response of a junior aviator. Maybe I'd have been more comfortable a few years later with more instrument experience under my belt.

Dick and I went to the crew's hooch after the meeting. Corporal McDevitt was there; Sergeant Storms had gone to chow. We told McDevitt what we knew and asked that the bird be ready by 0715. We mentioned we'd be in the clouds, if we could launch at all. But we were going to try to get the SOG guys. We also told him that Todt's section might be heading home after tomorrow, whether or not we were successful getting Nightrider.

"That's not too good, sir," was Corporal McDevitt's response. He knew, like we all did, what halving the gun support might mean. He told us the bird was rearmed, the guns had been cleaned, and the helo was ready. We parted. Dick and I went to chow.

The evening was unremarkable: food, a shower, a beer, and the sack. It was cool to the point of cold, unusual for Vietnam in March. The weather was wet, raining off and on with a heavy mist. In short, the weather was shitty, the kind nobody likes, especially pilots who like to fly with some visibility. I didn't sleep well. I was chilled, but wouldn't have slept well if I'd been warm and the weather'd been super. I knew there were many bad guys where we were headed. They were well trained and well armed, and there's no such thing as "cover and concealment" in a big, noisy helo. The world knows you're coming. If we could get to Nightrider, the world would erupt again in shooting from both sides.

It's one thing to know you might be shot at. It's another to know it with certainty. You stare at your mortality a bit more. I believe I understand what the Marines and Army guys experienced the night before the landing at Okinawa and Iwo and elsewhere in World War II campaigns. This reaction must be timeless, uniform among Roman Legions, Napoleon's Grand Armée, the Rebs and Union soldiers, and the guys at Verdun. It's a warrior's lot.

After we'd turned out the lights I stared into the darkness overhead. I listened to the rain on our corrugated metal roof, felt my heart pulse slowly in my chest, and thought. Tomorrow my comrades and I would stand and deliver, as military men had since earliest times. Technology differed, but little else. It was Waterloo or Hastings, Guadalcanal or Sebastopol. It was war. Sleep finally came, as it does to all tired young animals.

I was up early for my cold-water shave, my ten-dip mantra. After breakfast, Dick and I and the rest of the pilots eased into the ready room. We were seated by 0700. Carver stood up and our final briefing began. It was a review of the previous afternoon's information. Nightrider's frequency had changed, which we all noted on our kneeboards. The weather was crappy, but we could expect to break out between cloud layers. We would execute individual takeoffs and climb outs to VFR conditions about four thousand feet overhead. We were to collect at a Phu Bai TACAN fix to the west, fly out as a gaggle of twelve, and try to find a hole in the clouds somewhere around Nightrider. Then get through the hole, pick up the team, climb back out of the hole, come home, and shoot individual instrument approaches into Ph Bai. Piece of cake!

When Carver was finished with his review, one of the Bonnie Sue captains asked, "What about the downed 46?"

"We're leavin' it," came the short answer from Carver. "At least for now. Our priority is recovering Nightrider; the senior guys are considering when we might secure the area so the riggers can get the bird ready for external lift. Today we're trying for the people. I'm sure we'll get more on this later."

"One last thought. There'll be no designated SAR bird going along. If someone goes down out there, we'll have to get the crew and troops ourselves, without SAR help. If it's after the pickup, it's gonna require several birds going down, each pulling out as many as his helo can lift. We'll maintain division integrity for SAR purposes. If someone in my division goes in, my division will get them. If it's from the second division, then the second division leader, Captain Trask, will coordinate and execute the pickup within his division. Got it?" We did.

"One more thing, and this is a reminder. If, heaven forbid, you have to shoot an auto in or into the clouds, watch your RADALT for your flare altitude. Check you TACAN fix on your way down. After you're clear of the bird, if you clear the bird, call us on your survival radio with the TACAN radial and distance. But gettin' you will be a problem unless the weather breaks or until it does. Stay near the helo if you can. We can spot that better."

The SAR SOP for Klondike was section integrity. So we didn't need to talk about it. If I went in, Olson was my savior and vice versa. The same was true of Todt's section.

We broke up and walked to waiting helos and crews.

After a quick huddle with Storms and McDevitt, I signed off the helo. Then Dick and I preflighted. An uneventful start and run up followed. We checked in with Andy on the FM and listened as the Bonnie Sue helos came on line and checked in with Carver. Then, "Phu Bai Tower, Bonnie Sue Lead, taxi for takeoff and IFR departure; flight of eight CH-46s; mission 1623. Over."

The flight of eight was cleared onto the runway, heading northwest. Then Tower switched them to Phu Bai Departure Control for the individual takeoffs.

"Phu Bai Departure Control, Bonnie Sue Lead ready for departure. Over."

"Roger, Bonnie Sue Lead, you're cleared to VFR on top. Maintain runway heading until passing one thousand feet. Then turn left to heading three hundred degrees. Expect VFR approximately four thousand feet. Squawk 1412. Maintain Departure Control frequency. Call VFR on top. Over." (Transponders are well known to aviators. It's electronic gear that responds to ground radar inquiry and allows the ground control agency to identify, from coded pulses on a radar screen, one aircraft from another. You dialed in the number of the assigned "squawk" on the transponder control box, squawk, 1412 for the Lead helo, 1414 for Dash two, and 1416 for Dash three, and so forth. The ground guys could then watch on a radar screen each individual helo.)

"Roger, Departure, Bonnie Sue Lead to maintain runway heading until one thousand feet; then left to three hundred degrees, squawk 1412, remain Departure freq, and call on top. Over."

"Read back correct, Bonne Sue Lead. You're cleared for takeoff." The first of eight CH-46s pulled into a hover, nosed over, and started down the runway. Carver disappeared into the soup at three hundred feet.

Two minutes later, Bonnie Sue Dash two took off with a different "squawk" and a different heading after one thousand feet. After six were airborne, Olson called for our taxi onto the runway. When all the Bonnie Sue birds were swallowed into the gray, low clouds, our Klondike birds were sequenced into the clag at two-minute intervals, just as the Frogs were before.

I accelerated to eighty knots, held that speed, and raised the nose. We flew up into the gray. Early in our climb I allowed my right "wing" to dip which induced a slight right turn, away from runway heading. I experienced mild vertigo. I simply did not fly instruments much and was not great at keeping my instrument scan pattern going: airspeed, wings level, nose slightly up on the gyro-horizon, arrow up on vertical speed indicator, ball centered, power up.

"Dave, you're drifting right," Dick said calmly into the ICS.

"Okay," I responded, but in my mild vertigo, it felt just right to be ten to twelve degrees right wing down. I fought it and forced myself to level the wings on the gyro-horizon. After thirty seconds or so, everything felt sorta right. I got my scan working better; we held heading, gained altitude, and were stable at eighty knots.

Passing through one thousand feet, we turned to an assigned heading and continued in the cool gray. Nothing outside the cockpit mattered, just the instrument panel and my response to any indication that we were not on heading, at eighty knots, wings level, ball in the center, and climbing. We knew the Bonnie Sue birds were out on top of the clouds from radio calls.

We were in the clouds for six minutes. It seemed longer, but predictably the clouds first lightened, then we flew out to a wide vista and openness. Puffy, gray beneath us, and high, thin overcast well above. I turned left and headed for our rendezvous point at eight-mile fix on the two seven zero TACAN radial.

We saw the other helos, dots and silhouettes against the clouds. Shit, training is wonderful; you train, you train, you practice, and then you do. You're no longer a trainee. I was happy to be out of the gray stuff, even though I knew I'd be heading back in soon. Like most folks, I'm most comfortable with the familiar.

"Phu Bai Departure, Klondike Dash two is VFR on top and has a tally on the other helos. Over," I radioed. Departure Control acknowledged. Andy, clearly distinguishable from the Frogs, was nearing the CH-46s. I headed his way. We were at 4,600 feet.

"Dash two, Klondike Lead has you in sight. Over," Andy called. Within six minutes, Todt's section was also above the clouds and closing in on the rendezvous fix.

Out we went. Beneath was solid overcast. Although Bonnie Sue Lead switched us to Nightrider frequency and made contact, even though they could hear us overhead, there was no hole anywhere, no getting down. We loitered for thirty-five to forty minutes, drilling around, four gunbirds, eight CH-46s, burning gas, waiting for an opening. Nothing.

Eventually Carver, with some resignation in his voice, realizing we'd all have to shoot individual approaches back into Phu Bai, called it a day. He contacted Nightrider and provided the news.

"Nightrider, Bonnie Sue Lead. We can't stick around longer; we don't have the gas. If the weather breaks out here let your headquarters know immediately. Maybe we can give it another go later today. Over."

"Roger, Bonnie Sue Lead. We'll call if this starts breakin'. Thanks for tryin'. Talk to you later. Nightrider, out."

We left the area, flying east toward Phu Bai.

Phu Bai Approach Control cleared the flight for individual GCAs and brought us down at three-minute intervals. More than a half hour was required to get twelve birds on the deck. We landed to the northwest, the same direction we'd taken off.

GCAs are simple compared to other options; you establish radio contact with a controller who watches you on a radar screen. He gives you headings to fly, tells you when to begin your "normal rate of descent," and whether you are on, above, or below the glide path and left or right of course. You listen and do, and after about eight minutes of farting around where you'd rather not be, that is in the clouds, you ease out the bottom, all lined up nicely with the runway. After we were down, we taxied to the fuel pits, topped off, then went to our parking spots and shut down.

After my bird was still and during the postflight, I said, "Well, guys we'll do this again and probably keep doing it until those SOG guys are out. I'll get information to you as soon as we know something. Lieutenant Todt and his section may be headin' back to Ky Ha. It might just be Captain Olson's Huey and ours. I guess you can just preflight her again, Sergeant Storms."

"Yes, sir, I'll look her over. McDevitt or I will either be here or at the hooch if you need us. I'll find you if I discover anything bad on post or preflight," Storms answered. We talked a little more. The gloomy weather was a downer, gray and drippy. But the impending unfinished mission also hung heavy. It was necessary, but not a joyous prospect.

The four-letter word "duty" is one of the most powerful in the language. Ask an audience, "Who'd like to go get shot at?" and only a fool would stand. But bathe the audience in a sense of duty, pose the question differently, and few would remain seated.

Perhaps the apogee of life is to have and fulfill duty. Without it, pallor seeps in, prevails. Military organizations in war have prominent, pronounced, and serious duties. The sense of responsibility to 'brothers" (and now sisters), to nation, and service is huge, and, when the duty is discharged, military people feel a genuine and heightened sense of contribution as well as pride at living up to demanding institutional expectations often in threatening environments. After war, nothing is as rewarding in such a pronounced way. It's because few activities are as challenging, nor do they have a keen sense of duty and contribution attached. Duty, contribution, and challenge provide psychic income. Since Vietnam I've often wondered, "Where's the meat?" There ain't much.

The weather continued to be lousy for the rest of the day, three-hundred- to four-hundred-foot ceilings at Phu Bai, and ground-hugging over Nightrider. All efforts to keep the second gunbird section failed. At 1600, Bob Todt took his helos south. They stayed under the overcast and swung off the coast just north of Danang, not chancing the Hai Van Pass in crappy weather. (More than one helo has smeared itself along the ground just below the summit of a pass from a pilot's conviction that he could "get through.") Then they drove south along the coast past Marble Mountain to Ky Ha. I figured it was down to Olson, me, and our crews. I was wrong again.

Although we had ready room meetings two more times that day, the best we could do was wait until tomorrow and hope for the best. Dick and I kept the crew informed, and we hunkered down for another night.

In the morning three Army UH-1B gunbirds arrived. Enough hell had been raised and concern voiced that the seniors cut three helos out of Pleiku, a hundred and fifty miles south. They'd made it partway the day before and came taxiing in from a Danang overnighter at 0730. Their call sign was Gunslinger, and they were great guys, full of piss and vinegar, loose, friendly, and led by a first lieutenant. Except for the lieutenant, the pilots were warrant officers. If I'd been an Army pilot, I'd have been a warrant. I felt perfectly at home with them.

This day brought a new wrinkle. The weather was still not good, but the commands decided we should reposition to Khe Sanh, a beleaguered airstrip in the extreme northwest corner of South Vietnam with a Marine infantry regiment dug in on its perimeter. (Much has been written about Khe Sanh. It was truly a place of war. Death and heroism attended daily activity. Give a nod to any who served there. I met one vet from that corner of the war who said he'd made no important decisions since he was nineteen and a fireteam leader there. Oh, he'd since made plenty of decisions, but none of them carried life and death as a consequence. After Khe Sanh, all was pretty easy for him.) Khe Sanh was closer to Nightrider than was Phu Bai. If the weather broke, we could make the extraction more quickly, at least that was the thinking.

We briefed, flew up through the clouds at Phu Bai, once again on individual departures, then out to Khe Sanh on top of the cloud cover, and shot individual GCAs to the Khe Sanh runway.

Because the Army crews were not instrument-qualified, they flew to Khe Sanh visually! They said they'd get there by just following Route 9, which ran west to Khe Sanh out of Dong Ha. At this announcement, the Marine pilots sorta looked at each other with the, "Ya gotta be shittin' me" expression. The weather was not good and especially bad at Khe Sanh. But that's exactly what the Army bubbas did. Even though they were virtually air-taxiing over the road for part of their journey, they got there. The old adage that IFR means "I follow roads," was perfectly true for these guys. They made it happen Army-pilot style. We were impressed.

We farted around at Khe Sanh, but the weather did not break. Shrill words filtered down to us from Nightrider. They had wounded and now KIAs, and they needed, at the least, resupply. We could do nothing. The day was grim; our people needed us and we were trapped by shitty weather.

The Vietnamese Air Force came to the rescue. Early in the afternoon a single CH-34 arrived. The crew had been sent to try to get resupplies to Nightrider. They'd volunteered for a low-level, under-the-clouds attempt from Khe Sanh to the SOG location. Most of us were amazed at this, but these pilots were handpicked. They knew the country. C rations, ammo, medical supplies, and water were loaded. Off they went, single bird, below a low overcast in mountainous terrain, searching for Nightrider. Our collective opinion was skeptical.

An hour later they returned smiling. They'd found the team, kicked out the supplies, and taken holes; some were made by 12.7-mm. They'd not be going back, and recommended we not go either, but their mission was a success. Nightrider would not starve, dehydrate, or be easily overrun from lack of ammunition. They'd have to hold out longer, but some tools had been provided.

Later that afternoon, we flew out of Khe Sanh and back to Phu Bai, again, up through and down through clouds. We were getting good at this. The Army jocks followed the road again and beat us to the fuel pits.

CHAPTER 22

Extraction II

We did not go back to Khe Sanh the next day, and we were still on weather hold.

Mid-morning, Andy found Dick and me, "Group wants us to take a 53 pilot (CH-53s were the Marine Corps' heavy lift helos) out to look over the downed Frog. In this shitty weather, I doubt if we'll be able to see it. But Group wants us to try. They need to know how hard it'll be to retrieve the 46. No need in both of us goin'. I'll take him out. Probably be gone about an hour. We'll take a look, if the weather lets us. I'll launch about 1030."

"Okay, sir. We'll be here," I answered, thinking Andy'd be able to give us a PIREP (pilot report) on weather when he returned.

He launched and, as he predicted, returned before midday. A solid pattern of low clouds covered the west as it did Phu Bai. He'd been unable to get beneath it. Retrieval assessment for the Frog would have to wait.

The weather guessers were guardedly optimistic that the whiskey–x-ray was improving. It didn't look any better at Phu Bai, but word from Nightrider late that day was that a few holes were opening in the mountains.

The next morning we were briefed again, a brief nearly identical to previous ones, except the extraction grid coordinates had moved and Nightrider had changed Fox Mike frequencies again. We waited until afternoon to give the weather even more time to improve.

The Army gunbirds had no road to follow. Willing though they were and as welcome as their support would have been, they could not join us. This would be a Marine effort and our two gunbirds would have to do.

At 1430, March 6, 1967, eight HMM-265, CH-46s, and two VMO-6 armed Hueys taxied, took off into low overcast sky, climbed to four thousand feet, and popped out on top again in between cloud layers. We rendezvoused and headed west. As we flew, we saw first breaks in the clouds, then huge swaths of exposed terrain. Because I was a helo guy, I began to think we were way too damn high. I liked terrain plus one thousand, maybe fifteen hundred, feet max. This shit was for the jets. I liked to see individual trees instead of expanses of green. As usual nobody consulted or cleared anything with me.

We drilled out; Andy and I eased ahead of Bonnie Sue again. We knew we'd go down and snoop before the Frogs landed. The weather had given us a break, now if the NVA would, all would be well.

"Bonnie Sue Lead to flight. Switch Nightrider. Over." During the brief, Andy'd told us to follow Carver's radio instructions on frequency shifts. We all acknowledged. Dick swiveled some knobs and held out his right hand, thumb up.

The flight, including me, rippled in on the new Fox Mike frequency. I felt a hair lonesome when just two Klondike birds responded. I liked it better when the other section was with us. It's partly the old safety in numbers idea, but we could keep a lot more heads down with two more gunbirds.

"Bonnie Sue flight, let's lose some of this altitude. Over," Carver called. I liked that and I expect most of the guys did. Andy had already led our gun section lower. Without a call he reduced power and dropped farther. I was loose as hell at Olson's right rear and followed suit. We leveled at about 2,800 feet MSL, 700 feet above the high points of undulating terrain. The RADALT needle swung up and down with the varying ground clearance.

"Nightrider, Bonnie Sue Lead. Over."

Nothing. A minute passed; Carver repeated his call.

"Bon . . . Su . . . der. Over," came a broken answer. First nothing, then something meant we were closing. Trees and terrain interfered; soon we could expect good comm.

"Roger, Nightrider. Bonnie Sue Lead. You're broken, but readable. We'll call again in a minute. Over." We kept drilling.

Before Carver tried again we heard, "Bonnie Sue Lead, this is Nightrider. We can hear your helos. Over." This was both good and bad, but either way, it was a helo crew's lot. Everyone could hear us. A bunch of guys named Nuygen were getting off their asses, grabbing their AK-47s and heavier shit, chambering rounds, and searching the skies to the east. Officers and NCOs were issuing instructions. Here we go again.

"Roger, Nightrider. Bonnie Sue Lead, reading you five square now. We're estimating your position in five. Do you have an LZ, and what's the enemy situation? Over."

"Bonnie Sue, Nightrider. We have a zone at grids DX743297. It's a treeless ridge like the original LZ. We've had light contact off and on this morning, but nothing for the last couple of hours. We have fifteen WIAs and three KIAs and five are missing. We have a perimeter around the LZ. Over." The pilots in each helo were checking the grids transmitted by Nightrider against those briefed. They had not changed.

"Roger, Nightrider. Understand a ridgeline LZ at DX743297, and you have WIA, KIA, and a perimeter. Can you tell us approximate wind direction and speed? We'd like to avoid smoke. Over."

"Bonnie Sue Lead, Nightrider. The wind is easterly. We have some sway in the treetops. I'm guessin' ten miles an hour. Over."

"Roger, Nightrider, ten from the east. I think we have your LZ in sight. Are you broken into sticks for load? Over."

"Bonnie Sue, Nightrider's in sticks. We'll put WIAs and KIAs in the first two birds. Over."

"Roger, Nightrider. Break. Klondike Lead, you guys have the zone? Can you take a look? Over."

Andy was way ahead on this, as were Dick and I. Klondike SOP was always to "take a look." Dick was flying at the time. I'd pen-circled the zone on my map at the brief and found it on the approaching terrain. I gave Dick a thumbs-up. I pointed to the ground well out the front left through our Plexiglas windscreen."Got it, Dick?" I said into the ICS.

"I guess that's it about a mile or so out there," he answered.

"Yeah, that's gotta be it." Once again the Frogs had a small, but usable landing area perched atop a ridge.

"Bonnie Sue, Klondike Lead. We have the zone and will make a recon pass. We can head in now, if you'd like. Over," Andy answered.

"I'll take it, Dick," I said into the ICS and we went through the standard "You have the aircraft; I have the aircraft" sequence. Once on the controls, I reduced power and held altitude. I slowed to put tactical separation between Andy and me.

He pulled ahead. I surveyed the zone as we closed. It looked small, but lift guys lived by judging zone size from altitude. Carver would make the right call.

"Klondike Lead, Bonnie Sue. We'll overfly the zone and keep going west a minute, then do a one-eighty and land into the wind, headin' east. Looks like another four-bird LZ. Will that give you time to recon and get in position for support? Over."

"Roger, Bonnie Sue," Andy responded. "We can recon and be ready. Break. Dash two, after our pass, stay low. Look west a bit, then climb out. I'll cover the north side; you take the south. No shootin' around the zone. I'm heading down. Over." He nosed over, not in a gun run, but to recon. But recon could be converted to ordnance delivery with the flick of a switch.

"Klondike Lead, Dash two copies. Recon the zone and to the west; cover south on the Bonnie Sue approach. Over," I answered and crossed to the left of Andy's descending Huey. We had a quarter-mile separation and were closing on the ridgeline.

I held my altitude for a couple of heartbeats, then, "Klondike Dash two's in for recon." I lowered my power setting slightly and eased the stick forward, keeping my speed up, not slowing like I would have before an ordnance delivery run. Down we went; the terrain became more distinct.

"We set for guns, Dick?" I asked.

"You're ready," he answered.

On our way down I said, "Don't shoot around the zone, guys, but protect us away from it. Keep your eyes peeled."

"Okay, sir," answered Storms. McDevitt responded as well. They were standing in the doors hunched over their M-60s, alert, ready to start slamming.

We flew over the left side of the LZ at ninety knots with fifty feet of terrain clearance. It was quiet. No shots and no movement. We drove west, straight ahead, the direction from which the Frogs would approach.

"Klondike Lead is climbing right. No activity. Over," Olson radioed.

"Roger, Klondike Lead," Carver responded.

I started up and left. Dick threw the switch putting our guns safe. Storms and McDevitt reported they'd seen nothing. I radioed, "Klondike Dash two climbin' left. LZ's quiet. Over."

"Roger, Dash two," answered Carver. "Break. Bonnie Sue flight will make division landings to the east. Break. Nightrider, are your people ready? We want this fast. Over."

"Roger, Bonnie Sue, Nightrider's more than ready. We'll be movin' to you on touchdown. The first two sticks will be slower with the KIAs and WIAs. We're in a tight perimeter at the LZ. Over."

"Roger, Nightrider, Bonnie Sue Lead is heading down in about thirty seconds. Break. Klondike, you ready? Over."

Andy had gained attack altitude and I was closing. We'd each turned slightly away from the LZ, Andy north, me south, and climbed at max power. Andy was ahead; he'd be ready first.

"Klondike Lead, Roger, Bonnie Sue. Break. Klondike Dash two, you gonna be ready? Over."

"Roger, Lead. We'll be in position," I radioed. Although we weren't quite in position, I knew we would be before the lift birds neared the zone. Still in a climb, I began turning back toward the zone; I lined the bird up for a gun pass south of the approach corridor. I lowered the sight reticule from its stowed position overhead.

"Sergeant Storms, the LZ will pass on your side. No shootin' close to it," I said into the ICS. "And, guys, everywhere else is a target if it moves, shoots, or looks suspicious."

"Bonnie Sue Lead is inbound to the LZ," Carver radioed from the first division. I was almost ready, but it would do. I made last adjustments and brought the Huey around to the target line.

Within five seconds Andy radioed, "Klondike Lead is in hot."

"Let's go hot, Dick."

Boston threw a console switch. "You're ready," he answered.

"Klondike Dash two is in. Over," I radioed and down we came. I passed south of the descending 46s and began spraying red-orange balls first along their approach corridor and then south of the LZ. Storms and McDevitt pumped bursts.

We passed over the terrain just south of the zone. Andy was off target, gaining altitude. Both of us, in sequence, called off target. After I'd added climb power and began a right turn, I noticed two men among some trees on a knoll about one hundred meters southeast of the LZ.

The lift birds settled in the zone. No one reported fire. Not yet.

"Guns safe," Dick offered.

We crawled back toward the perch and I radioed, "Nightrider, this is Klondike Dash two. You guys have anyone separated from your main body, maybe southeast? We saw two guys on a knoll. Over."

After a pause while Nightrider mentally adjusted to a call from someone other than Bonnie Sue, he answered. "Klondike, Dash two, we lost contact with our MIAs due east about two clicks up the valley. Those guys you see are NVA. You're cleared to fire. Over."

"Roger, Nightrider. Dash two will take 'em on next pass. Over." We were gaining altitude, straining for position again.

"Bonnie Sue Lead is lifting. We'll climb left. Over." The second division was already starting down.

"Bonnie Sue Dash five is inbound to the zone. Over." These guys were well-oiled, one division lifting the other closing fast on the zone.

While they descended, Olson radioed in with guns. Ten seconds later, we were in position again. "Klondike Dash two in with guns. Over." Down we went.

"Bonnie Sue Lead is taking fire east of the zone. Over." Shit, here we go again, but I already had the trigger depressed providing suppressive fire for the second Frog division.

"Klondike Lead, Roger. We'll put some rounds out there. Over." Andy was about out of his run on the north side of the LZ, but, rather than climbing, he stayed low extending his attack to the east.

I fired not just into the area south of the approaching Frogs, but bent the Huey around and sprayed into the knoll where I'd seen the two guys. Then, staying low like Andy had, I extended firing east. But we had birds in the zone to cover too, so I pulled in power and began a right climb again.

"Sir, two guys just came from behind trees on that knoll; they're wavin'," McDevitt said.

After a pause to compute I radioed, "Nightrider, this is Klondike Dash two. We've discovered your MIAs. Over."

No response. Nightrider was either in a 46 or hauling ass to get that way. In either case, he was not answering the FM.

"Bonnie Sue Dash five is lifting. We have everybody. We'll be climbing right to avoid the fire from the east. Over."

I climbed up and to the right again, but this time leveled with five hundred feet of terrain clearance. Then I bent back around farther to the right to get a visual on Andy. He was still climbing to the left, no longer providing suppressive fire for the first division of Bonnie Sue, since they were above an altitude typically vulnerable to small arms.

"Klondike Lead, this is Klondike Dash two. I think we discovered the MIAs. They're on a hill just southeast of the LZ. Over."

After a pause, "Dash two, this is Lead. Take a closer look; let's make sure. I'll get in position to cover you. Over."

"Roger, Lead," I responded, then into the ICS, "Okay gents, we're going down there and we'll be slow. If these folks even look cross-eyed just start hammering. We won't be able to get the main guns trained, so it's up to you guys in back. Be damn alert." I made a 360-degree turn to kill time while Andy climbed to a cover position.

"Dash two, this is Lead. We're ready when you are," he called.

"Roger, Lead. We're heading down." I raised the Huey's nose, reduced power and slowed, then turned directly at the knoll. We started down, this time from a northerly direction. As we neared, several men stepped into the open from low growth and trees. They were Nungs; they waved again. We passed directly over them, both Storms and McDevitt waved in response. I added power and climbed to the west again.

"Klondike Lead, those guys are ours, but we don't have a Frog-sized zone, maybe not even a Huey-sized one. Over."

After a pause while Andy considered options, he responded. "Okay, Dash two. We gotta try. See if you can get in there. We'll cover. Over."

"Roger, Lead. We'll fire our rockets and jettison pods, then give it a try. Over." There was no zone there, no place to land, but we might fit in between the trees. It would be snug.

"Roger, Dash two."

Bonnie Sue was heading east overflying their downed 46 from several days earlier. They'd monitored our transmissions. "Klondike Lead, Bonnie Sue Lead. We have fuel considerations so can't loiter while those guys get to a better zone. We might hoist 'em out, but you guys can do that. We probably ought to head for Phu Bai. Can you handle them? Over."

"Bonnie Sue Lead, Klondike. We'll know in a couple of minutes. If we can't get close to the ground, maybe we can hoist 'em if we have the power. If we can't get 'em, guess we'll come back," Andy responded.

"Roger, Klondike. Bonnie Sue concurs. We'll be back if you're unable to pull 'em out. Over."

I climbed and turned, lining up with the area east of the LZ, the area from where Bonnie Sue had received the fire on climb out. "Dick, give me rockets."

He turned knobs and threw the switches. "You're set, Dave." I nosed over and pulled the trigger seven times. Two rockets, one from each pod, came out at split-second intervals until all fourteen rockets whooshed, spewed, and swirled into the jungle east of the LZ. They exploded gray-black in green trees.

I added power and climbed again to the right. "Let's jettison the pods, Dick." He reached for the armament panel and threw the switch to jettison stores. The rocket pod on Dick's side fell away immediately. The other hung. He reached for the manual release handle next to the panel and worked the lever several times. Nothing.

"McDevitt, looks like you're gonna have to tromp on yours," I said into the ICS.

"Okay, sir," and Corporal McDevitt, secured to the helo by his gunner's belt and exposed to a slipstream of sixty knots, stepped out on the gun racks and began stomping on the pod. Dick continued pumping the jettison lever. After four stomps and pumps, it fell away. I was unwilling to lighten our load further by tossing the door-mount M-60s and what was left of our ball ammunition. If we went down, we may need these to defend ourselves. We were as light as we ought to get. Time for a try.

I climbed up but not high and circled back over the knoll looking for the best place to lower the Huey. Smoke, yellow and swirling came billowing. The guys down there were trying to help, but they'd also given away their position and our intended point of landing. The winds were easterly, gusting a little, bouncing in the mountainous terrain. High stumps and low growth covered the knoll and a mix of living and limbless dead trees bristled the crest. The trees precluded an approach from the west into the wind. I'd have to come in heading southeast; a quartering wind was as good as it got. I curled to the north.

"Lead, we're settin' up to approach from the northwest. The wind's easterly, but there's so damn many trees, our best chance is toward the southeast. When I'm outta this turn, we'll start down. Over."

"Roger, Dash two. Lead's in cover position. Over."

I kept my speed low; the blades popped. We headed back toward the knoll. This time I set up for a steep, precision approach into the stand of trees. I raised the nose further, slowing more and drew an imaginary line between the Huey and the site where I intended to settle. I'd take her down on a forty-five-degree angle from the earth's surface. I intersected the line, lowered the collective slightly, and raised the nose even further. We began settling. I kept the rate of descent low and the power high.

The terrain at the knoll was 2,100 feet and the slope of the terrain would wash out any ass-saving ground effect I might have enjoyed from a flatter surface. (Ground effect is a bounce-back air cushion helos create from rotor-wash. It helps hold you in the sky and begins one rotor diameter from the ground, forty-four feet in a Huey, increasing in intensity as the helo descends.)

Engines are less powerful and rotor blades less effective as elevation increases. I was alert, creeping down, monitoring the engine, watching the ground foliage and trees. We settled into the only space available. The last sixty feet of the descent was vertical. I tried to squeeze licorice from the black plastic handgrip of the stick. All control inputs had to be small, smooth, and immediate.

The crew, apart from listening for the snap of cracking bullets and watching for the flash of muzzles, gave me verbal cues as we went into the trees.

"Okay on the right, sir."

"Six feet clear on the left."

"Tail's clear."

"Right a little."

"Steady. Stop. No farther down."

And we brought the bird into a hover five feet from sloping ground. I couldn't land. The slope precluded its as did low trees and stout under-growth. I held position by watching outside at fixed objects: tree branches, bushes. My job was to freeze the helo in space. Wind made the effort more difficult. It tried to kick us around as it played against the fuselage and through the rotor head, making blades more or less effective with even the slightest change in velocity. I was on autopilot. My responses were unthinking reactions, programmed by many hours in the Huey. A year earlier and I might not have been able.

Once we were stabilized in a hover, Sergeant Storms turned his attention away from giving me voice information on our descent and back to potential enemy action. He hunched over his machine gun in the cabin opening behind Dick and watched the terrain for bad guys and muzzle flashes. Corporal McDevitt, on my side and closest to the SOG guys, motioned them to get their asses to and on the helo. There were five, not two or three. They approached and clustered in powerful rotor downwash beneath the right skid. Up they reached, and one by one they clambered up, first pulling themselves onto the skid tube, then in the small space just forward of the gun barrels and with McDevitt's help, into the cabin. Each time one added his weight to the Huey, I adjusted control input to compensate for the added weight and lateral center of gravity displacement.

I glanced at the engine's performance. "Dick, help me monitor the engine." Each time a man got into the helo, the power demand increased, and we'd have to lift straight up sixty feet to clear the treetops. Only then could I nose over and feel my way toward God's gift to helo jocks, translational lift. After the second guy, I knew we'd be unable to get all five and still pull the bird up out of this hole. Andy would have to pick up at least one, maybe two. "Klondike Lead, we can't get 'em all. Don't have the power. Over."

"Roger, Dash two. Get what you can and we'll pick up what's left. Over."

I held the helo steady. After the third SOG guy crawled on board, I judged it was dangerous to get anymore. "Dave, you might be pressin' it with another one." Dick offered. His opinion reinforced mine.

"McDevitt, motion to 'em that Captain Olson will get the last two," I said.

"Okay, sir," and McDevitt, using whatever charade of arm and hand signals that occurred to him, made the last two SOG bubbas know we could not take them, but the other Huey would come to their aid.

"They know, Lieutenant," McDevitt said.

"Okay, gents, I'm pulling her up. Keep me clear." I raised the collective slowly, just a little at a time, but I kept it coming to max power. I didn't have far to go; we were near it anyway. Up we crept. I watched the trees around me and monitored the engine and rotor RPM. I was beginning to droop the rotor RPM a little, but the Lycoming engine pumped out what was needed. Straight up, out of the hole we came, slowly, steadily, but surely.

Once again I relied as much on relative motion as on comments from the crew. Both Storms and McDevitt were hanging out of the helo's sides. "Drifting right." "Clear left." "Tail clear."

Forty, fifty, sixty feet, and we cleared the treetops. I dropped the nose a hair and started inching forward, inching toward translational lift and flying speed. I swung slightly left more into the wind and to where the terrain fell away. The airspeed indicator first bounced, then registered steadily. We were no longer hovering, we were taxiing. Then we were no-shit flying. Now to avoid the assholes out east who'd shot at Bonnie Sue on their way out at sixty knots, I swung south and started my climb. I reduced power a little. The tension knotting my thighs and shoulders began to subside.

"Dash two, any advice on the zone?" Andy radioed.

"Roger, I think the only way in is the one we used. Before you try, get really slow. The last part is vertical, zero airspeed. Keep your power up, none of that bottoming collective and saving it at the end with a fistful of power. You'd just crash. You can't set down, but can get close enough for the SOG guys to grab a skid. It's tight as hell in there, Captain."

We climbed to 2,800 feet and circled. When Andy knew we'd be unable to get them all, he had picked a likely target area, as we had, pumped his rockets into the countryside, then dropped his pods.

"Dick, you want to drive awhile."

"Sure, Dave." I felt him on the controls. "I have the aircraft."

"You have the aircraft," I responded and loosened my tight-as-hell grip. I slid my legs to the rear; my feet came away from the rudders. I relaxed some. Dick circled; we watched Andy.

"Gents, if they get shot at, we're gonna attack, even though we have guests. Be ready," I said.

When everyone acknowledged this, I glanced at the switches and made sure I had only one to throw to activate guns for Dick. He had us in cover position for Captain Olson.

Andy set up for an approach. I glanced back into the faces of three Nungs. One smiled. I tried to imagine what their lives must have been like for the last several days. I couldn't.

Well into his approach, about the time he was over the vertical part of the descent, he called, "Lead is waving off."

I was not surprised. Before I went in I'd had three chances to look at the area. He was shooting the approach almost cold. I figured it was his recognition pass. He'd had a look; he'd make it next time. And he did.

After five minutes, Andy had the other two SOG guys. He pulled vertically out of the hole in the trees. His engine was not as strong as mine, and his rotor RPM decayed as he came out. Still, he was able to milk enough. By stages, Andy nursed the helo to flying speed and began a climb.

"Klondike Lead is out, climbing southeast. Over."

Dick kept us in position to shoot, but no one was shooting at Andy. We loitered, waiting for him to gain altitude.

"Roger, Lead. Dash two has you. We'll follow in trail," Dick answered.

Bonnie Sue was gone, a few specks well ahead nearing their individual descents into the coastal overcast that still socked in Phu Bai. Andy gained altitude and turned east. We followed, drilling along at three thousand feet. After a while he added power and climbed to four thousand feet, three hundred feet above the cloud tops over Phu Bai.

Even though Andy'd briefed five hundred pounds as bingo fuel, we were well below that. I knew we'd be landing with the twenty-minute fuel light illuminated on the panel. It blinked on as we climbed to four thousand feet. Dick and I saw it and glanced at each other, but said nothing.

"Bonnie Sue Lead, Klondike Lead. We have five MIAs. We're well behind, but heading your way. Over," Andy called.

"Roger, Klondike. Break. Bonnie Sue flight and Klondike, let's go Bonnie Sue Fox Mike and Phu Bai Approach. Over," Carver responded.

We all rippled acknowledgment, then checked in on the new FM frequency. After we reported in, he radioed again. "Bonnie Sue flight, we'll shoot individual approaches as briefed. I'll head down first. Over." No response was needed nor given.

"Phu Bai Approach Control, Bonnie Sue Lead. Flight of ten, eight CH-46s and two Hueys, we're approaching the eight-mile fix on the two six zero radial Phu Bai, requesting individual approaches to Phu Bai. Over."

Then a stroke of genius: "Bonnie Sue Lead. This is Approach Control. We're going to bring the flights down individually at one-minute intervals on different headings. You'll break out underneath the clouds and fly to Phu Bai VFR. Report the six-mile fix, two seven zero degree radial, Phu Bai. Maintain VFR. Phu Bai is reporting two hundred feet overcast; visibility varies one to three miles in light rain showers. Over."

After Carver paused, "Roger, Approach. Understand we're doing individual radar-monitored letdowns to VFR beneath the clouds. Then fly to the airfield VFR. We'll not, repeat not, be shooting approaches to the runway. Over."

"That's affirmative, Bonnie Sue. We have no traffic in the area. The sky is ours. When you break out beneath, Approach will clear you to switch Phu Bai tower for VFR landing at the airstrip. Bonnie Sue Lead, squawk 3614 and ident. Over."

"Roger, Approach. Bonnie Sue Lead squawk 3614 and ident. We're closing on six miles, two seven zero. Break. Flight, go trail and string it out. I guess you heard, we're going down at one-minute intervals, separate headings, separated squawks, then VFR for landing. Over."

We were still distant but high enough to hear it all. What a great piece of headwork. Each of the Bonnie Sue helos and our Klondike section could expect to simply dive into the clouds, separated by time and heading; some minutes later we'd ease out the bottom, and visually fly to the field. It was art.

We hit the fix ten minutes after the last Frog disappeared into the clag. Andy copied his assigned squawk and heading and disappeared. Dick and I were last. We spent a lonely minute over gray-white rumpled and puffy cloud tops. I felt isolated, tied to the world only by the periodic reassuring radio contact of Approach Control and hearing other bird providing or receiving information.

"I'll take her down, Dick." We went through the, "You have the aircraft; I have the aircraft," exchange. Shortly after, we tucked into the billows and were once again surrounded by gray mist, cool and moist in the openness of our doorless gunbird. I held ninety knots and seven hundred feet per minute in descent. I'd had a hell of a lot of practice in a short period and was getting better.

I glanced in the face of the Nung sitting on the floor just behind the center console. Flying in clouds was new; his eyes were large with uncertainty. Eventually the gray-white began to thin. We registered 350 feet on the RADALT. First we saw the ground periodically; then we were through. Mother earth!

"Phu Bai Approach, Klondike Dash two is VFR three miles zero nine zero radial. Over," I called on the UHF.

"Roger, Klondike Dash two. You're cleared to contact Phu Bai Tower for landing. Over."

"Roger, Approach, Dash two, switchin'. Good day."

Dick switched us to the tower and we were cleared to land. As we closed, I saw Andy ahead of me. The other birds were on the deck. We were the last. We landed with low, low fuel, taxied, refueled, and repositioned to the parking apron.

Dick and I shut her down. It was quiet. We unstrapped, got out, and chatted a bit, but were less talky than usual. We'd just pulled it off. Each had done his part, each felt fulfilled. Success in the dangerous and difficult, in some perceived great endeavor is singularly satisfying.

The Nungs were especially relieved. They smiled and extended their hands. We shook and they walked away toward their companions with only their weapons, which was all they'd brought from the jungle. The crew and I looked the helo over. It was okay.

Later we learned that the CH-46 crewchief had survived the ordeal with the SOG folks and, as a temporary grunt, acquitted himself remarkably well. He even engaged in some hand to hand!

We also discovered eventually that the abandoned Frog was destroyed by airstrikes. It was just too damn dangerous to go get it.

We had a beer at the bar that night and listened to the club's reel-to-reel Akai. Predictably, Johnny Cash wailed about walking "the line" and hearing "that train a'comin'." In the morning we were first out of the gate. The Frogs were getting ready; we were pulling pitch. The weather had improved, so we didn't have to fart around in clouds. Andy led us home and to a more routine existence.

It was nice to get back to Ky Ha. For one thing, we'd all run out of clean clothes.

PART 5

Heading Out and Epilogue

CHAPTER 23

Checking Out and the Journey

I was relieved to leave. I'd learned Vietnam was a deadly, injurious place. A number of aircrewmen were dead, others wounded, including hoochmates, and I'd lost a commanding officer. Self-preservation alone made leaving a good idea. Yet I was ambivalent: I also felt sheepish, like I was abandoning my partners and the situation midstride.

My last two weeks, in April of 1967, Ops took me off the flight schedule. It was squadron policy; all who'd made it that far were going home alive and unhurt. Lieutenant Colonel Maloney was responsible for this, but it may have been common practice among the helo squadrons. It would have been bad to "buy the farm" with only a few days left in a war zone.

For those days, I was lost and felt mild guilt. Everyday I heard and saw the gunbirds and slicks lift, head out, and return. My job was flying Hueys, not reading, writing, hanging out, and listening to my new portable. I browsed the slowly expanding PX and got in some exercise. Yet something was not quite right; I was a Huey pilot. The birds were launching and I was ass-sitting.

New pilots, new crewchiefs, new gunners, and the whole panoply of Marines required to operate the squadron had slid into the slots of the old hands. They'd trickled in piecemeal each month, just as Waters, Ross, Wilson, and I had in March of 1966. At the end of my tour, I looked around and every pilot was a FNG, at least compared to me. But they weren't really; they'd just been "Klondike" for less time: Kufeldt, Buchanan, Murphy, Andrews, Boston, Thatcher, Rankin, Saunders, Peckham, Peterson, and the others. They learned the in-country "how-to" as copilots, and as they came up on the learning curve, they signed for the birds, flew wing, then led sections and divisions. The squadron rolled along. I'd flown with them all and knew they were ready. It was my time to look ahead.

The good-byes were mostly individual, and we each had a short one-on-one with the CO. At formation one week, our names and those of others were mentioned as rotating. I "small-talked" with the guys and pressed the flesh around the squadron. I made a special effort to see as many of the door gunners and the crewchiefs as I could and thanked them for saving my ass. I had a beer or two some nights at the O club to see the lift helo guys.

I managed to squander the time, partly with the checking-out process itself. The Admin Chief, Staff Sergeant Brandt, gave me a checklist of places to go and initials to get. Among them was the post office, medical, Group admin, and CO. I made those rounds and, once finished, I checked out around the squadron and turned in my .38. Brandt then let me have my orders. They were to VMO-5 at Camp Pendleton, California. I'd known this for several weeks and was pleased. I'd still be flying Hueys.

Near the end of the two weeks, I packed, took a short truck ride to Chu Lai, and a C-130 to the Marine Corps processing center at Danang Airbase. Two days later I joined a long line of Marines boarding a chartered civilian airliner headed for the Marine Corps Air Station, El Toro, California. To a man, the occupants erupted in shouts and applause the second the jet's landing gear cleared the Danang runway. We had survived. We were going home.

It was an all-Marine flight with a cross section of ranks. Some were veterans of earlier wars, Korea, even World War II. But my war, like all wars, was fought mostly by the young. Marines in their late teens or early twenties were greatest in number. More than half in our plane were younger men; I was twenty-six.

Everyone was lean. Vietnam is so hot and humid that even keeping weight is difficult. Getting tubbed up was out of the question, quite apart from people riding you and putting you on the "sumo wrestling team." It was hard enough to lug a skinny ass around.

Six beautiful women were aboard the airliner; everyone agreed. American gals were rare and exotic creatures in Vietnam. In those days only women were attendants and they were screened for personality *and* looks. Usually they married and settled down well before middle age, so their ranks were constantly replenished at the bottom with young beauties. They were called stewardesses rather than flight attendants, and it was before all the concern about equal opportunity. Now, of course, they can be most any age or shape and even guys.

To see a fistful of them together, prancing about, was highly entertaining and the women knew it. They smiled and joked, fetched us beer, drinks, pillows, and served chow. It was promise and luxury compared to the life we'd had, especially for the Marines who'd lived in the field. The young women were eye candy, a sample of what one might hope for somewhere after the end of the flight.

RECEPTION

We landed once for fuel and a leg stretch. It was either Alaska or Washington and eventually we arrived at El Toro. (Marines are no longer stationed there, but in the 1960s it was a humming Marine Corps jet base.) After the plane was parked on the apron near station operations, some movable steps were rolled up, we collected our carry-on gear, and deplaned. The station band played some martial music, you know, the John P. Sousa, "monkey wrapped his tail around the flagpole" stuff.

We hung around the bottom of the stairs for a few minutes, then were asked to move to an area close at hand and face a lectern. Once we'd organized ourselves, an officer stepped to the microphone and provided a welcome home spiel. We were given instructions about what awaited us in the terminal and allowed to go mingle with anyone who'd come to meet the plane. After some paperwork, I made travel arrangements to visit home and my life went on.

Something tugged at me a little at the time and more over the years. I didn't quite understand it then, and maybe I have it wrong now. I was young with few comparisons and an underdeveloped set of expectations, but a couple hundred Marines were stepping back into the American culture. They'd been off doing the nation's bidding in a corner of the world most rank-and-file citizens had never heard of before 1963. The Marines had endured privation and danger; some had seen more brutality than most citizens would in a lifetime, and *they* had been brutalized as well. War is not possible without the repression of civil sensibilities: People must be killed and hurt; most sensible and civil people would not be able to do this without themselves becoming the brute.

Our Marines had changed, some of them dramatically. We had received a brief prepared pitch and listened to some band music. But reentry was much more serious business than that. More psychic axle grease might have been applied, especially to the grunts. Maybe eventually it was, but it did not start at the El Toro reception.

Another idea that grew in me was that not enough of a big deal was made over the returning men. I am amazed this thought occurs to me, since I am not huge on pomp and circumstance; in fact, ceremony often strikes me as ludicrous. But we'd gone off to war for thirteen months, not twelve like the other services, thirteen, the Marine Corps way. And we were back. It was a right of passage for everyone, even though we might not have realized it at the time.

More hoopla was probably warranted. I realize that since many of us came back one planeload at a time, this was likely impractical. But an officer reading and a band playing were thin reward. Something was missing. Maybe I'm thinking of national gratitude. And this ground, once lost, cannot be made up by an eventual parade for the Vietnam Vets. The nation tried that. Odor clings to afterthought.

The El Toro reception was a small thing and did not affect my life, but for a long time I've pondered that nongreeting. I'm pleased that Marines and Soldiers returning from the Middle Eastern troubles of the early twenty-first century seem to be fussed over a bit more than we were. It is fitting.

I was home and life came at me, though at a different and nonthreatening pace. I was back, but one who goes is never quite *back*. War is a singular experience; it follows you around.

CHAPTER 24

Life after 'Nam

VMO-5

I blended back into the Stateside Marine Corps, assigned to VMO-5 at Camp Pendleton, California. Some of my mates from VMO-6, Waters, Wilson, Garner, and a couple of the gunners and crewchiefs, Sergeant Hockenbury for instance, joined me there. We trained pilots destined for the Hueys in Vietnam.

Initially I was assigned to squadron operations as the Reports Control Officer. It was not a good fit. I did my best, but controlling reports both for the squadron's records and for higher headquarters at the Marines Corps Air Facility, Tustin, was no fun. I kept checklists and hounded people for input. Once the report was complete, often at the last damn minute, I'd forward it through the front office for the XO's chop and the CO's signature. If it were truly the last minute, I'd have to "walk it through." Then I got to explain to the XO why it was 1400 and the report was due at Group Headquarters at 1600 the same day. I'd get caught in the middle of the thing. That captain this or major that or gunnery sergeant whoever could not be moved off his lazy ass to get his stuff in so I could complete the report mattered not. That I was gaffed off, despite begging, pleading, cajoling, ass-kissing, and even threatening, was not a concern of the XO. If you've ever had the coordinator's job, you know this drill. Maj. P. Upschulte, the XO, would eye me sternly, more interested in the bottom line than the bullshit in between. He'd been affected by the *Message to Garcia*, a small book Marine officers and SNCOs read about a guy who, hell or high water, got a really difficult task done. I didn't care for the reports control job.

The only good thing about the assignment was this: If we were truly down to the last damn minute with a report bound for Group Headquarters, I could call maintenance for a helo. Then a crewchief and I could leap off in mid-afternoon, just the two of us. We'd fly directly northwest, across the scenic Case Springs area of Camp Pendleton, get clearance from the MCAS, El Toro tower to fly through their airspace, and ease into nearby Tustin. We'd land at the base of the tower and hand the report to a jeep driver, who'd been prearranged to meet us. He delivered it. This air delivery option probably saved my ass and precluded someone making a big deal out of a late report to our CO, Lt. Col. Don Tooker. Then, of course, I'd have been explaining myself to the boss, one-on-one.

I liked the flight to Tustin, single pilot in a slick with a crewchief over some impressive terrain. Sometime we'd take the coastal route south back to Pendleton and watch for whales making their lazy swim south to Baja for the winter or north to cooler climes for the summer. On the trek north, calves often swam alongside their moms.

After eight months of monkey-in-the-middle with reports control, I went to aircraft maintenance and worked again for Waters, who'd been recently promoted to major. I was the Shops Officer, but SNCOs or warrant officers ran the individual shops. Although I represented them at maintenance meetings, they did the heavy lifting. What I really did was serve as perpetual test pilot. That's where I belonged. I tested Hueys and, in between tests, flew instructional hops with new and transitioning pilots. Life was pretty good.

OFFICER CAREERS AND DEGREES

Although I liked my job, my future in the Corps was not promising. I had no degree and, although I took night school college classes when I could, I had no assurance of completing one. The Marine Corps had a program called "boot strap," which, if you were selected, let you go to college to complete a degree. But at that time, nondegreed officers had to be within one year of completion. I had about seventy hours, not close enough to even apply. Without a degree, if I kept my nose clean I might make major, but getting past that was tough sledding.

I didn't mind the prospect of failing promotion in a test of competency. I figured I was as good as half my peers, but I rankled at the thought of entering the contest on an unequal footing. No degree was a huge dose of unequal footing. After soul-searching, I opted to get off active duty and go to college on the GI Bill. In the summer of 1969, I stepped over the side.

In college I decided to be a college professor, and after six years at two different universities, I was writing a doctoral dissertation in European History.

BACK TO THE GREEN MACHINE

I looked around for a college job in the 1970s and could have papered my apartment with letters that began, "Although your credentials are impressive." My wife was pregnant and I needed a job. I started sifting through alternatives to the academic field: Enter the Marine Corps to save my sad ass from who knows what chicken-shit reports control officer–type job in corporate America. I'd stayed active in the Reserves, which helped. I put my hat in my hand, shuffled a bit, and wrote my best letter to the Green Machine, asking for a return to active duty. They let me. I was to work with the Reserve Community on three-year contracts. If I screwed up or ever failed promotion selection, my contract would not be renewed, and I'd be sent home short of retirement.

I was elated! If I could just piece together enough years of this, I would have a profession and a future in a respected institution. I returned to active duty in the winter of 1976, a rookie major, but an educated one.

I served at Camp Pendleton, a Reserve Air Group Headquarters, where I flew the CH-53A; at Marine Corps Headquarters in D.C.; at Quantico's Doctrine Center; and finally at an administrative headquarters in Kansas City, where I retired in 1989. This last assignment was perfect for a Kansas man.

I didn't like my second stint as a Marine nearly as much as I liked the early years of machines, missions, and aircrews, the days of rocket, rotor, and gun. I became a coordinator, XO, action officer, administrative assistant to generals, chief of staff, and deputy director. My education came into play in staff assignments, unlike in the cockpit where it's systems and aviation knowledge, physical skill, and headwork. I survived fifteen years of this coordinator-type work. It was a blessing in a way, but not in the way of my younger years.

IMPACT

Recently I saw another mediocre war movie. It was about the Marines' part in pushing Iraqi forces out of Kuwait in the Gulf War. As usual, the Hollywood effort to reflect the Corps was not good, but the movie's ending was perfect. It was a scene of the central character a few years after the war. He sat in civilian clothing in an office somewhere, a little puffy from lack of exercise, his hair longer. He looked a bit lost, but somehow sober and knowing. As he stared out an office window, the movie's director used the trick of voiceover to reveal the character's thoughts. The narration offered that once you've had your hand around a rifle in combat, you never quite let it go. Amen. To the rifle I will add the cyclic and collective for a helo jock and the grip of an M-60 for a crewchief or door gunner. We can never go back, never let go. It's okay. We'll just never be the same, and sadly what follows this sort of high adventure is a bit flat, the ho-hum mellowness of everyday life. After you've finished a no-net high-wire act, the clown suit doesn't quite fit.

In the coming years as a civilian and as a Marine I expected the sort of association I felt with the VMO-6 pilots, crewchiefs, and gunners, indeed with all my squadronmates. But there was none of that. Combat is a special catalyst. The tightness of our squadron has never been reproduced. Not everyone in VMO-6 was my bosom buddy, but they were my kith and kin. I could and did rely on them, and I in turn felt inordinately responsible to them. I liked the feeling of belonging, of interlocking responsibility. Teamwork in business is a joke compared to combat. You probably don't often find that sort of reciprocal commitment except in a unit in war.

The tense episodes had amplitude unlike most Stateside jobs and activities. Maybe police work can be this way, but after Vietnam nothing was close. There is something mildly seductive, even addictive in this ultimate gamble, in doing the difficult in an environment of danger. I've heard that some men miss the adrenaline surges so much they become mercenaries, although this was not my response nor that of anyone I knew. I just got the shit scared out of me here and there. It's a test, in a way. After Vietnam, life has been much less challenging, less exciting. Surprisingly, I've missed that.

I believe once you've known mortal fear, the other kinds are less fearsome. Showing up late and unprepared, for instance, although embarrassing, is decidedly in a different class than fear from people using you or your helo for target practice. Not too much scares me, but the experience has not made me a foolhardy tempter of fate either. I am just steady. I know when situations are dangerous, when the alarms should sound. Usually they should not; I don't go to battle stations over the small and annoying. I think Vietnam is responsible for this.

The distinctness of high purpose has also been missing. Our job in war was to act in behalf of the nation. I believed I was about the business of the United States of America. That's a rare, lofty assignment and very heady stuff. We were acting for the red, white, and blue in some great cause. At least that was my conviction while I was there, and, even though this idealism was well in the background, hidden behind the reality of the daily missions and routines, I was aware of its presence. You don't find that in most jobs.

Finally, Vietnam may be responsible for a keener awareness of the world and a heightened appreciation of things large and small: The patchwork of eastern Kansas fields sliding beneath my low-flying Piper, hearing my wife sing or laugh in the next room, watching my children advance from infancy to adulthood, and seasonal retreat and renewal. Although I'm uncertain, since I can never know the alternate me, the one who did not go to 'Nam, I suspect opposites really do help define each other. If knowing hot helps me understand cold, then maybe knowing death and danger helps me understand, and appreciate, life.

Military folks come together in units and go in harm's way to do the government's will, believing their actions protect our people. Then we disperse back into the nation's common culture. On return from war, we are far removed from what was our recent routine. We become bewildered, stunned by the lack of order and discipline in the general ways of the world, annoyed, for instance, at pettiness, at small issues raised for discussion at meetings. We miss our people, our old military units, our routines, and our very distinct, lofty, and pronounced national purpose. We are out of place. I've shaken my head, at least inwardly, at much of the bullshit that passes for serious endeavor in my nonmilitary life. I don't feel superior; I am just periodically astonished. But we humans must be occupied, must earn a living, must sell goods and services.

Our longing for a spark of the old cohesive brotherhood and a chance to reflect on what was both tragic and magnificent is noticeable in the institution of reunions. These can be a little maudlin, a bit corny, and maybe sad, but veterans like to be around each other. We watch ourselves grow old at periodic intervals. I think I go, not because I expect to be well entertained by what's said, but to be in the presence of this special group of men. I feel comfortable and at home with them in a way I do not elsewhere. We have a common secret, a secret that cannot be known to others even though we often try to include them. Some things must be lived, must be endured, for there to be true understanding, true community.

FINAL THOUGHTS

I was a Klondike pilot and for that I will ever be glad and proud, though not struttingly so. If tomorrow I could walk to an awaiting Huey for a mission, joined by others who have chosen my way, tumblers and gears would again mesh. I would be satisfied having a perfect, specific, and even noble purpose in a remarkable association.

When I fly my rag-wing Piper across the plains and fields of Kansas, I am usually alone. But sometimes without straining, just by listening intently, I am once again in a green shape suspended from whirling blades. The ICS crackles with the voice of a crewmember who makes some observation about the aircraft, our mission, or the terrain below. Seniors have ordered us to perform a needed task, and we are off again to help our people in some way. I smile. Once more my purpose in life becomes vivid, clean, and clear. Though alone, I am not. *They* are crowded in just behind my eyes. I have full pods and ammo cans; Boston, Storms, and McDevitt are with me. I am in the heart of a great organization going about the business of the Corps and the nation. And I am whole. I am Klondike once more as I will be forever.

Though I wait, I know it will not come.

VMO-6 Deaths in Vietnam

*(statistical source: USMC/Vietnam Helicopter Association website,
www.popasmoke.com accessed December 29, 2007)*

Cpl. Paul Allen
LCpl. Walter Armstrong
Sgt. Daniel Bennett
Capt. Norman Billipp
LCpl. William Brencich
Cpl. Frederick Cain
Capt. Leon Chadwick III
Capt. James Cawley
Capt. Alan Dean
LCpl. Michael DeMarco
Capt. Bobby Galbreath
Cpl. Rudolpho Gonzalez
Maj. William Goodsell
LCpl. Benny Hack
Maj. John Hagan
First Lt. William Hall
First Lt. Ralph Hunt Jr.
Capt. David Jacobsgaard
First Lt. Paul Jensen

First Lt. Edwin Keeble Jr.
First Lt. Robert Kimmel
First Lt. Richard Krupa
First Lt. Richard Latimer Jr.
Pfc. Edgar Laye Jr.
First Lt. Glenn Mann
Capt. Bruce McMillan
GySgt. Donald McPhee
First Lt. James Reese
First Lt. Ronald Riede
LCpl. Edward Sanchez
Cpl. Harry Schneider
Capt. Jack Schober
Pfc. Brock Schramm
Cpl. Joseph Scruggs
Capt. Brooke Shadburne
Cpl. Alvin Slaton
SSgt. Jimmy Tolliver
Capt. Barton Uplinger

INDEX

ABOUT THE AUTHOR

DAVID BALLENTINE joined the Navy after high school in the late 1950s and attended the University of Florida. After two years, he joined the Marine Corps and attended flight school in Pensacola as a Marine aviation cadet, earning a commission as a naval aviator in 1965. From March 1966 to April 1967, then-Lieutenant Ballentine served in Vietnam and flew armed UH-1Es in Marine Observation Squadron Six, stationed at Ky Ha, north of Chu Lai along the coast, fifty miles south of Danang.

Shortly after Vietnam he returned to college and earned a PhD in European history. He returned to active duty in 1976, later serving in Headquarters Marine Corps and then as chief of staff/deputy director of the Marine Corps Reserve Support Center. Colonel Ballentine retired in 1989 and worked for Northrop Grumman with the Army at Ft. Leavenworth. He lives in Overland Park, KS, with his wife, Dana. He teaches at a local community college and has written for the *Marine Corps Gazette*. His personal decorations include the Legion of Merit and the Distinguished Flying Cross. He still flies a Piper Colt.

THE NAVAL INSTITUTE PRESS is the book-publishing arm of the U.S. Naval Institute, a private, nonprofit, membership society for sea service professionals and others who share an interest in naval and maritime affairs. Established in 1873 at the U.S. Naval Academy in Annapolis, Maryland, where its offices remain today, the Naval Institute has members worldwide.

Members of the Naval Institute support the education programs of the society and receive the influential monthly magazine *Proceedings* or the colorful bimonthly magazine *Naval History* and discounts on fine nautical prints and on ship and aircraft photos. They also have access to the transcripts of the Institute's Oral History Program and get discounted admission to any of the Institute-sponsored seminars offered around the country.

The Naval Institute's book-publishing program, begun in 1898 with basic guides to naval practices, has broadened its scope to include books of more general interest. Now the Naval Institute Press publishes about seventy titles each year, ranging from how-to books on boating and navigation to battle histories, biographies, ship and aircraft guides, and novels. Institute members receive significant discounts on the Press's more than eight hundred books in print.

Full-time students are eligible for special half-price membership rates. Life memberships are also available.

For a free catalog describing Naval Institute Press books currently available, and for further information about joining the U.S. Naval Institute, please write to:

Member Services
U.S. Naval Institute
291 Wood Road
Annapolis, MD 21402-5034
Telephone: (800) 233-8764
Fax: (410) 571-1703
Web address: www.usni.org